Sticks AND Stones

Sticks AND Stones

*Defeating the Culture of Bullying
and Rediscovering the Power
of Character and Empathy*

Emily Bazelon

Random House
New York

Published in the United States by Random House,
an imprint of The Random House Publishing Group,
a division of Random House, Inc., New York.

RANDOM HOUSE and colophon are registered trademarks
of Random House, Inc.

Library of Congress Cataloging-in-Publication Data
Bazelon, Emily.
Sticks and stones : defeating the culture of
bullying and rediscovering the power of
character and empathy / by Emily Bazelon.
p.   cm.
Includes bibliographical references and index.
ISBN 978-0-8129-9280-9—ISBN 978-0-679-64400-2 (ebook)
1. Bullying.   2. Bullying—Prevention.   3. Bullying in schools.
4. Bullying in schools—Prevention.   I. Title.
BF637.B85B39 2013
302.34'3—dc23   2012022773

Printed in the United States of America on acid-free paper

www.atrandom.com

1 2 3 4 5 6 7 8 9

First Edition

Book design by Diane Hobbing

For Paul, Eli, and Simon

Contents

Sticks AND Stones

Prologue

WHEN I WAS IN EIGHTH GRADE, MY FRIENDS FIRED ME. TWO and a half decades later, I can say that wryly: it happened to plenty of people, and look at us now, right? We survived. But at the time, in that moment, it was impossible to have that kind of perspective. Being rejected by the girls I loved left me crawling with insecurity and self-doubt—what had I done wrong? I disappeared from the lunchroom and hid during free periods. I dreaded the words "choose a partner" in class, especially gym, where you could either pair up and scamper away or stand there alone. At home I cried. On some level, I guess, I knew that I wasn't the only lonely thirteen-year-old in the world, but how did that help, really? Instead of finding some inner source of comfort, I picked myself apart—was I too bossy? Irritating? Self-absorbed? What was it that had driven them away? *What was wrong with me?*

My parents asked why I would care so much about friends who acted this way, and suggested gently that I make new ones. In retrospect, it was good, rational advice, but I couldn't take it, not then. I couldn't see past my own flaws. I couldn't imagine that anyone would want to be my friend ever again.

I was eventually rescued from my exile by someone else's travails. Allie, a girl in my grade I didn't know well, had been close friends with two girls, Heather and Lucy, who, in the span of one summer, had grown into tall and beautiful Madonna acolytes, and knew it. Suddenly they had the attention of every boy they beckoned. This sounds like the script of a John Hughes movie, I realize, but it's true. Heather and Lucy, newly emboldened, decided to drop Allie much as my friends had dropped me—only they didn't stop there. Because they had status, they could really make her suffer. When they started calling Allie "squid," as in nerd, everyone began calling her squid. (Never mind that we went to a progressive Quaker school: in eighth grade, good grades were social death.) They sat behind her in assembly and threw bits of paper in her hair and laughed. Some of the popular boys joined in, too, one-upping each other in their efforts to make Allie miserable—and to prove their allegiance to Heather and Lucy. One group of boys, whenever they passed Allie in the hallway, would stick their thumbs and forefingers to their foreheads in the shape of an L, chanting "L, L, L—loser." Then, one day, she was walking through school alongside a boy whom she'd been friends with for a year, and as they pushed through the doors to go outside he lunged, knocking her down onto the leaf-strewn walkway. He laughed. "I was scared," Allie told me, remembering. "No one had ever done anything like that to me physically before. It was so out of nowhere. I don't remember there being people around, so it wasn't like he did it to impress anyone—it was just the two of us. I was so shocked I don't think I even said anything."

Allie's mother had the same logical response my parents did—when your supposed friends turn on you, make new ones. She convinced Allie that what was happening to her wasn't her fault; she just needed allies. She persuaded her to call me. We hadn't talked much before that, but our parents knew each other and we had plenty in common, since I was a squid who'd been dumped, too. We both remember those first hesitant moments on the phone in those late fall days of eighth grade—not what we said exactly, but the exquisite relief of connecting. We talked forever that night. "I remember going into my parents' bedroom and closing the door, and lying on their bed and twisting the phone cord between my fingers," Allie said. "It was like we were therapists for each other, talking out our situations, trusting each other to understand what was happening."

Out of some combination of survival instinct, genuine affection, and pure need, we became a unit. We sat next to each other in French class, slept at each other's houses on weekends, listened to David Bowie, and took pictures of each other, our faces expressionless and too close to the camera.

I'd like to say that we rescued each other, but that's only partly true. Just before their friendship ended, Lucy had invited Allie to a slumber party and given her a pair of jeans to wear home and keep, because that's what good girlfriends do. Post-jilting, Lucy asked for the jeans back. The problem was, Allie had gotten her period in them and stained them. When Allie returned the jeans—and on this point her mother gave her bad advice—Lucy was furious. She told all the boys what had happened, and then she and Heather paid the boy in our class with the loudest voice to walk into the lunchroom and scream, "Allie bled all over Lucy's jeans!" "We were going down those dark steps into the cafeteria, and he was ahead of me, and then as we went through the doors he yelled it at the top of his lungs," Allie remembered. "It was definitely planned. It was the peak hour for lunch, with everyone there to see and hear, and at the bottom of the steps there was a platform area, so it was as if I was standing onstage. It was just horrendous—I wanted to die. And I don't remember anybody helping me. I think I ran into the bathroom by myself."

Listening all these years later, I tried to picture myself in the lunchroom that day, next to Allie. I'm sure I was there. I'm also sure I didn't do what I wish I'd done—I didn't stand up for her. No one did. I remember feeling like I should have followed her when she ran out of the lunchroom, offering her assurance and solidarity. Yet I didn't move.

I can't claim to have been bullied, at least not like the teenagers you are going to read about in this book, but I know the feeling of watching powerful kids rip a vulnerable one apart and not knowing how to blunt their power. I have kids of my own now, and I can see the old patterns beginning to assert themselves among some of their peers. My own eighth-grade cowardice makes me want to figure out how to help other kids do better.

Today, Allie's word for that year is *raw*. "It was pretty hellish, and yes, raw, like this wound that was incredibly intense and painful," she told me. "Talking about it makes some of that creep back—that vulnerable, weak feeling, like there's something wrong with me. I have my whole life experience to tell me that's not actually true, so I know that now, but those feelings are still there. I can still tap into them."

In the course of reporting this book, I was constantly amazed by how many of the adults I talked to could access, with riveting clarity, a memory of childhood bullying. It was as if they could reach inside themselves and, almost with a sense of wonder, conjure their hurt or confused or shocked or resentful younger selves. This was true for former bullies and bystanders as well as for victims. These early experiences of cruelty were transformative no matter which role you played in the memory reel.

I was particularly struck by this when I spoke with a pair of thirty-year-olds named Adam and Brad. They knew each other from childhood. Adam remembered noticing Brad's outie belly button in the kiddie pool—that's how far back they went. Adam was a kid who tried hard but was always on the outside, the boy who would secretly rather play Barbies with someone's younger sister, the one other boys made fun of for being girlish. His father had a code word, *lamb,* that he used to signal Adam when his voice was getting too high pitched. He kept at his son to be friends with Brad and the other boys, but Adam could never convince them that he belonged, that he could be tough, that he got their jokes. They would tease him and lure him into traps: a group of boys in the neighborhood would gather, one of them would ring a girl's doorbell, and then they'd point to Adam to take the blame. He always came back for more.

One morning in tenth grade, Adam got to school early to check his grade on a precalculus exam. He'd done well. Mark, a friend of Brad's who'd also come in to check, had not. Adam felt a rare rush of superiority. Caught up in the moment, he said something like, "You'd have done better if you hadn't smoked so much weed."

Mark lost it. He dragged Adam out into the hallway and slammed him into a locker while Brad and his friends stood around, laughing. As the group walked away from Adam, Mark was still fuming. "We should kick that kid's ass," he said to his friends. And so they made a plan. A few hours later in the gym, in front of a crowd of students, Brad snuck up quietly and got down on his hands and knees behind Adam. Mark pushed Adam backward, and when he tripped over Brad, landing hard on his back, Mark pounced on him and started punching. His friends joined in. Adam tried to hit back, but it was futile, four against one. When the fight was broken up and Adam got up to limp away, a final punch leveled him from behind. "I was heaving, trying to catch my breath, trying not to cry," Adam told me. "I couldn't believe how public it was and how far they'd gone. I was just completely overwhelmed."

Adam came out after high school. Today he works as a middle school counselor on Long Island, not far from where he grew up. He's convinced that Brad and the other boys turned on him because he was gay. Not long ago, he found Brad on Facebook and asked what he remembered about their history. Brad, who has become an anthropologist in Alaska, wrote back:

> *Even now, years later, I can't understand what was going through our minds or even why we felt the need to do this. . . . I knew it was wrong, but that didn't seem to matter at the time. I remember going up to you and apologizing, in part because I knew I would be getting suspended, but also because I was really affected by the way everyone was reacting. It was only in this context that it really hit me. I had positioned myself as something of a ringleader and gave up a substantial part of "me" in the process. I began to realize later in high school how wrong I was, and I still think about it to this day.*

Many of us have had a similarly indelible experience of bullying— of being predator or prey, of taking or failing to take a side, or being humiliated or ostracized or worse. We're deeply affected by these encounters. They helped make us who we are, and the visceral memories and feelings stay with us, giving us a window we can actually see through, one that takes us right back to our childhood selves. Adam and Brad, Allie and I: we're still trying to understand what happened to us and why, and what lessons we should draw from it all, about ourselves and about other people. Why is that? What makes this particular aspect of growing up affect us so deeply?

For centuries if not forever, children have bullied each other, and for almost as long, adults have mostly ignored them. The concept that children deserve special protection—as opposed to serving as a source of cheap labor—didn't exist until the nineteenth century. At that point, child-rearing manuals began urging parents to teach their children Christian kindness, making clear, for example, that an older brother who scalded his little sister's kitten (after she used his kite to make a muff for it) was to be sternly instructed in the wrongness of his ways. Even then, though, bullying wasn't considered worthy of much comment by adults—with the exception of a few sharp-eyed novelists. Only in the fiction of the era have I found tales of bullying that read like the real-life stories we tell today. Charlotte Brontë, for example, made her readers feel Jane Eyre's misfortune by showing her cowering before a vicious older cousin: "He bullied and punished me; not two or three times in the week, not once or twice in the day, but continually: every nerve I had feared him, and every morsel of flesh on my bones shrank when he came near." A decade later, in 1857, *Tom Brown's School Days* launched a thousand British school novels with its account of eleven-year-old Tom's thrashings at the hands of a seventeen-year-old tormentor named Flashman ("Very well then; let's roast him," Flashman calls to his buddies before knocking Tom into the fireplace). Looking back on her American frontier childhood in her *Little House* books, Laura Ingalls Wilder anticipated the modern-day mean girl in her character Nellie Oleson, who wrinkled up her nose at Laura's and Mary's homemade dresses. " 'Hm!' she said. 'Country girls!' " And, "Don't you wish you had a fur cape, Laura? But your Pa couldn't buy you one. Your Pa's not a storekeeper." Laura tells us that she dared not slap Nellie, who "went away laughing."

These fictional kids—stand-ins for the real children left out of the history books—suffered their cuts, burns, and hurt feelings while the adults stood by. No teacher or parent helped Tom or sympathized with Laura. When Jane's aunt interceded, it was to lock up her niece for defending herself. Fiction reflected a cold underlying fact of life: bullying was a matter of course. A battery of sayings would arise to dismiss its significance: *Boys will be boys. Just walk away. Ignore it. Sticks and stones may break my bones but words will never hurt me.* This basic stance remained largely unchanged in America for the next hundred years: bullying was an inexorable part of life, a force of nature, and the best thing to do was to shrug it off.

And then on April 20, 1999, that bedrock principle of child rearing collapsed in this country. That morning, at 11:19, two seniors—Eric Harris and Dylan Klebold—walked into Columbine High School, in a suburb outside Denver, and opened fire on their classmates with semiautomatic weapons. When the forty-nine-minute rampage was over, twelve students and a teacher lay dead, with two dozen more students injured. It was a dreadful awakening, for many of us, to the devastation that disaffected but normal-seeming middle-class teenagers can wreak. In the aftermath, a nation that had treated bullying as a rite of passage suddenly started to rethink its indifference. Harris and Klebold weren't themselves targets of bullying (or known bullies). But when a subsequent nationwide investigation revealed that most kids who turn into school shooters have previously felt persecuted, bullied, or threatened, the lesson was driven home: to brush off bullying was to court disaster, by ignoring a deadly serious threat.

For the first time, Americans made a concerted effort to address the problem. In state capitols from California to Mississippi to West Virginia, laws were written ordering schools to come up with policies to stem bullying. Schools instituted prevention programs, with weekly announcements, occasional assemblies, and posters in the hallways. But after an initial burst of energy, this first effort never quite materialized into a national campaign. It became the province of a small group of educators and psychologists. Bullying hadn't made it onto MTV or a cereal box.

The second wave of awareness about bullying we're in the midst of now, however, has built the kind of momentum that drives issues to the top of the national agenda. This time the problem isn't just confined to schools; it's on our computer screens and phones for all to see. As the Internet became a huge part of our lives, parents faced a new set of challenges and worries. At first, we focused mostly on the danger posed by strangers. The threat of "stranger danger" seemed scariest to the parents of young children, and I count myself among them. But it turned out that while child seductions and abductions do begin online, and of course are devastating, that is exceedingly rare. Far more commonly insidious is the harassment and humdrum cruelty that kids inflict on other kids. And so, with the constant connectivity of cell phones and laptops, bullying started to feel omnipresent, inescapable. Coming home from school was no longer a refuge from torment: you could always check Facebook or Twitter to see what other kids were saying about you, and a bully could find you on IM if he missed you that day in the hall. The barbs and jeers and ganging up never stopped, and all too often, bullies were able to needle their victims under a cloak of anonymity.

The electronic incarnation of bullying also changed the equation for adults by leaving a trail. Name-calling and intimidation are not new, of course: kids have called each other *slut* and *whore* and *faggot* for, well, what seems like forever. But much of the meanness took the form of the spoken word—there and then gone, ephemeral and untraceable. On social networking sites and in text messages, by contrast, cruelty among kids is on display via printouts and screen shots. This makes bullying more lasting, more visible, more viral. The consequences have infinitely expanded. It's not just the kids who happen to be on the playground who see it—it's any of hundreds or even thousands of Facebook friends.

The Internet multiplies the risk in another way as well. Sitting at the keyboard alone instead of talking face-to-face, often shrouded in anonymity, teenagers (and adults) sometimes strike a pose and write in a kind of text-speak that's harsher than what they would dare say out loud. Stripped of tone of voice or eye contact, the meanness often hits harder than intended. Here again, the electronic trail only increases the blow's impact. Read again and again by the target, a tossed-off insult can become exponentially more painful. Girls tend to feel this particularly acutely. They spend, on average, more time social networking and send more texts—ninety a day compared to fifty for boys—which can mean more gossiping, name-calling, and hurting.

The Internet and the cell phone don't *cause* bullying on their own, though, and they haven't created a new breed of bullies, as scare-mongering headlines such as "Out of Nowhere Comes the Shadowy Cyberbully" suggest. While you can find the word *cyberbully* in the *Oxford English Dictionary,* you can't walk into your local middle or high school and observe a new and distinct creature who slinks around only online and would be harmless without her iPhone. In reality, the way kids treat each other on the Internet is merely an extension of the way they treat each other in person. The depersonalized features of technology can exacerbate the cruelty, but its roots are in the real world rather than the virtual one. Social network sites and texting are a new, amped-up venue for the gossip, exclusion, and ganging up that have always unfolded in person—and continue to do so. But bullying, wherever it takes place, isn't on the rise. It feels more pervasive only because the Web is pervasive.

What *has* exploded is our interest in the harm kids can inflict on each other. Parental concern about bullying is one strand of our hyperattention to kids in general. We are a generation that can debate forever the merits of helicopter parenting versus free-range parenting, of minute-by-minute scheduling versus benign neglect, of tae kwon do versus soccer versus swimming. Bullying plus technology sets off old alarms and new ones, a pairing practically designed to obsess us. As I worked on this book and my older son crossed the line into teenager-hood while my younger one became a tween, I had endless conversations with friends and family and experts about how to both unleash my sons and protect them. Maybe every generation of parents feels like they're making it up as they go, but for ours the technological shifts are certainly unsettling. So often it feels like we're scrambling. Is there something we should be doing that we're not? Or is the problem that we're interfering too much?

Much good has come from all the heightened awareness. It has shone a spotlight on kids who are in need of protection from cruelty—because they're gay, for example, or Muslim, or overweight. It has prompted a growing number of parents to talk to kids about the on-line risks posed not only by adult strangers but by their classmates as well. At some schools, the push to prevent bullying has intersected with the recognition that kids need to be *taught* how to treat each other right, and even how to empathize, and that character building is a community-wide project with academic as well as social benefits. It used to be that "safe schools" meant schools without guns and knives. Today parents, and school officials, too, equate safety with their children's emotional well-being.

All of this has the potential to fuel the kind of sustained and transformative effort to reduce bullying that has previously fallen short in the United States. Before 1999, no states had laws that clearly addressed bullying; now forty-nine do. If we can tackle this issue wisely and well, the benefits to our kids will be real: bullying has been linked with depression, substance abuse, poor health, delinquency, and suicide—among both victims and the bullies themselves. And if we beat it back, even incrementally, perhaps we can begin to tame some of those bigger monsters, too.

Doing this right, though, means recognizing that there is truth in the old sticks-and-stones chant: most kids *do* bounce back from cruelty at the hands of other kids. They'll remember being bullied or being a bully; they'll also learn something useful, if painful. "Children need to encounter some adversity while growing up," says Elizabeth Englander, a psychologist who is the guru of bullying prevention in Massachusetts. "Even though it's normal for adults to want to protect them from all meanness, or to rush to their defense, there's a reason why Mother Nature has promoted the existence of run-of-the-mill social cruelty between children. It's how children get the practice they need to cope successfully with the world as adults." Allie and I both got to this place. Eighth grade taught me not to take anyone's good-will for granted, and even though I failed my own test in the lunchroom that day—or maybe because I did—my experience as a whole gave me bottomless appreciation for loyalty. I wouldn't give back the pain of that year if I could. This is how Allie, who has taught middle school and still works in education, thinks about her experience: "The part I wouldn't take away was that in the end, my parents helped me see that to be cruel like that you have to feel awful inside. And then it was like, *Ohhh, I understand—they're struggling, too.* I wouldn't want my daughter to have to go through all that, but at the same time, it was transformative."

The catch, and it's a crucial one, is that a smaller number of kids involved in bullying won't recover so well. And we're not very good yet at knowing who will emerge stronger from taunting and who will be seriously harmed by it—or, God forbid, succumb to it. Meanness that leaves one kid unscathed in the long run can destroy another one. Which means that, for the sake of the vulnerable, we can't shrug it all off and say simply that what doesn't kill you makes you stronger.

Thankfully, when it comes to finding ways to address bullying, we're not starting from scratch. We've learned something in the last half century of working with and thinking about adolescents. By many measures, the kids of this generation are better off than their predecessors. Rates have fallen for teen pregnancy, smoking, alcohol abuse, drug abuse (except for marijuana), and drunk-driving fatalities. Teenagers today are less likely to commit crimes—and to commit suicide—than they were in the 1980s. They're far less criminally violent. More of them are finishing high school.

There are many complicated reasons for these positive shifts, but it's fair to say that to a degree, prevention campaigns and increased awareness have played a role. Think about drunk driving. When I was in high school, I confess, I saw taking this risk as a tiny bit cool rather than taboo. The teenage equivalent of me today would likely disagree. It's now drummed into kids' brains, long before they get their licenses, that drunk driving is socially toxic as well as stupid. Binge drinking has declined by almost 50 percent since 1980. Mass media campaigns have had a hand in this, and so have school-based programs, including an approach called social norming. The idea is that students often overestimate how much other kids drink and drive, and when they find out that it's less prevalent than they think—outlier behavior rather than the norm—they're less likely to do it themselves. One of the lessons here is that it's crucial to remind kids that bullying, too, *isn't* the norm. Everyone *doesn't* do it. Though bullying is a problem that cuts across lines of class, race, and geography, the reality is that most kids aren't directly involved—either as perpetrators or as targets. And when kids understand that concerted cruelty is the exception and not the rule, they respond: bullying drops, and students become more active about reporting it.

If real change can and has come from a concerted effort to stop bullying, there's also a risk that the search for solutions will end up doing more harm than good. This could happen in two ways.

The first is that by prying too far into the lives of teenagers, we impinge on the freedom they need to grow. We stifle development when we shut down unstructured play at recess, for example, or censor their every word online, in the name of safeguarding them from each other. We risk raising kids who don't know how to solve problems on their own, withstand adversity, or bounce back from the harsh trials life inevitably brings. Teenagers, and even young kids, *have* to have their private spaces. It's a tricky balance to strike, the line between protecting kids and policing them. But we have to keep trying to find it.

The second danger in bullying prevention is in our zeal to punish. Too often, adults attempt to fight bullying by making examples of a few kids and declaring victory. It's a natural impulse: who doesn't want to wring the neck of the thug who punches a weaker kid in the face, or the mean girl who starts a hateful gossip thread on Facebook? And when bullying is associated with a far greater harm, such as suicide, it is especially tempting to demonize the kids who seem to be at fault. Punishment, after all, is easier, and more immediately satisfying, than the longer-term labor of prevention.

But in its extreme form, the rush to punish can lead to overreaction. We can forget that kids *are* kids and shouldn't necessarily be held to the same standard of accountability as adults. In the last twenty years, scientists have shown that the adolescent brain is not fully developed. The frontal lobe, which governs impulse control and judgment, is particularly late to mature. These findings have led us to think differently about how to hold kids accountable when they commit violent crimes. The Supreme Court began relying on this neurological research in 2005, when it ended the death penalty for juvenile offenders, and invoked it again six and seven years later in barring the sentence of life without parole for most minors. But when a bullying incident blows up into a media frenzy and one teenager comes to stand for malice writ large, we lose sight of our own standard for giving kids a second chance. Instead, we indulge our primal urge for revenge.

That's in part because bullying is supposed to be clear-cut. There's a bad kid and a victim, and once you know who's who, you know whose side to be on. In our complicated world, that comes as a relief. The problem is that much of the time, when you dig into the facts and the context, stories of bullying become more complicated. Some victims retaliate, or themselves have a history of bullying or of psychological problems. Some kids (and parents) use the word *bully* when they really mean *rival* or *adversary*. Some kids who bully lack empathy not only at thirteen but at thirty-three or fifty-three; a few will grow up to be full-fledged psychopaths, and perhaps no amount of parental love will cure that. But far, far more will outgrow, and come to regret, their worst behavior. It hurts them and us to write them off as bullies and make this label the defining feature of their identities. The key is to remember that almost everyone has the capacity for empathy and decency—and to tend that seed as best as we possibly can.

This book begins with the stories of three kids—two girls and one boy—in three communities. Bullying isn't monolithic; there is no single type of experience, so I looked for people who would give me a chance to explore its different facets. Monique McClain, whom you will meet in Chapter 1, was a seventh grader in Middletown, Connecticut, when her mother finally pulled her out of school after months of taunts and exclusion, in person and online. Jacob Lasher, who arrives in Chapter 2, was a gender-bending eighth grader who sued his school in upstate New York, arguing that officials there failed to protect him from physical attacks, threats, and slurs based on his sexuality. And Flannery Mullins, whose story begins in Chapter 3, was one of six students at South Hadley High School in western Massachusetts who faced criminal charges related to bullying after the suicide of Phoebe Prince, a fifteen-year-old who'd recently emigrated from Ireland.

Understanding Monique, Jacob, and Flannery as individuals—along with the supporting casts of teenagers in their stories—matters a great deal if we want to truly make sense of what happened to them. The same is true of understanding how their families, schools, and communities function. If you zero in only on the personal flaws of the kids caught up in bullying—the bullies and the targets—you miss the way they respond to the environments they find themselves in. One of the lessons of this book is that kids often bully because they stand to gain by it, in terms of social status. Maybe they're after a laugh from another kid they want to impress, or induction into a clique; maybe they want to publicly distance themselves from a friend they sense is now seen as a loser. How can families and schools dismantle that kind of informal reward system? How do you convince kids that they can do well by doing good?

Another lesson of the book is that, for better or worse, adults play a crucial role in bullying stories. When the narrative spins out of control, it's usually not because of the errors and wrongdoing of kids. They're the originators, the first movers. But when their private screw-ups turn into public debacles, it's often because adults either did too little or too much in response. The mishandling can start with parents, teachers, or principals and can wind up drawing in the police and the courts. In Part II, I trace the escalation of Monique's, Jacob's, and Flannery's problems into community-wide wars—largely waged by adults.

Part III is about solutions. Too often, journalists (including me) focus only on crisis. I've tried here to give equal billing to successful resolutions and interventions, to what we've learned about how best to deal with and prevent bullying. We can't end bullying, of course, but we *can* take steps to diminish it. In Chapter 7, I write about the visionary psychologist in Norway who launched the first movement to stop bullying more than a generation ago—and about an American school that is successfully employing his method today. In Chapter 8, I explore a different approach, developed by the field of special education, which focuses on turning chaotic schools into calm and orderly ones and has been shown to reduce bullying as it tackles a host of other social problems. Chapter 9 is about social networking sites, the new locus of bullying and harassment. In particular I focus on Facebook, the elephant in the room, with more than twenty million American teenagers who use it for good and for ill. What does a company such as Facebook—which let me in to observe its methods—do about policing its users? What should it do?

Part IV offers guidance, advising kids, parents, and educators about where they can turn and how they can help. I also pull policy makers and big technology companies into the discussion, because if we're going to tackle the issue of bullying effectively, we all need to share the load—whereas at the moment, we're mainly asking schools to shoulder it. As I hope you'll see throughout this book, the responsibility for preventing and addressing bullying falls increasingly on teachers, counselors, administrators, the lunch line lady, the bus driver, and the playground monitor. Parents, of course, remain accountable for kids' behavior, yet we are ever more inclined to blame schools when kids behave badly, even when they're acting out online. Schools are the social institution left standing. And so, at the same time that academic expectations are rising, many schools have also been forced to take on more and more of the task of teaching students social and emotional skills.

To a degree, this makes sense. Schools *are* our remaining universal social institution. The many smart and conscientious principals, teachers, guidance counselors, and social workers I met in the course of my reporting said that in order to thrive, schools *have* to help students better manage their behavior. A school will fail if it has too many kids of unsteady character or with a need to dominate through conflict. For the sake of the institution as well as the students, it makes sense to conceive of bullying prevention, and the social and emotional learning it entails, as a school-wide project. As one of the principals in this book puts it, "We are raising these children. School has to be a place kids come to be safe, to be happy, and to learn. Being happy is what I focus on the most, because if they have that, the rest will fall into place."

As we look to schools to help solve our kids' problems, we also have to reckon with the burden this imposes. If we want schools to raise our kids along with us—refereeing their disputes on the Internet as well as on campus, teaching them the skills of conflict resolution, and enhancing their capacity for kindness—then it's on us to make sure they have the resources and the know-how to do it well.

This is easy to say and much harder to accomplish. For starters, there's the basic conundrum of teenagehood: it's the time of life when people care the most about what their peers think—but those peers can lead them in the wrong direction. Adults see this and exhort teenagers to come to them for counsel—but then often don't come through with good solutions. One of the most important markers of a successful school and community, I've found, is that kids learn how to help themselves and each other through the rough patches, and are *also* made to feel that if they bring a problem to an adult, things will get better for them, not worse. How do we—teenagers, parents, teachers, counselors, principals, police, lawmakers, Internet entrepreneurs and engineers—make that happen?

That's what this book is about. Along the way, I'll try to sort through the question that resonates most from my own childhood: why does bullying have the power to shape us—for bad, but also—if what we learn is resilience—for good?

Part I

Trouble

Chapter 1

Monique

Monique McClain wanted a new hairstyle for the first week of seventh grade.

She got the idea from her mother, Alycia, who had her long dark hair done up in a sweep over the summer, so that it lay braided smooth on one side of her head and fell in a cascade of curls down the other. Monique, who was thirteen, had her mother's long dark hair and wanted the sweep for her first week at Woodrow Wilson Middle School in Middletown, Connecticut. She thought it would look grown-up.

A friend of Alycia's who does hair came over and went to work on

Monique. When she was finished and Monique's hair was sleek and shiny, her mother snapped a photo of her daughter in profile, a stud earring in the shape of an M gleaming below the braids and a shy half smile on her face. She looked like a more glamorous version of her old jeans-and-ponytail self. Monique didn't usually like to strut, but that morning she let her curls swing on the way to the bus stop. "I was excited to go to school," she said. "I liked how my hair looked. It felt special."

But Monique's head was down when Alycia looked out of her fourth-floor apartment window that afternoon and saw her daughter walking home from the bus stop. Alycia called from the window to ask if the hairstyle had been a hit, and Monique said nothing, just shook her head. At the door she followed her mother's rules by stopping to take off her sneakers, then came inside to tell what had happened: two eighth-grade girls on her bus, Destiny and Cheyenne, had mocked her for being a "biter"—a copycat. It turned out that Destiny's cousin had gotten the same hairstyle the week before. Monique hadn't known that. Still, in Destiny's and Cheyenne's eyes, she was a biter, and biters were fair game.

The older girls, who were known for being tough, kept at it the next day. They trailed Monique when she got off the bus, walking a few steps behind her and taunting her all the way down the street and onto the grounds of her apartment complex. Monique didn't know why they cared so much about a hairstyle. She just wanted it to stop. She went to her room and called her friend Sonia. "The eighth graders are in my face on the bus and I can't take it," she said. Sonia didn't ride Monique's bus; none of her friends did. She had no one to sit with, no one who could be a buffer against Destiny and Cheyenne.

Listening, Alycia felt bad for Monique, but she figured it would blow over. It was just girls being rude; it was just a hairstyle. They'd forget the whole thing by morning. Wouldn't they?

But the next afternoon, Monique's head was hanging again: Destiny and Cheyenne had taunted her for being a biter on the way to school and on the way home. Alycia walked Monique to the bus stop in the morning, stayed to make sure Destiny and Cheyenne didn't bother her, and at noon headed to Woodrow Wilson to report that her daughter was being bullied. Alycia met with a Middletown police detective who was stationed at the middle school. He called in Monique and assistant principal Diane Niles. Niles told Monique that if the girls made fun of her again on the way home, the school would take action. Principal Charles Marqua came in for a few minutes and also assured Alycia the school would not stand for this kind of behavior. "They said they would handle it," she told me later. "That they would not tolerate those girls going after Monique like that."

And so when Alycia met Monique at the bus stop later that afternoon, she expected to hear that the ride had gone smoothly. But Monique was blank-faced and silent. When the other kids streamed away down the street, she mumbled to her mother in a low voice that the eighth graders were now calling her a snitch as well as a biter. No one—not one kid—was sticking up for her. Alycia called the police on her cell phone to make a harassment complaint. She also called Niles, handing the phone to Monique right there on the sidewalk so she could describe how the bus ride had been worse, not better, than the day before.

Niles listened sympathetically and said she would call Destiny's and Cheyenne's parents. But later she called Alycia back to say she hadn't reached the girls' parents, which meant she couldn't tell them to stay off the bus. Niles suggested that Alycia drive Monique to school the next day. Alycia, who is a home health aide trained to care for disabled patients, was working the night shift. She asked her mother, Alexa, to drive Monique in the morning. But this didn't strike Alycia as a viable long-term solution, since Alexa lived a few miles away and Alycia usually borrowed her car to get to work. And why should Monique be the one forced off the bus?

Niles told Destiny and Cheyenne to sit away from Monique on the way home that day and from then on. Over the next several days, the girls didn't do as they were told. Some afternoons they got off at the same stop as Monique and followed her home, yelling insults along the way. Smoking cigarettes at the bus stop, they blew smoke in Monique's face.

During the last week in September, principal Charles Marqua boarded the bus in the afternoon before it left school and admonished Destiny and Cheyenne to sit in the back, away from Monique. Marqua was new to the school. He hadn't had time to establish his authority, and Destiny and Cheyenne decided to test it. Telling Marqua that only her mother could tell her where to sit, Cheyenne turned her back on him and walked down the aisle. Marqua told her to behave and got off the bus. As soon as it left Woodrow Wilson and rounded the corner, the girls moved to seats right behind Monique, cursing her for snitching, and then shadowed her on the walk home from the bus stop. "We don't totally control the bus," Marqua would tell me later. "We can only do so much."

Monique didn't know what to do or where to turn. Over the weekend, she did her best to shake off the dread she felt about riding the bus. She saw her friend Sonia and a couple of other girls, and tried to make sure that the bullying didn't infect the rest of her life. "My friends weren't jumping into it," she said, talking about the trouble she was having with Destiny and Cheyenne. "I always had a lot of different friends at school. I never had a problem like this before." In fact, Monique had thrived in school, doing well in math and reading and in fifth grade even winning an academic achievement award. Signed by President Obama, it hung on a wall in her grandmother's apartment next to the invitation Alexa, a devoted Obama supporter, had gotten to the president's inauguration.

Alycia and Alexa went back to Woodrow Wilson repeatedly in September to press Niles about why Destiny and Cheyenne had been allowed to keep riding the bus and to keep sitting near Monique. Alycia suggested that the girls be suspended from the bus for a month. Niles finally said she would tell them to stay off the bus. But when they didn't listen to her and went to the bus stop anyway, it turned out that for liability reasons, the bus drivers had orders to let on any kids waiting at the bus stop. Destiny and Cheyenne kept riding and sitting where they pleased.

At last, at the end of September, the girls got a one-day in-school suspension, which they were supposed to spend in a supervised study hall, isolated from the other students. But in the afternoon, Destiny saw Monique walking by on her way to science class, and from the doorway, hissed, "You think ISS"—in-school suspension—"is gonna *stop* me?"

Back on the bus, Destiny and Cheyenne tried to provoke a showdown. Instead of sitting apart from Monique as they'd again been told to do, they stood in the aisle, berating her, as a bunch of eighth-grade boys started calling, "Fight, fight, fight!" Monique kept her face turned toward the window, putting every bit of will she had into stopping herself from crying. When the bus driver told them to sit down, Destiny and Cheyenne moved to the back and threw pens and food at Monique, persuading a few other kids to join in.

All of this behavior broke the rules for riding the bus. At the time, though, Connecticut didn't officially require schools to address bullying on the bus or at a bus stop (the law changed the following year). The administrators at Woodrow Wilson tried to help Monique, but their half measures were no match for Destiny and Cheyenne's determined meanness. At the end of September, assistant principal Niles returned the bullying complaint form that Alycia had filed weeks earlier, checking off the box saying she'd investigated the case and found that Monique was in fact the target of threats and intimidation. She recommended a mediation meeting between Monique, Destiny, and Cheyenne.

Niles meant well, but sitting all three girls down together was likely to backfire. Mediation works well when kids of equal status are having a two-way conflict, not as an antidote to bullying. Putting a victim and her bullies in a room together and asking them to make up doesn't recognize the power differential between them. Kids who bully are good at manipulating this kind of setting: they often say what adults want to hear in the moment, then retaliate later. One review of anti-bullying programs found that programs that urged peer mediation were associated with *more* victimization, not less. And if intervention isn't skillful, bullies can use it to their own destructive ends. No one had to tell Alycia this. "I said absolutely not," she told me. "It was common sense. You don't stick a child who's been bullied in a room with all these girls and expect any real change. There'll be all this fronting and pretending and then they'd walk out and say she's a snitch again." The day after Niles finished her investigation, Cheyenne blew smoke in Monique's face at the bus stop again.

After a full month of bullying, Alycia was worried about her daughter. Monique was turning inward, losing weight, and sleeping for long stretches—signs, her mother and grandmother feared, that she was depressed. When I met Monique that spring, it was hard for her to talk about the previous fall. Monique had a composed steadiness and could flash a high-wattage smile when she was pleased, but she shut down when I asked her to tell me about her experience at Woodrow Wilson. Her eyes dulled and her voice flattened. She said she didn't remember much. She avoided saying Destiny's and Cheyenne's names. "Yeah, I was crying a lot," she said, staring at the floor of her living room. "Not in front of anyone, but coming home, talking to my mom, thinking about it. At school I didn't go to the second floor where the eighth-grade classes are. I tried to stay away from them, but it didn't work." At that point, Alycia and Alexa took over telling the story, and Monique got up, went to her bedroom, and closed the door.

Thinking that an activity outside school might help, Alycia signed up Monique for a local boxing program. Monique liked it at first, but then she started to feel excluded because one of the girls on the team was turning the others against her. That girl was Brianna, the cousin of Destiny whose hairstyle Monique had been accused of imitating at the beginning of all the heartache. On one bad afternoon, Monique was drinking water when Alycia came to pick her up. A younger girl on the team whom Monique knew well playfully tapped the bottom of the cup Monique was holding, spilling water on her chin. Monique asked the girl to stop. She did it again. Monique threw the cup down and screamed, "Leave me alone!" She ran out of the gym, and by the time Alycia caught up with her, Monique was doubled over by their locked car, sobbing. "Why does everyone keep messing with me?" she asked, over and over. "I just want everyone to leave me alone!" Alycia had never seen Monique break down like that. She realized how much her daughter was holding inside, behind her blank expression and affectless speech. The next day she took Monique to see a therapist.

Alarmed, Alycia now tried everything else she could think of to stop the bullying at school. She called the mother of Monique's friend Sonia to ask if Sonia would be willing to ride the bus with Monique and sit next to her. That helped for a day or two, but then Destiny and Cheyenne complained to the bus driver that Sonia didn't belong on this bus, snapping a picture of her so they could prove it. Sonia had to go back to her own bus. Alycia tried calling the police the next day to report Destiny and Cheyenne for harassing Monique on the way home. An officer came to the house and took down the complaint but said there was nothing he could do: the girls hadn't broken any laws.

Alycia didn't know Destiny's and Cheyenne's parents, but she had a friend who knew Cheyenne's mother, and he offered to broker a meeting. "He said, 'We're going to solve this,'" Alycia remembered. She drove to Cheyenne's house, and her mother came over to the car. But she quickly got defensive, said her daughter had done nothing wrong, and threatened to have Monique suspended from the bus.

Sick with frustration, Alycia turned away. Monique would be waiting for her at home, hoping for relief, and she had none to offer.

Why do strong kids like Destiny and Cheyenne go after weaker kids like Monique?

I started asking myself this question soon after I met Monique. It also happens to be the starting point for the first research ever done on bullying, more than forty years ago. A Swedish graduate student named Dan Olweus had just finished his PhD in psychology in 1969 when he decided to study aggression and victimization among boys. At the time, few adults considered meanness among kids to be a subject worthy of academic attention, but Olweus shuttled from school to school in Stockholm and the town of Solna, asking one thousand sixth- and eighth-grade boys to tell him which of their peers started fights or teased other kids, and which kids were targets. Uncertain about the reliability of the boys' answers, he checked their responses against the impressions of their mothers and teachers. He then asked what aggressors and targets looked like: How did they talk and behave? Were they physically strong or weak? He gave the boys Rorschach-like psychological tests, and went into their homes to gather information about social status and child-rearing practices. How much education and money did the boys' parents have? How strictly did they discipline their children? Finally, Olweus collected data on the school setting and climate. Did the size of a school or a class matter? Did students' attitudes toward their teachers and their schoolwork?

With the answers he collected, Olweus could identify the form of aggression that children told him they found particularly wounding. Boys suffered most acutely when they were the targets of repeated acts of aggression over time, acts from which they felt they couldn't defend themselves. A fight between equals wasn't the problem. The real damage was done by consistent domination to inflict pain.

Olweus cemented the significance of this central finding with a definition of bullying that is still standard among academics and educators. Bullying, he said, had to satisfy three criteria: it had to be verbal or physical aggression that was repeated over time and that involved a power differential—one or more children lording their status over another. "A special thing about bullying is that kids do it even when the victim seems helpless," he told me. A onetime episode of meanness or violence could be bad in the moment, but it was the repetition and the power imbalance that were most often associated with lasting, scarring impact. Bullying, as Olweus defined it, was the behavior that constituted real abuse in the eyes of the children themselves: a serious rupture in their lives with potentially devastating consequences.

Like a lot of crucial insights in social science, it seems obvious once you lay it out, because it so closely tracks the experiences many of us have had. At the time, though, there wasn't even a word in Swedish that captured what Olweus was describing. And so he turned to an English word that dates to about 1600: *bullying.*

Which kids got caught up in bullying, though, and why? Olweus combed through his data for clues. He found that about 5 percent of the boys in his study were "pronounced bullies," and another 5 percent were "whipping boys," his term at the time for the targets. Whipping boys weren't often marked as outsiders or deviants by the way they walked or talked or dressed; instead, what they had in common was that they were physically weaker and more sensitive and anxious than other students. A parade of follow-up studies has generally confirmed his findings. Among girls, meanwhile, physical strength hasn't proved important; they typically bully by more subtle and indirect means.

The field of research Olweus launched—let's call it bullying studies—has filled out the picture from his early study. For victims, both boys and girls tend to show higher levels of insecurity, anxiety, depression, and low self-esteem than other kids. Sorting out cause and effect here is tricky—a kid's insecurity can make her an easy target, or it can be the result of being picked on. Still, there is a relationship between being bullied and having trouble making friends, to the point of isolation and rejection. One analysis of bullying in twenty-five countries found that in adolescence, victims had more health problems, poorer relationships with classmates, and higher alcohol use.

You can catch a glimpse of Monique here. Talking to a psychologist for an evaluation months after her troubles with Destiny and Cheyenne, she described herself as peaceful and passive. Asked to draw animals for a personality test, she chose small and harmless ones. "She sees birds, she sees rabbits, she sees insects, and they carry very little power or aggressive tendencies," the psychologist wrote. The significance of this? Monique "seems to identify herself much more like a prey than a predator."

Kids who bully, by contrast, have more varied profiles. This is one reason why bullying is such a stubborn problem for schools: the perpetrators aren't a monolithic group, so they don't lend themselves to a one-size-fits-all fix. I learned this from talking to Susan Swearer, a school psychologist at the University of Nebraska–Lincoln (UNL) who did her dissertation in the early 1990s on adolescent depression and conduct disorder—how depressed kids act out in violent or antisocial ways. She was interested in the intersection of two kinds of troubled behavior that are often seen as separate: being withdrawn and anxious, and lashing out aggressively. In 1997, during Swearer's first year teaching at UNL, a middle school counselor took her class and asked for help with a problem plaguing the school where she worked: bullying. "I realized she was talking about the same dynamic as conduct disorder—kids threatening and intimidating other kids," Swearer told me.

Swearer surveyed the students at the counselor's school about bullying, and asked the ones who were caught up in it questions about depression and anxiety. Her findings revealed bullies of at least two distinct types. "What I found was that some kids who bully feel fine, and other kids have very high levels of depression and anxiety," she said. "That second finding really struck the principal of this middle school. He said he'd never really thought of the kids who bully as having mental health problems. His realization allowed the counselor to make the case that if we could treat the depression, maybe we could help them stop needing to make themselves feel better by making someone else feel worse. It was an argument against suspension as the only alternative for dealing with them. I think of it as myth busting about who these bullying kids are."

As I dug into more research, a taxonomy of bullies started to come into focus. I've come up with five basic types. Let's start with the traditional bully: the thug in training. In fiction, he's familiar—Nelson in *The Simpsons,* Crabbe and Goyle in Harry Potter, Scut in *A Christmas Story.* He takes advantage of his superior strength to beat up other kids and steal their stuff. He picks you up by the scruff of your neck and plows you into a snowbank. He shakes you down for your lunch money. This type helps account for the oft-cited statistic that suggests bullies are four times more likely than other kids to become criminals. (According to Olweus, 60 percent of childhood bullies wind up with at least one conviction; between 35 and 40 percent have three or more.) Bullies are also more likely to have a drinking or drug problem, fare poorly academically, and have negative feelings about other people, school, and their lives. "Many bullies seem to continuously come into conflict with others, to run against the world," the psychologist Philip Rodkin has written.

The second type of bully is the kid who tries to act like a thug not out of malice but because he's clueless. "These kids just don't get it," Swearer told me. "Maybe they're on the autism spectrum, or maybe they're just not socially adept. They may think bullying is the way to get ahead, but they're just not very good at it." This made me think of a bumbling seventh grader I'd met who repeatedly called other kids fat without seeming to realize how unlikable this made him.

The third type of bully has more serious problems. He or she is both a bully *and* a victim. These kids experience "the worst of both worlds," as one researcher put it, in that their peers take turns rejecting them and goading them into making trouble. Bully-victims, as they're often called, tend to have deeper psychological problems than other bullies or victims, and they're more likely to consider suicide. Bully-victims are more likely to be boys, and often they harass girls.

They tend to see themselves and others negatively, perform poorly in school, and feel isolated and rejected. They're more likely to report physical or sexual abuse and conflict with their parents at home. Sometimes they have a disability, such as attention deficit disorder, that makes them a classroom irritant, alienating the kids around them and often the adults, too. Dan Olweus called bully-victims "hot tempered and generally irritating" and "often unruly and distractible." The modern gloss on this, from Elizabeth Englander, the Massachusetts research psychologist, puts these kids in a more sympathetic light. "They're not good at protecting themselves," she said. "They end up deeply involved in these behaviors, and they're victimized just as often, or more often, than other victims. The kids who only bully, who I think of as the sharks, their social functioning is much higher. They're the higher-status, higher-skilled kids. The bully-victims are not."

The fourth type of bully is the opposite of a misfit. These kids tend to score higher than their peers on tests for social cognition. They're good at reading the emotions of the people around them, and at manipulating them. They report more, not less, ease at making friends than their peers. In other words, they're popular. That's not exactly the same as being well liked; as early as preschool, kids say they don't like other kids who try to dominate by being coercive. Still, as they grow up, the fear that these kids instill can bring them power and social standing. That's what they're looking for, and they've made a rational (if unfortunate) calculation about how to get it. As one teenager I visited outside Atlanta said of the boy who taunted her relentlessly throughout middle school, "Whoever came up with the theory that kids who bully lack self-esteem was on some drug. Because the opposite is the case. He was happy with his life. His parents have money and he has the respect of a lot of people." Unlike the thugs, popular bullies are sophisticated enough to be subtle. Their methods of choice are whispered gossip, freezing out a target, or finding a minion to do their dirty work for them. As a result, kids often have a keener nose for sniffing out popular bullies than adults do.

Often girls are cast as the popular bully, in life and in the movies, but in fact most victims—boys and girls—report that they've mainly been bullied by boys. Put another way, boys tend to bully other boys *and* girls, whereas girls usually bully other girls. Boys are more likely to bully physically, and some of them are obviously trying to prove their masculinity, but they do their share of gossiping and manipulating friendships, too.

To be honest, this surprised me: it flew in the face of my own assumptions, in which the backbiting mean girl is, well, a girl. Most researchers would in fact say girls can be just as aggressive as boys—they just express their hostility differently. When academics made this point in the 1990s, it resonated: girls tend to use their highly attuned social antennae, instead of their fists, to wage war against other girls. "Girls can better understand how other girls feel," the Scandinavian psychologist Kaj Björkqvist wrote, "so they know better how to harm them." But the gender difference Björkqvist put his finger on isn't innate. Until the age of four, girls grab toys, push, and hit just as much as boys. At a certain point, social expectations to be nice drive their attacks underground.

When you look at how bullying has migrated to cyberspace, you see girls more often using technology's latest tools of social manipulation. Girls who are aggressive online tend toward "threats, blackmail, destroying friendships, gossip and rumors," according to Englander. The stupid risks boys tend to take on the Web are sexting and clumsy pranks—boneheaded, for sure, but not all that prevalent. Girls socialize more via the Internet and the phone, spend more time on social networking sites, and send and receive more text messages. No wonder they're the ones whose cyberbullying woes we tend to hear about most often.

The last type of bully, the Facebook thug, comes directly out of this new world, a product of the increasingly connected lives kids live. Many of the kids I spoke to in the course of my reporting talked about girls who tried on brasher, meaner personas online than they'd ever displayed in person. A senior from the Connecticut suburbs named Andrew told me about a girl he knows who is quiet and shy in person, and an unabashed trash-talker on Facebook. "She is totally different online," he said. "It's very strange when you see her walk down the hall, looking at the floor. It's hard to believe she's the same person." It was the students at Monique's school who taught me the term *Facebook thug* for a kid—usually a girl—who acts threatening online and meek in person. "You're all mouthy on Facebook, and then you see the person you started the beef with, and you don't want to fight them," one thirteen-year-old girl explained. "That's when people are going to be like, 'She's a Facebook thug because she's all up in your face on your wall but she's not gonna go through with it.'" Another one told me, "Everything starts on Facebook because it's easier to talk junk to someone. People get keyboard happy. They talk junk on Facebook, then someone confronts them, and they have to decide if they're a Facebook thug or if they're for real."

Monique got an unexpected reprieve at the end of October. Destiny's and Cheyenne's families moved out of Middletown, the girls left Woodrow Wilson Middle School, and just like that, Monique stopped worrying about getting on the bus or being harassed on her way home. She began reconnecting with her friends. "I felt this wave of relief," Alycia said. "It was like my daughter was back to her old self." Monique even said she wanted to go to a school dance, a sure sign of her returning confidence. It turned out, though, that she'd missed the deadline for buying a ticket. So Alycia asked Principal Marqua if he could make an exception, given the difficulties of the past two months, and let Monique buy her ticket a few days late. Marqua said no. It was a small thing, but it made Alycia seethe. Couldn't anyone at school give her daughter a break? Alycia tried not to dwell on it, though. She threw a birthday party for Monique at the local Courtyard Marriott.

"Seventeen kids came," Alycia remembered. "We rented a hall, we put up balloons, the kids swam. Monique was happy. It was maybe the only time that fall she had a big smile."

The good feeling didn't last. Destiny and Cheyenne's departure turned out to be a reprieve rather than the end of Monique's troubles. She'd started dating a boy named Jordan, and in November the relationship touched off a new round of conflict, this time with a group of seventh-grade girls. "There's an after-school program called SWAG, where you can do things like cooking and boxing," Monique said. "Jordan was in it, and all the eighth-grade girls liked him, but he didn't like them because they were bullying me. So they got mad, and they told these seventh graders who wanted to be friends with them, and then those girls"—the seventh graders—"came after me."

Suddenly Monique had a new group of tormentors who were in her classes, on her seventh-grade floor, and at her lunch period. One girl followed her down the hall, calling her a dog and a pig. Another smacked her fist against her palm in class while staring at Monique and counting down, as if for a fight. Monique reported this to Niles. She also said that a girl named Gianna was calling her a snitch.

Monique and Gianna had been friends the year before, when Gianna was new to Middletown, where she'd moved at the start of sixth grade. That year Gianna even came to Monique's birthday party. But now it looked to Monique and her mother as if Gianna and the other seventh graders were picking up where Destiny and Cheyenne had left off. "Monique comes home every day and tells me they're saying stuff, messing with her, and it was like, 'Oh no, oh please no, not again,'" Alycia said.

In mid-November, Monique fell in the doorway on her way from gym to the locker room, scraping her knee and hitting her head on the door. She told the school nurse that she thought a friend of Gianna's named Jasmine had tripped her. Jasmine denied doing anything wrong; she said Monique had been running in a game of tag and tripped. Other girls in the locker room backed up her version of the story. Jasmine admitted to laughing, but said that everyone else had laughed, too, even Monique.

Still, Alycia was sure that Monique had been tripped deliberately, and that Jasmine and the other kids were lying. Alycia's suspicions only deepened after a food fight broke out in the cafeteria on the day before Thanksgiving. Syrup was poured in Monique's hair, and a sausage and a waffle were thrown at her. Monique said that Gianna poured the syrup while another friend of hers, Aminah, threw the food. But Gianna denied it again, and none of the other kids who were there said she'd done it. (The teachers in the lunchroom hadn't seen what had happened.) A couple of kids admitted throwing food when Marqua questioned them, but they said that Monique wasn't a target. The principal repeated this to Alexa and Alycia. They didn't believe it, and, not knowing where else to turn, they called the police again.

A week before winter vacation, Alycia had a good meeting with Niles and a representative from the school district, both of whom reassured her that they wanted to help Monique. "They were saying, 'You know what, we're going to handle this. We all want this to stop,'" Alycia remembered. "There were moments when Niles got teary-eyed. I thought maybe the new year will be good."

But over the Christmas vacation, Monique got a notification on her phone that she'd received a message on MySpace. This was a surprise: she'd signed up for the site at the beginning of sixth grade to message with her friends, but she'd stopped using it after her mother found out and told her to stay off. The other kids at Woodrow Wilson had since migrated from MySpace to Facebook. Alycia didn't want her daughter on Facebook, either, so Monique didn't have an active social networking account.

She found her old MySpace password and logged on. Her last status update from the year before, "Luv my life," came up on the screen. Below it was a note from Gianna:

I fucking hate yhu with all my heart. Yhur a bitch & + I just wanna like ughh. Yhur a fucking snitch & + I just wanna like beat you the fuck up. The more yhu keep snitching on me in school the more it makes me tougher. All yhu doo is tell yhur lil ass mom like she gonna do something. Yeahh okay probably just bring me to court butt IDC [I don't care]. Keep on Imma show ya something. The more you keep snitching the more Imma keep wanting to fight yhu & + and when I doo Imma demolishing yhu, yhu H [ho].

Monique showed Gianna's message to her mother and grand-mother, who called the police, since school was out of session, and also emailed it to Niles. "This is horrible," the assistant principal wrote back. "Please let me know what the police do. I will do every-thing I can to protect her at school. I am so sorry your family has to go through this." Niles called in Gianna when school started again in January, and she admitted to sending the message. The police also came to talk to her, warning that she could face criminal charges for sending threats over the Internet. They told her not to have any more contact with Monique, in person or online.

Gianna's formal punishment, however, was mild—a one-day in-school suspension. The police asked Alycia whether she wanted the local district attorney to press harassment charges against Gianna. Alycia was about to say yes, but then hesitated. She thought of Gian-na's mother, whom she'd met the year before when their daughters had been friendly, and decided to send her a note on Facebook first, to let her know she was sorry things had turned out this way.

Gianna's mother called Alycia and asked her to reconsider. "She said the school hadn't told her anything about what was going on with Monique," Alycia told me. "It wasn't like she was apologizing, it was more like, 'I have little ones at home. I'll have to send Gianna down south to her father if it comes to this—I just can't take time off work to deal with court cases.' She kept saying, 'Just please don't press charges. I'll make sure my daughter never looks in your daughter's direction again. I'll handle it.'" Alycia was torn. She knew what it was like to be a working single mother. She decided to talk it over with Monique before calling the police back. Monique told her mother she thought they should give Gianna's mother a chance to deal with her daughter. Alycia decided not to ask the police to move ahead with the charges.

Gianna's mother yelled at her and took away her access to Facebook for a couple of weeks. The punishment, along with the police's warning, had an effect: Gianna stayed away from Monique at school. But the hassling from other girls started up again. More of them were calling her a snitch, and Monique heard they were planning to beat her up. "I got a five-minute pass, where you stay in the classroom for five extra minutes after the bell rings, so you don't have to walk in the hall with everyone," she said. She started eating lunch in the office of Melissa Robinson, a social worker for the Middletown Youth Services Bureau who worked on campus, so she wouldn't have to sit alone in the cafeteria. Her friend Sonia had been avoiding her since winter vacation.

Other girls who'd come to Monique's birthday party, less than three months earlier, also began to fall away. "That was a big shock, seeing everyone switch up on her," Alycia told me. The stress started to get to Alycia, too. On her drive to work she'd hear stories on the radio about suicides linked to bullying, and she'd have to pull over because she was crying and shaking so hard. She couldn't sleep, and so she'd get out of bed and start looking at what the kids were saying about her daughter on Facebook. The harassment had moved online, and the worst series of posts Alycia found was on the wall of a seventh grader named Davina. As a status update, Davina had written, "lol cant wait to end this cause its gone too far." Seven kids checked the box on Facebook to show they "liked" her post. The thread continued as a conversation between Davina and a girl Monique barely knew:

Other girl: lol what the hell you gonna do?

Davina: deal with problems UGLY PIG LOOKING PROBLEMS.

Other girl: is it what you told me about on the phone?

Davina: uhmm I think so bout the girl I dn't like? it's the girl
   that I threatened . . . well so she says.

Other girl: yeah that girl; & oh dam lol.

Davina: lol lk she stays talking but dnt do ishh.

Other girl: smh [shaking my head], she all talk then, if she
   hits you BEAT HER ASS!

Davina: it aint even dat she wont get no hits cause goinh up
   to her right wen I get off the bus den ima punch her in
   dah face point blank no talking what so ever.

Monique soon got a text from Davina saying that a group of girls were planning to jump her outside the cafeteria. The next morning, Monique told her mother and grandmother she didn't want to go to school. Alexa appealed one more time for help. "She is sooo depressed at this point," she wrote in an email to Niles. "Please protect my Granddaughter at school. . . . I am begging you." Niles responded by reviving her idea of mediation between Monique and the girls arrayed against her, but to Alycia, this was the opposite of helpful. It shredded her last bit of faith in the school and the district. On January 26, she pulled her daughter out of Woodrow Wilson.

At the end of 2009, I proposed a series on cyberbullying to my boss at Slate. After doing a few stories, I realized that I was writing about something quite different from what I'd imagined. Cyberbullying, it was becoming clear, was a new incarnation of an old phenomenon. The Internet was changing the nature of teenage cruelty, but I couldn't write about online bullying without writing about face-to-face bullying, too, because Facebook and other social networking sites aren't a discrete, walled-off universe. Instead, they're like planets that teenagers (and adults) visit, bringing their baggage, good and bad, along with them. Most kids who report being bullied online are also bullied in person. Kids who identify as bullies also say they operate in both spheres: they don't distinguish "when it comes to who they mistreat and where," as the researchers Sameer Hinduja and Justin Patahin told me.

What also became obvious, the more I talked to people who studied bullying, was that it wasn't a problem of suddenly epic proportions—it's a real problem, but it's not necessarily on the rise. Since Olweus' foundational work in the 1970s, most surveys in the United States and abroad have found that 10 to 25 percent of kids are involved in bullying, as perpetrators or targets or both—and these statistics have remained more or less constant. When the surveys include questions about online bullying, the numbers tend to rise, but that's generally because freewheeling questions encompassed online harassment of any sort, rather than hewing to the Olweus definition: repeated meanness by someone who has more power than her target. The bottom line is that no one knows whether the Internet has spawned more bullies.

What we do know is that for the bullies who *are* out there, going online provides a new, never-ending opportunity to make trouble. The Internet makes bullying feel like a far bigger problem than it used to be for five reasons:

1. The connectivity of the Web makes bullying harder to escape. It used to be that the end of the school day brought relief, that home was the one place where you knew you could be safe. Now kids log on when they get home, and stay online into all hours of the night. If they think other kids are talking about them on Facebook, they can't resist checking. If they find they're under attack, they can respond right away, and that can be the beginning of a vicious cycle.

2. The Web changes the experience for the attacker, too. It allows him to operate at a remove, pressing a button to send a cruel post

or mocking photo without looking his target in the eye. He can do this with the illusion of privacy and, if he's writing under a made-up handle, even anonymity. The result is that bullies gain an unfortunate measure of distance from the cruelty they're inflicting. "The Internet depersonalizes everything," Andrew, the Connecticut senior, told me. "Sitting at their computer screen, people don't think anyone can see them. It doesn't let them see that the person they're talking about is someone they see all the time in school, not a Facebook profile."

3. Then there's the audience. The number of potential witnesses to an online humiliation can be exponentially higher than for almost any face-to-face encounter. Because teenagers often have hundreds of Facebook "friends," rumors and slights can rapidly spread in a way that wasn't possible in the era of landlines. Add in friends of friends, as Facebook's privacy settings for teens automatically do, and the audience for a cruel post easily expands into the thousands. The cleverer and more cutting the insult, the more likely it is to go viral. This can happen when someone gets hold of a message that was intended to be private, too: in 2010, girls at the Connecticut prep school Choate were suspended and expelled after a months-long thread among a half dozen of them, which they were having over Facebook's internal message system, was forwarded to the whole school (probably by someone who knew one of the girls' passwords).

4. The viral nature of the Web means that with a single click, a mean thread or photo or video can be endlessly forwarded, cut and pasted, printed out. The bits of content also live on forever in digital memory. Most of the time, of course, none of this matters, because only a small circle of people are paying attention. But any post *could* go viral; the threat is always looming, whether kids realize it or not. And if that happens, it can mean ten minutes of the worst kind of fame, plus a long tail of lingering notoriety: *Are you that kid who . . . ?*

5. The Web is toughest on subgroups of kids we think of as more vulnerable—twelve- and thirteen-year-olds (as opposed to older teens), lower-income kids (as opposed to higher-income kids), black (as opposed to white), girls (as opposed to boys). In a Pew Research Center survey, more than 30 percent of twelve- and thirteen-year-old girls said that kids were mostly unkind to each other on social networking sites, significantly more than the 20 percent of teens who reported this overall. This stat was also higher for African American teens and for those whose parents earned less than $50,000 a year. The survey followed up with this intriguing question: *Have you had a bad experience online that made you nervous about going to school the next day?* More than 25 percent of twelve- and thirteen-year-old girls said yes, again a higher rate than any other group.

Another study by two Stanford researchers of about thirty-five hundred girls ages eight to twelve found that the girls who used online media heavily had fewer good feelings about their friendships than other girls their age, and more friends whom their parents considered a bad influence. The single predictor of healthy emotional interactions was lots of face-to-face communication. All told, the data suggest an unsettling digital divide: young girls in particular seem to suffer from bad online behavior, or even just tapping away too much on their screens. "Girls who spend more time interacting via a screen than in person do not get sufficient practice in observing and experiencing true emotions," one of the researchers, Clifford Nass, wrote by way of explanation. "As a result, they are less equipped to navigate the social world." He had more to say when I called him for a Slate story: "Face-to-face contact is the best way to learn to read other people's emotions. It's how kids learn empathy. So it's as if the in-person socializing is the healthy food, and Facebook is the empty calories. It's like junk food, and the more of it kids have, the less time they may have for the healthy stuff."

No wonder the Internet has amplified the impact of teenage meanness. "Bullying has the same dynamic, but it's become 24/7," says Susan Swearer. "What's increased over time is the prevalence." Swearer is the mother of two daughters who grew into teenagers as she continued her research, so she's always seen bullying through the prism of parenthood as well as psychology.

When Catherine, Swearer's older daughter, was eleven, she started lobbying for a Facebook account. Swearer told her no, she wasn't old enough. When Catherine turned thirteen, the age when it's legal to sign up on the site, she went to a slumber party where her friends set up a Facebook page for her. At this point Swearer gave in—80 percent of thirteen-year-olds are on Facebook—and tried to make sure her daughter understood the new terrain she was venturing into. "I spent a lot of time talking to her about privacy settings, what blocking meant, how defriending worked, and what good online behavior should look like," Swearer said. She friended her daughter, but didn't stop there. "I also have her password, so I can log on as her. Periodically I scroll through her text messages. People say I'm invading her privacy, but she doesn't have that kind of privacy under our roof. And since we've always done it that way, she takes it for granted. It's just part of living in our family."

Swearer sees phones and the Internet as a conduit to other people, for good and bad—not so different, in that sense, from walking down the street or going into a store—and she doesn't give Catherine more freedom in the virtual world than she would in the real one. Her rules may not be for everyone, but they have the virtue of being clear and consistent.

I've heard other approaches to monitoring that also work for particular families. One lawyer-writer I know has a "probable cause" standard for checking her daughter's phone and online accounts: if she gets wind something may be amiss, her daughter loses any entitlement to privacy and is subject to the technological equivalent of a search warrant. Another friend talks about "trust and verify": she generally assumes her kids aren't up to trouble, but periodically checks up on them to make sure. I also have friends with older teenagers who used to monitor their kids' phones and Facebook pages but have stopped. At this point, they say, they trust their teenagers to live out the values they've spent years inculcating. These aren't parents who take a laissez-faire approach to child rearing in general; to the contrary, they rely on the close relationships they've built with their kids over time rather than scrolling through a week's worth of text messages.

Often in my reporting, I asked parents whether they take the same approach to online and smart phone monitoring as other parents they know, curious about whether communities develop a shared consensus. Instead, I found that parents tend to make individual choices, which is one reason I've sketched out various approaches rather than settling on a single right answer (or, as the experts would say, best practice). There's a spectrum of alternatives, and you may try one when your son is twelve and shift to another when he's a few years older. The one thing that's clear is that it's almost always better to stay away from the far ends of the spectrum—ignoring the challenges technology poses for kids, or trying to control their every move. To state the obvious, kids need some guidance. You have to figure out how best to offer it. One way to do that is to present the issue and ask your kid what she thinks a good system would be. You don't have to do what she says, but in talking it through, you may learn something.

Of course, teenagers are not the only ones who get themselves into trouble online: adults harass and stalk and bully and humiliate themselves as well. The Web's depersonalizing features make it hard for people to empathize and control their worst impulses no matter their age, as the flame wars in online comment sections (especially if they allow anonymity) attest. But teenagers may be particularly susceptible to the pitfalls of online communication because it hits them exactly in a neurological weak spot.

Adults have despaired over the rash and callow nature of youth since at least the days of ancient Greece, when Aristotle wrote that "the young are heated by Nature as drunken men by wine." In the eighteenth century, Rousseau observed that a person on the cusp of adulthood "becomes deaf to the voice he used to obey; he is a lion in a fever; he distrusts his keeper and refuses to be controlled." But only in the last two decades has cutting-edge neuroimaging given us biological proof for what the philosophers suspected all along: it turns out that the brains of teenagers aren't fully developed yet.

The prefrontal cortex, the part of the brain that governs what's called executive function—which includes impulse control, planning, taking stock, and weighing risks versus rewards—isn't entirely mature until the early to mid-twenties. And a key part of the brain's reward circuitry—a small area called the ventral striatum, which scientists recently identified as a kind of switching station for emotional, arousal, and motivational signals—is more active in adolescence than adulthood. The upshot is that the teenage brain is much more likely than the adult brain to give in to impulse rather than to resist temptation. "There's a constant back-and-forth between the brain's control system and its reward-processing system—it's like a teeter-totter," Laurence Steinberg, a psychologist at Temple University, explained to me. "The more oomph you get from the reward system, the easier it is to overpower the system that puts the brakes on."

That doesn't mean teenagers are uniformly prone to screwing up; there's nothing uniform about adolescence. The point is that they are more likely, neurologically, to throw caution to the wind, on average, than adults are. As the science writer David Dobbs has written: "Teens take more risks not because they don't understand the dangers but because they weigh risk versus reward differently: In situations where risk can get them something they want, they value the reward more heavily than adults do."

This isn't all bad. Dobbs points out that if the teenage propensity for recklessness and thrill seeking was a total loser in evolutionary terms, natural selection would have weeded it out long ago. The makeup of the adolescent brain nudges teenagers to try new things, meet new people, and go (gulp) new places. Still, the potential risk to the individual is undeniable. The drive to seek out novelty leads to unforgettable adventures, and also bouts of binge drinking, reckless driving, and, most lethally, the two in combination.

As if these aspects of teenage neurology weren't dangerous enough, teenagers have one more weakness: they're highly influenced by their friends. Peer pressure is a real force for teenage ill, and for this, too, the developmental path the brain takes may share the blame.

Consider the results of an ingenious lab experiment conducted by Steinberg. In 2010, he and his colleagues ran lab tests on fourteen teens between the ages of fourteen and eighteen, fourteen college students, and twelve adults between the ages of twenty-four and twenty-nine. All forty subjects were hooked up to functional magnetic resonance imaging machines—fMRIs—while they played four rounds of a driving game that lasted about six minutes. They had to approach a series of intersections and, at each one, decide whether to cross. The goal was to whiz from start to finish in as little time as possible. At random points, the traffic lights at the intersections would turn yellow, forcing the players to decide whether to zoom through or brake. They could win more for beating the red light than for stopping. But if they tried to zoom through and didn't make it in time, they crashed—a bigger penalty than if they'd stopped. In other words, the game goaded the players into taking risks but tried to dissuade them from going too far.

While the fMRI machines vibrated and beeped, each player drove the course alone. Each one also drove another time while two friends of the same sex, whom they'd been asked to bring along, watched from another room. The players knew when their friends were watching and when they weren't. Steinberg found that adults and college students drove the same way, with the same degree of risk taking, whether or not their friends were watching. The fourteen- to eighteen-year-olds, on the other hand, ran more yellow lights and crashed far more often when their friends could see them. What's more, the ventral striatum and a part of the prefrontal cortex that's also associated with reward became more active when the teenagers played in front of their friends than it was when they played on their own. For only the teenagers, the presence of peers—even sitting in the next room—apparently overrode the warnings their brains would otherwise have sent out. Steinberg called this "one very plausible explanation for why adolescents do a lot of stupid things with their friends that they wouldn't do when they are by themselves."

You can apply the same science to bullying—a behavior that peaks in middle school, continues to some degree in high school, and then declines significantly in college. "To the extent teenagers think bullying will elevate their status in the eyes of their peers—the immediate reward—they may not be paying as much attention to the longer-term cost," Steinberg told me. "Bear in mind that a lot of bullying occurs in front of other kids. I think you can easily make the case that the main reason bullies bully is to get the attention and admiration of others. That explains why they're not thinking about future consequences, not only for the victim but for themselves."

Gianna has a soft voice, a gap between her two front teeth, and dimples. She wears sweatpants and tank tops with brassy jewelry: stud earrings with her mother's name in loopy cursive, big enough to cover her earlobes, and a gold necklace plate with her own name. When she moved to Connecticut from the South, the first friends she made were Aminah and Jasmine, both girls her age who grew up in Middletown and had known each other since they were small. "I was friendly," Gianna said when I asked her how she'd found a place for herself in the tumult of middle school. "Middletown seemed more city to me, but I didn't really have to change myself to make friends."

With a population of only fifty thousand, Middletown feels urban without being big. The city had its moment after the Revolutionary War, when its location on the Connecticut River, in the heart of New England, made its port nearly as important as New York's or Boston's. The town's prosperous merchants built up a brisk trade with the West Indies and then, in the nineteenth century, made Middletown central to gun manufacturing, the home of a factory that churned out ten thousand pistols a year. But that was a long time ago. The city's consequence then is hard to imagine now. Downtown today is a few unassuming blocks, an assortment of hole-in-the-wall restaurants and municipal offices. Median family income is about $60,000 a year, and only a third of the city's residents have finished college. Wesleyan University is here, supporting its quota of coffee shops, but most of the faculty either live in more upscale towns nearby or send their children to private school. This means that the demographics for the public schools are poorer than Middletown as a whole, with more than a third of the students meeting the state's definition of economically disadvantaged. About half of Woodrow Wilson's 750 students are white, one quarter are African American, and the rest are Hispanic and Asian American.

I started visiting Woodrow Wilson a month after Alycia pulled Monique out of school. I wanted to know what the school was doing to combat bullying and how Gianna and some of the other popular seventh-grade girls who had been accused of harassing Monique saw themselves. I first met Gianna in the Middletown Youth Services Bureau, which operated out of three small rooms at the end of one of Woodrow Wilson's cinder block hallways. Melissa Robinson, the social worker who'd let Monique eat lunch with her, worked there and had tried to make her windowless office a refuge from the jockeying for power in the lunchroom and hallways. She tacked notes from students along with pictures of her three-year-old daughter and her boyfriend to her bulletin board. She knew how to be warm with the kids without going soft. One day I watched her break up a fight and then scold a boy when he asked who'd won. "Nobody wins in a fight," she told him, bending to look him in the eye.

Robinson sprang Gianna and her friends Aminah and Jasmine from gym class so I could talk to them about Monique. The girls pulled up chairs, sat down, and passed around a pack of blue gum. They wore the same wide headbands, Gianna and Jasmine with ponytails, Aminah over tight brown curls. Gianna had on a black North Face jacket—the same one I'd seen Jasmine wearing earlier. Aminah explained its significance to me. "Basically it's like, the school is split up into maybe three groups of people," she said. "You've got the popular kids, the nerds, and the floaters. The popular kids, they're divided into two. Some are super cocky; others like to still be friends with people not in their arena. You can tell who's the in people and who's not that at all. It's the way we dress, the way we articulate ourselves, the way we put ourselves out there. You'll see us in North Face." Popular girls could be of any race; most but not all of Aminah and Gianna's friends were black.

Monique, in the eyes of these girls, was a floater. She didn't wear a North Face jacket. She didn't strut. Most crucially, she hadn't learned how to play the game: how to mock other kids and be mocked in return. This was the key to scaling the social heights of middle school, if that was your goal. If you wanted to be one of the popular kids in Aminah's mental chart, you had to learn to trade barbs, to give as good as you got. The girls had words for this, which they'd learned when they got to Woodrow Wilson—gunning, flaming, or cracking on someone. The eighth graders had gunned, flamed, and cracked on them at the beginning of the year, and they'd learned to do it back as a necessity. "You have to defend yourself," Gianna told me.

The gunning that Gianna was talking about reflected a pretty deep culture of combat at Woodrow Wilson. The fight I saw Robinson break up later that day was one of several during the year. The number wasn't huge, but it was high enough to be a cause for concern among the teachers and some students. Sexting had also arrived at Woodrow Wilson, with girls feeling pressured to send naked pictures of themselves to boys to prove they wanted a dating relationship. It was the latest form of combat pitting boys against girls, and somehow the boys always seemed to have the upper hand. One seventh grader had sent a shot so compromising she'd acquired a horrific school-wide nickname. Another trusted her boyfriend with a topless photo only to find he'd shown it to all the boys on his bus. These were cautionary tales, passed around among the girls, which somehow didn't quite deter others from making the same logic-defying leap.

With notable exceptions, the relationships between staff and students were also tainted by a culture of mistrust. "The teachers curse," one seventh grader told me. "They can be real rude. The drama with the kids here is just too much and the teachers have come to not care." I asked for an example, and she told me that she and some other students put their book bags into empty lockers near the cafeteria one day, only to have them dumped on the floor and then taken to the front office, where the kids had to line up to reclaim their possessions. "We all missed our bus," she said. "We were so mad. And this teacher was like, well, you should have used your *own damn lockers.*" On another visit, while I was sitting with Robinson in her office a guidance counselor came in to complain that one girl had called another "white trash." With gusto, the counselor repeated to Robinson and me the comeback she'd suggested to the girl who was bothered by the insult: "Do you know what it means to say, 'The pot is calling the kettle black'?"

The day-to-day of Woodrow Wilson replicated itself on Facebook. Just as Swearer said, the site functioned like a 24/7 parallel combat zone. Along with mean threads on their own pages—such as the one Davina started about Monique—students also signed up en masse for anonymous "voting pages" with names like "Middletown Hos," "Middletown Trash Talk," and "Middletown Too Real." The biggest page, with more than five hundred followers, was called "Let's Start Drama."

The creators of the voting pages used fake email addresses so they could stay anonymous, which violated Facebook's rules. A typical contest on "Let's Start Drama" featured two girls in suggestive poses, with the question "WHOS PRETTIERRR?!" Below the pictures, a stream of commenters would heckle and vote. Facebook founder Mark Zuckerberg would surely understand the impulse. When he was a Harvard student, he hacked into the university's computer system, copied the directory of student ID photos, and started posting pictures of two women side by side with the caption: "Who's hotter?" He called his website Facemash and invited others to join in the judging. "I almost want to put some of these faces next to pictures of farm animals and have people vote on which is more attractive," Zuckerberg wrote at the time. At least the students at Woodrow Wilson hadn't added pigs and cows to the "Let's Start Drama" mix.

A "WHOS PRETTIERRR?!" contest between Jasmine and another girl drew 109 comments over three days. When it became clear that Jasmine was losing, she wrote, "Honestly i would care that i loss bt i actionally dnt! nt even tryinqq to b funny or smart." To which her rival answered, "lol ' juss mad you losss ' ok ppl voted me ! If you really loooked better they wouldve said you but THEY DIDNT ' sooo sucks for you." Jasmine threatened to fight her but Aminah talked her out of it.

For boys, the typical "Let's Start Drama" contest was even more primal: dueling photos above the caption, "Who would win in a fight?" This was also bait. "COOL I DONT CARE ILL FIGHT ANYONE WHO HITS ME," one boy wrote under his picture. "Ndd yhu will gett yoo ass beat niggah," the boy he'd been pitted against retorted. This reportedly led to a real fight outside the school grounds one day after dismissal.

Clicking through "Let's Start Drama," I could see what Aminah and Gianna meant: to have social clout at Woodrow Wilson—to be popular rather than a floater or a nerd—you *had* to be aggressive. You couldn't afford to seem weak by backing away from a fight, verbal or physical, in school or on Facebook. When someone gunned you, you had to gun back.

For some kids, gunning wasn't a hard sell.

"Sometimes it really *is* fun," Aminah told me. "I'm not gonna lie. I see something funny, I'll say it."

Aminah stipulated, however, that you weren't supposed to crack on someone who was much weaker than you or whom you didn't know. *That* was bullying, and she disapproved of it, and she disapproved of Destiny and Cheyenne for doing it to Monique at the beginning of the year. To Aminah and her friends, the eighth graders had violated the unwritten rules in a way that made them feared but didn't earn them respect. "They were the type of people that were just bad," Aminah said. "They didn't care. I don't think their parents did, either." In her view, it was Monique's bad luck to be on the bus with eighth graders who were looking for someone to pick on. "We all thought that was dumb. They went way too far over a hairstyle. Sometimes, yeah, we all join in, like on 'Let's Start Drama' if someone puts up pictures. But not this."

The girls had a way to distinguish and justify their own meanness toward Monique: they called it drama, not bullying. The term gets lots of play among older teenagers, to whom *bullying* can sound babyish and old-fashioned. *Drama,* on the other hand, is the word for the sparks of conflict that flare up on reality TV shows such as *Jersey Shore*. For a study about teen conflict online, the researchers danah boyd and Alice Marwick interviewed high school students throughout the country and found that the kids opened up about drama, but had less to say about personal experiences of bullying or cyberbullying. *Drama* was their word for conflict that was broader and not necessarily one-way. To frame a conflict as drama was to withhold judgment, at least at the outset, about who was to blame. Drama allowed for shifting power dynamics and competition over social status. As the kids used it, the word described far more teenage conflict than

the narrower definition of bullying, with its settled hierarchy of powerful and powerless.

It was a sociologist at the University of California–Davis named
Robert Faris who helped me understand this. In 2004, Faris decided
to explore the relationship between teenagers' level of aggression and
their social status over time. He persuaded public health researchers
who were surveying thousands of high school students in several
North Carolina schools to add a question asking the kids to name
their five closest friends. Faris then used their answers to map out a
giant social network for each school. He could see which students
were at the center, based on their friendships, and where everyone else
stood in relation to them. He decided that certain kids had "elite status," as he called it, because they were varsity cheerleaders, or football
or basketball players, or homecoming or prom king or queen, or had
been chosen for yearbook awards such as "most likely to be famous"
and "most likely to succeed."

Next, Faris asked all the students to name peers who "picked on
you or were mean to you" or whom "you picked on or were mean to."
He asked whether the aggression involved physical violence, or attacks on another person's reputation, through verbal harassment, gossip, or exclusion. Faris took all the responses and, on his social
network map, located the kids identified as aggressive, either by themselves or by other students. They turned out to be about 30 percent of
the student body.

At the end of the year, Faris repeated his questions in a follow-up
survey. This allowed him to see how social positioning had changed
over time: who'd moved toward the center of the network and who'd
slid toward the periphery, who'd become an elite or a friend of an elite,
and who'd become more or less aggressive as his or her position
shifted. He found that the kids who'd advanced toward the social hub
tended to be the ones who attacked other kids' reputations. Physical
aggression didn't do the trick—but verbal harassment, rumor spread-

ing, or exclusion did. If you attacked someone else's reputation, you doubled your chances of becoming friends with an elite. And you were also more likely to move up socially if you lashed out at another kid who was close to you on the map, or close to an elite. Faris explained this, too, in terms of self-interest: "Aggression is instrumental for social climbing," he said. "But it's hard to imagine a lot of kids rising to the top based on picking on the isolated nerds. The way I think about it is this: We definitely have situations—and these are greater tragedies—of chronic torment of isolated kids. The majority of what's going on, though, is status rivalries."

In other words, drama.

Faris' insights helped me make better sense of Monique's troubles with Gianna. When I'd first asked Gianna about Monique in Melissa Robinson's office, she'd started by saying they'd been friends in sixth grade—close together on a map of Woodrow Wilson's social network. Then at the outset of seventh grade, the girls didn't hang out, but Gianna saw her as "a floater who was trying to be popular." At this point, Monique was still only a rung away on the social ladder, a near equal.

It hadn't dawned on Gianna that Monique was actually much more vulnerable. She'd misjudged Monique by failing to take into account the toll that Destiny and Cheyenne's bullying had taken on her, how it had left Monique depressed and unsure of herself. She didn't see that Monique was a girl who wouldn't be able to fight back. The problem was that once a kid like Gianna used aggression to advance her own social standing, she could wind up crushing her target.

In Gianna and her friends' eyes, Monique had made a few crucial mistakes. The first was trusting Jordan, her boyfriend. "He put Monique in a lot of drama," Gianna said. "He was trying to help her, but he made things worse." Jordan ferried insults back and forth between Monique and the other girls who liked him, Gianna said. And this led to Monique's second, bigger failing: she'd reported all these minor conflicts to the adults at school. "She'd snitch about *everything*,"

Gianna said, and Aminah and Jasmine agreed. The code at Woodrow Wilson was to report major blow-ups, not the smaller stuff. Monique had violated that rule.

But the biggest mistake of all, Aminah and Jasmine said, was that Monique had gotten it wrong when she accused them. "She just made stuff up," Aminah said. "I'd never had a problem with her before. Then there was that food fight and she got syrup in her hair, and this boy threw something that stuck in it. I thought, I'd want someone to take that out of *my* hair. So I did. The next thing I know, I'm being called into the office for throwing something in her hair." Questioned about the food fight, Aminah owned up to laughing at Monique. "If the principal asks me, and I did it, I'm gonna say that," she said. Aminah's perception of herself as honest made her angrier that Monique hadn't believed her. "Don't accuse me when I didn't do it. That's the thing that makes me mad. I got detention and missed basketball and the school dance because of her."

Jasmine harbored resentment, too. When Monique accused her of tripping her in the hallway, school officials investigated and then cleared Jasmine. Frustrated by what she saw as the school's unwillingness to act, Alycia called the police. A policeman came to Jasmine's house and knocked on her door when she was home alone. "He said, 'Do you know why I'm here?' I said no. He said, 'Are you sure you haven't been tripping people?'" The officer, she said, warned her that if Monique committed suicide, it would be her fault.

All the girls rebelled strongly against this idea. "If she killed herself, it would be her own insecure problem," Aminah said.

I flinched at this: it sounded so coldhearted. The scariest aspect of bullying is the utter lack of empathy. "Kids say, 'He deserved it' or 'Other kids started it,'" Dan Olweus told me. "They are making it easier for themselves." Olweus said the excuse making can involve a chilling cognitive shift: they come to see the victim as worthless. For a small number of kids who bully, this is a harbinger of worse to come. The inability to feel empathy is the hallmark of a psychopath—

someone who can inflict pain without feeling an ounce of compassion or remorse. But true inability to feel empathy, luckily, is exceedingly rare. Most kids, including Aminah, are pitiless one moment, then soften the next.

"I feel like Monique was just depressed, because she didn't have a lot of friends," Aminah told me in a more reflective moment. "She had some friends, but not as much as in sixth grade. I could see that she'd walk in the hallways with her head down." The problem wasn't that Aminah had no compassion for Monique. It was that she didn't act on that compassion; she did what it took to maintain her status. As Susan Swearer puts it, "In some schools, there's a lot of value in bullying others."

The key word in that sentence is *some*. It's a reminder that the culture of a school plays an important role in the social choices students make. This is another finding of social science that's obvious once you think about it. School culture (also called climate) is about how calm and orderly the classrooms and hallways and cafeteria are, how well the staff treats each other, and how much respect students feel they get on campus. In an environment such as Woodrow Wilson, where conflict was frequently in the air, Aminah and Gianna had more reason to steel themselves against feeling compassion for a weaker girl such as Monique. Plenty of people around them were doing this too, in ways large and small. Their behavior didn't stand out; it wasn't surprising.

It was also no surprise that most students at Woodrow Wilson were allergic to snitching: they could see that when kids *did* report bullying, the situation often worsened for them. This is sadly true for the majority of students who tell an adult at school they've been bullied, according to their own reports in surveys. Only at schools that have a real handle on bullying and drama does telling an adult seem to help.

Monique had lost faith that Woodrow Wilson could be such a place. "I don't want to go back to that school," she said that spring. "I just want to start over."

Chapter 2

Jacob

WHEN JACOB LASHER REALIZED HIS CRUSHES ON BOYS WEREN'T going away anytime soon, he went to his room, logged on to his computer, and took an online quiz called "Are You Gay?" It asked him to name his favorite sport (tennis, basketball, football, ice skating) and his favorite movie (*The Godfather, Rambo, Brokeback Mountain, Say Anything*). It asked him whether he thought fuchsia was "OMG, like the best color ever" and whether he went to the ballet. Jacob, who was eleven, decided that the quiz was dumb by the time he finished. Also, that he already knew the answer.

Gay teens often report feeling the first spark of same-sex attraction between the ages of nine and twelve but tend not to identify as gay until they're around fourteen, if not older. But Jacob had a sixteen-year-old sister, Tiffany, who had recently come out, and she helped him make sense of his own feelings. "My sister said she liked girls," Jacob remembered. "I was like, I don't like girls. I *wish* I did, but I like guys."

Jacob found videos on YouTube that offered advice about how to talk to his parents about his sexuality. Though his mother and father had accepted Tiffany's declaration, he wasn't sure if they'd do the same for him, since he was only in sixth grade and a boy. Jacob's mother, Penny, and his father, Robbie, had split up when he was four, so he told them separately. Penny wasn't surprised; Jacob had always been feminine as a kid, and she'd long ago made her peace with that. She hugged Jacob and told him she loved him the way he was. Robbie, though, wondered if his son was imitating his sister. By the time Jacob was thirteen, his dad acted like he'd forgotten about the whole thing. So Jacob had to come out to his father again: *Dad, I'm gay. I really mean it.*

At that point, Jacob was living with Robbie, Tiffany, and his stepmother in a trailer next to a creek in the town of Mohawk, New York. Robbie had previously worked at a meatpacking plant and as a bus driver, but a few years earlier he'd been diagnosed with Hodgkin's lymphoma and had to leave his job. (Later he developed a brain tumor.) The family was surviving on welfare, child support payments from Jacob's mother, and his stepmother's earnings at a bar. When the creek next to their trailer flooded in June 2006, the family moved to the nearby town of Utica, and for the year of seventh grade Robbie drove Jacob every day to Mohawk's combination junior and senior high school. The four hundred students came not just from Mohawk but also from the dozens of square miles of surrounding valley and foothills southwest of the Adirondacks. Halfway between Albany and Syracuse, the land there is mostly open country, dotted with woods, streams, and meadows. It's a place that feels more Midwest than East Coast, and a little slow-moving: in downtown Mohawk, one quarter buys an hour and twelve minutes of parking. Jacob and plenty of his classmates had parents who'd grown up nearby, and almost all of them were white, with about a third low-income enough to qualify for free or reduced-cost lunches.

Jacob was nervous about going to junior high in Mohawk because most of his friends lived in the neighboring town of Ilion. A few teachers at the school there were openly gay, but not so at Mohawk, where the climate was less forgiving. "Speak normally," one teacher chided him when his voice slid into a higher register. "You don't have to put on a show."

Kids called him "bitch" and "pussy" in the hallways. They said his voice was gay and that he should get a sex change operation because he was so girly. To Jacob, this made no sense. He didn't want to be a girl; he just wanted to be himself.

Jacob didn't see why he had to act like everyone else, and he didn't like the name-calling, either. His father called the principal, Edward Rinaldo, to complain, listing the slurs Jacob was hearing. Rinaldo didn't follow up right away, and at first Robbie didn't press it. He hoped the kids would tire of harassing his son on their own and move on. Instead, Jacob started finding notes taped to his locker with "fag" or "pussy" scrawled on them. Then near the end of the school year, a group of boys ganged up on him while he was changing in the locker room after gym class. Loud enough for the whole class to hear, they accused him of jerking off to gay porn. Jacob tried not to make eye contact. "I'm afraid of the locker room to this day," he told me.

When he came home, he was ashamed to tell Robbie what had happened, so his friend Alyssa told his dad for him. Robbie drove over to the school and reported the incident to Rinaldo in person. When he didn't hear from Rinaldo again, Jacob's father called the principal to ask what was going on. Rinaldo said he'd spoken to the students involved but they'd denied the taunting, so he hadn't punished them. "I interviewed kids who were in the locker room, but it was tough to have concrete evidence because there weren't adults who'd seen it," Rinaldo told me.

A few weeks later, an older student grabbed Jacob's iPod, threw it to the floor, and stomped on it. Robbie came in again to talk to Rinaldo. "The principal said, 'It'll all blow over soon, we'll take care of it,'" Robbie told me later. "He just didn't see too much wrong with it." Rinaldo said he *did* care about helping Jacob, but the reports of bullying were hard to prove. "Things would happen when he was going from one classroom to another, when no teachers or adults could see. The building had four floors and five or six stairways and there were a lot of places teachers couldn't see from their doors. Cameras in the school would have really helped, but we didn't have them. I was the only administrator—I didn't have an assistant principal."

The low-level harassment continued, and by eighth grade Jacob gave up trying to keep his sexuality to himself; instead, he experimented with self-expression. He covered the walls of his room with posters of Pink, the pop star. He started dyeing his hair purple, then pink, then a rainbow of colors. Some days he wore eyeliner or nail polish. "My mom always says, 'Don't give in to pressure, don't let them bring you down,'" Jacob told me. "She has that attitude: she doesn't care what anyone thinks. That's how I am, too. I was just going to keep doing my thing." Jacob had friends in Ilion who appreciated his flamboyance, and at school he had Alyssa, who considered herself bisexual, though she didn't talk about it to people she didn't know well. He also had his sister, Tiffany, who by now was living with their mother about thirty miles away.

Other students at Mohawk, however, were less forgiving. They took Jacob's hair and makeup as a provocation. "Jacob would go up to random people and give them a hug or high-five them, and they just didn't think he should be that way, since he's a guy," Alyssa said. "It got under their skin." A series of disturbing incidents unfolded. In history class, a student shoved Jacob and called him a faggot. Jacob, who was bigger, responded by putting the kid in a choke hold. A few days later, a boy grabbed Jacob's cell phone and stepped on it, breaking it. In October, Jacob went to his gym locker to find his clothes and shoes gone. They had been thrown in a trash can, and the word "faggot" and the phrase "I hope you die" had been scrawled on his shoes. Robbie went once more to Rinaldo; he says the principal told him that he couldn't "babysit" every student. (In Jacob's school file, a handwritten note next to this allegation states, "Not true.") Searching for practical solutions, Robbie asked for changes in Jacob's class schedule, so that he could stay away from the boys who were harassing him most. Eventually a couple of changes were made, but because of Mohawk's small size, Jacob was still stuck in classes such as Spanish with kids who were cruel to him.

By late fall, things were getting out of hand. Jacob was getting text messages from numbers he didn't recognize and anonymous calls to his house. Like a lot of Mohawk students, he had a MySpace account at the time, and dozens of kids he didn't know were sending him friend requests. "They seemed to want to know everything about me," he said. "Sometimes I'd be like, 'Who *are* you?'" Maybe if he came out publicly, he figured, everyone would move on. So in November, Jacob decided to explain himself on MySpace; he thought this would dispel the rumors and make it clear that he wasn't ashamed. Maybe people would just leave him alone.

"I was mad, and I was trying to be myself," he says. "I thought, 'Okay, if you want to be in my business, here it is.'" He changed his sexual orientation on the site from "not sure" to "gay," and posted a message on his wall that was frank, unapologetic, and, for a thirteen-year-old in Mohawk, dangerous:

Hey guys!
I'm gay.
Yes, it's true, OH MEE GAWD
yes, all the rumors are true

I like buttsex all night long
i think every guy is soooo hot.
I hate girls, they are sooo icky
Why am I even a Christain, GOD HATES FAGS Remember?!
I should hate myself for being gay
Fags go to hell
GOT HATES FAGS!
I like all men.
I do
It's true!
I like having fun on cam.
It's soo fun.
i like flirting with all guys.
And making out with every guy that walks down the school
hall. . . .

You know what?
I AM SO FREAKING TIRED OF HEARING THAT
Yes, I am gay.
So what?
I don't like girls like that.
I like girls as friends.
I dont think that every guy is cute or hot.
I don't want to make out with every single guy on earth.
I dont want to have buttsex every second of the day.

OKAY.

I am so sick of the labels you put on me, because I AM GAY!
YES, I AM GAY!
A BIG FLAMIN HOMOSEXUAL.
I LIKE MEN

GET OVER IT.
I am not going to flirt with you.
I don't like to flirt with anyone.
I am just me
LABELS ARE FOR CANS.
Leave the stereotypes out of this.
I've lost a few friends because, I am gay.
WHAT THE HELL!?
What is the reason for this?
People say:
GOD WANTS US TO MAKE BABIES!

The world is overpopulated
DONT TALK CRAP TO ME.
God, ignorance.

I won't stop being gay.
So bleh
i will always be gay
I don't care.

God will not be like,
"Jacob, you donated to charites, barely sinned, always prayed,
helped your friends, etc. UH OH!
YOU *are* GAY!
I'm sending you to hell."

My god, that I pray to, isn't like that.

GOD. IS NOT LIKE THAT.
The one I pray to, is not that cruel.
Stop with the labels.

Jacob showed me this post on his laptop three years after he'd written it. He'd moved in with his mother, Penny, about thirty miles north of Mohawk, in a small ranch house on a quiet road lined with pine, birch, and maple trees. The house number was painted on a yellow board tacked next to the door, along with Penny's name and a series of red hearts. Penny was at her cousin's house next door when I drove up, so Jacob padded off in bare feet to get her. He was wearing a gray zip-up hoodie, gym shorts, and eyeliner. His short hair was brown. It wasn't a rainbow day, he said.

A few minutes later Penny came over with her three-year-old niece, who drank chocolate milk and promptly fell asleep on the sofa. We sat at the kitchen table, and I asked Jacob about the reaction at school to his MySpace post. "It exploded," he said. "I was like a celebrity at school, and at other schools, too. Everyone knew who I was and where I came from. I felt like Britney Spears. Everyone knew my every move. I was doing YouTube videos, talking about being gay or just saying random things, and I had thousands of views. One boy at Mohawk came up to me and said, 'You're an inspiration for being who you are.' I was like, 'Aw, that's sweet,' and he asked to hang out, and then when Alyssa and I went to meet him he came up with a friend and a video camera and they were like, 'Oh ha ha, you suck.'"

Other kids told Jacob that his hair and makeup were stupid, and they spread rumors that he was giving oral sex to other male students. At lunch, they peeled bananas and sucked on them. "Kids smushed food on him and the cafeteria aide wouldn't do anything about it," Penny told me. "I went to school, I was in a rage, but it kept going on and on."

When I was growing up in the 1980s, boys learned early and often that it was not okay to act girly. When they flirted with crossing a gender boundary, they got called a fag. The slur was so common that it could seem meaningless, the generic word boys used to belittle each other. We took the word *fag* for granted without questioning the right or wrong of it, as rotten as that sounds. Jacob, by contrast, is part of a different generation, one that's caught between the closet and acceptance. Kids like Jacob can go online and get a message of celebration and support from Pink and Lady Gaga, only to be slammed by rejection when they try to translate it to their own lives.

In this in-between moment, teenagers who are gay, or thought to be gay, still come in for more abuse in school than other kids. A 2009 national survey found that 85 percent of kids who identify as LGBT said they'd been verbally harassed at school; 40 percent had been physically harassed, and nearly 20 percent had been physically *assaulted* because of their sexual orientation. The rate of harassment online is also higher for kids who are pegged as gay than for kids who are not.

The words do damage along with the assaults. Boys who are the targets of this kind of taunting have higher levels of anxiety and depression. For girls, being taunted as a lesbian is linked to social withdrawal. Students who are harassed because of their sexual identity miss substantially more school and, in one study, earned lower grades. Other research has shown that they drink and take drugs more often and are less likely to use condoms when they have sex. "The risk of HIV infection is an effect of school victimization that lasts into adulthood," said Caitlin Ryan of the Family Acceptance Project at San Francisco State University. "Schools that allow LGBT youth to be victimized are shirking their responsibility to protect these kids against future as well as present harm." In a study of young gay adults between the ages of twenty-one and twenty-five, the ones who reported being bullied frequently in middle school and high school were more than five times more likely to say they'd attempted suicide than the ones who hadn't been victimized. And a study in Oregon showed, not surprisingly, that gay teenagers who were raised in a supportive community were significantly *less* likely to try suicide than those who were not.

The important distinction here is that it's not coming out as gay but the damning social response this can elicit that increases the chances a kid will feel pushed to the edge of despair. Indeed, at his lowest points, Jacob said, he was "the most depressed kid in the world." He spent hours in his room writing songs and poems. "That's how I deal with sadness," he told me.

Jacob didn't become suicidal, though. We have to hold two ideas about gay teenagers in our minds at once: they're more at risk, and yet most of them will be okay. Parents make all the difference, says Dorothy Espelage, a professor of child development at the University of Illinois who is one of the leading researchers on the school experiences of gay youth. "Kids who have good communication with their parents, about their gay identity but also in general, show less depression and anxiety," Espelage told me. "It's clear that parental support has a crucial buffering effect." Ryan published a study in 2010 showing that gay kids with supportive families are far more hopeful about their futures, and far less likely than other gay kids to attempt or commit suicide, become depressed, abuse drugs or alcohol, or risk HIV infection. As she put it, family acceptance in adolescence had a "lasting, dramatically protective influence." The risks rise, on the other hand, when parents condemn or blame their gay children, or—in the name of protecting them from what they imagine will be a difficult lifestyle—forbid them from having gay friends. Like gay kids who are victimized in school, gay kids who feel rejected at home are more likely to drink and take drugs and to have sex without a condom, or with multiple partners. In this sense, Jacob was very lucky: he had his family's support.

Obviously, it takes some families time to get to this place of acceptance, but Ryan says that's okay: what matters is that LGBT kids see their parents trying, and eventually coming through for them. I thought about that when I went to visit Marina, a sixteen-year-old who got in touch with me when she learned I wanted to talk to gay teenagers for this book. Marina lived in the Atlanta suburb of Marietta, Georgia, and she was taunted beginning in sixth grade. "I had my hair cut short, I wore my older brother's hand-me-downs, and I was reading ninja comics," she said. "Kids called me 'Marina the man.' They said, 'Go shave your mustache,' even though I didn't have one. They would make fun of me in school and at the Dunkin' Donuts where we all went in the afternoon."

At the time, Marina didn't even know the word *lesbian*. When someone put a note with "go faggot die" in her locker, she tore it up without telling anyone. Her parents were immigrants from Moldova, and she had a lot of reasons for keeping the ugliness in school to herself. "It's not that my parents are homophobic, but where they come from, it's not spoken of," she told me. "I didn't want to seem weak to them. It was some really messed-up character building—that's how I thought of it. If people don't like the way I walked, then I'll walk differently. If someone was making fun of me, it was my fault. I never thought if I told my parents, it would stop."

Instead, Marina relied on a small circle of friends for support, especially the boy who was her best friend. "He was the one who was a lock, who would be there for the rest of my life," she said. "Then in eighth grade, I got confused. I thought maybe I felt something more for him. So we decided to try going out, even though I was also saying to him, 'I think I want to make out with girls.' I knew that, but I was also extremely scared—he was the only one I told, and I was also praying to God to take the feelings away." That summer, Marina had her first kiss with another girl at overnight camp. She told her best friend/"boyfriend," and he understood. "We had an official 'breakup' on Facebook," she said, using air quotes. "We stayed best friends."

We were talking in Marina's parents' gleaming kitchen, sitting on bar stools at a granite counter. Marina's father, a computer programmer, sat quietly nearby, tapping away on his keyboard. Her mother served us green tea with lacy cookies. "Marina knew to keep things inside," she told me. "She's not holding a lot of stuff outside her. You cannot read that. Inside, God knows what is going on. She never mentioned that she was not happy in some situations in school."

Marina told her mother about her overnight-camp kiss on the way home from the airport, but for a couple of years, her mother talked about her daughter's homosexuality as a phase. "You'll grow out of it," she would say. Her father wasn't comfortable discussing the subject at all. They kept it a secret from Marina's grandparents.

Marina's mother suggested a switch from public school to a private Jewish school in ninth grade, not because of the bullying, but because she'd heard about drugs and dissolute rich kids at the local high school and felt nervous about sending her daughter there. At first Marina resisted the move. In spite of the harassment, she didn't want to leave the friends who'd given her so much support. But at her new school, she came out and found herself becoming something of an activist. "If anyone has an issue with sexuality, I'm the person they come talk to," she said of her fellow students. The Anti-Defamation League launched a group at school to combat harassment that Marina helped lead. She made a moving YouTube video that was featured on local television, and she started going to gay pride youth events in Atlanta. Through Facebook, she met girls interested in dating and even brought one home for dinner. That was when she knew her family believed that she would find her way. "If you're a gay kid and your parents don't accept you, you think the world won't," she said.

Jacob kept the first episode of violence at school from his parents. He was pushed down the school stairs in November, and he fell without seeing who'd done it. He came home that afternoon, limping. Like Marina, he was embarrassed. "I wanted to cover it up," he said. "And I didn't think they could do anything about it." That night, when the pain in his ankle didn't go away, he called his father and said he'd hurt himself falling. Robbie took Jacob to the hospital. The ankle was badly sprained: Jacob got a cast and crutches, and when his father pressed him on how it happened, Jacob came clean.

He was still on crutches a few weeks later when a fellow eighth grader named Aaron tried to trip him in the hallway. Two teachers and a group of students were watching, but only Jacob's friend Alyssa tried to intervene. Robbie reported the tripping to Rinaldo, who suggested Jacob use the school elevator while he was recovering.

Aaron was Jacob's nemesis. "It's Adam and Eve, not Adam and Steve!" he would yell, for everyone to hear, when he saw Jacob in the lunchroom. To Aaron, these insults were just the latest salvos in a long-running battle that was very much mutual. "It started at the beginning of seventh grade when me and my friend were talking about gay marriage, and I said I wasn't comfortable with it," Aaron told me. "Jacob overheard us and got mad. He decided to sit there and harass me over what I'd said. Then in eighth grade, every time he got a new boyfriend, he'd tell me, 'Oh I guess you're not *comfortable* with it.' He made all these little comments."

The boys had a run-in in the lunchroom soon after Jacob got off his crutches. Jacob's version of the story is that Aaron said he was glad Robbie had cancer and continued, "Since your dad's probably a faggot like you are, why don't I go suck him off?" Aaron's version: "We were in the lunchroom and my friend made a joke, the same one we'd been making: 'It's Adam and Eve, not Adam and Steve.' We'd said it lots of times, but this time Jacob just started yelling." One thing is for sure: a fight broke out, and Jacob punched Aaron in the face. Both were sent to the principal's office and told to write down what they'd done. Jacob's handwritten note reads, "Yes I punched him on his left side of his face, but he is always starting trouble, and I wanted it to end, 'cause nobody here has been doing anything about Aaron." Jacob got a one-day in-school suspension and a five-day detention. Aaron also got detention, and instead of staying after school, the boys were ordered to eat lunch together for a week, just the two of them, in a classroom. "The principal told us to talk to each other," Jacob said.

"But we'd either be quiet or we'd talk crap to each other. We hated each other even more by the end."

For Aaron, eating with Jacob was irritating—who wants to spend five lunch periods with someone you can't stand?—and also embarrassing. Some kids, especially his football and wrestling teammates, were quick to pounce on the idea that Aaron and Jacob were now a pair, a couple. "He has to hear, 'So you're going on a date with your *boyfriend* today for lunch?'" Aaron's mother, Kimberly, told me. "People said it was terrible for Jacob to eat lunch with his perpetrator. But what about *my* son—what about that?"

Over that winter, Aaron's grades sank. He struggled to balance sports and his schoolwork, and in the end he failed enough classes to have to repeat the year. His record was also pockmarked with suspensions as he and Jacob continued to spar, even after the week of eating lunch together. Aaron's parents felt Jacob was more to blame for the ongoing conflict, not less. "Before Jacob came to school in sixth grade, the only trouble Aaron got into was a detention for getting into a Magic Marker war with a friend and for throwing an apple in the library," Kimberly said. "All the bad stuff that got him in trouble in school was between him and Jacob." We were having coffee at Denny's with Kimberly's husband, Tom, who owns a local salvage yard. They'd grown up in the Mohawk valley and had a cabin in the Adirondacks where they loved taking Aaron and his younger sister to hunt and fish on weekends.

Aaron has always been big for his age, and before he started wrestling and playing football, he got teased about his weight. "His whole life, he's been called 'fat boy' and 'Pillsbury,'" Kimberly said. In the cafeteria at school, kids dumped milk into his backpack. Jacob's friend Alyssa, who went to elementary school with Aaron, remembered Aaron getting pummeled as well as mocked. "There was a kid who constantly hit Aaron and called him all kind of names," she told me. "I think that was part of it for him, why he was always saying stuff to Jacob."

Aaron's parents dismissed this idea. They thought he'd learned to let the name-calling roll off him. "My son got to the point he could go with it," Tom said. "He got a T-shirt with the Pillsbury Doughboy on it that says 'Poke me.'" Aaron also minimized the bullying. "I slimmed down when I started playing sports, and anyway, everyone gets picked on. Kids are always saying, 'Let's fool with this other kid.' It's stupid stuff, just people trying to find ways to make themselves feel better."

Kids like Aaron are the ones who are called bully-victims in the psych literature, and as a group, they are considered especially high-risk for a host of problems, from low grades to depression and suicide. Sometimes they lash out because they're frustrated over how they're being treated, and sometimes they're trying to change how other kids see them, to make it clear they don't exist only to be picked on. As Alyssa put it, "Aaron didn't want to be the kid who took shit all the time."

Aaron's past probably helped explain his behavior toward Jacob, and so did their history of mutual antagonism. Philip Rodkin, a researcher at the University of Illinois at Urbana–Champaign, argues that patterns of "reciprocated dislike and animosity" between bullies and their victims don't get as much attention as they should. They don't fit with the idea that bullies are entirely culpable and victims entirely innocent. And yet, Rodkin has found, kids who bully tend to pick as targets the kids they don't like: "low-status peers whom they already dislike, and who dislike them." Sometimes the kids doing the bullying trump up a provocation, but often the conflict starts for a reason that feels real to them. This was true of Gianna and Aminah's behavior toward Monique as well as Aaron's toward Jacob. In other words, the conflict usually does not emerge from nowhere.

When a relationship is built on mutual acrimony, it's hard for parents of the teenager who is dominating, or the kid himself, to recognize when it's shifted from a fight between equals to bullying. That rift in perception ran deep for Kimberly and Tom because their son, not Jacob, had the backing of his school and his town. With his eye makeup, rainbow hair, and incendiary online presence, Jacob flouted all the local norms for boys. In Mohawk, no teachers were openly gay, and only a few other kids, including his sister, had come out—"and we were quiet about it," Tiffany said. Several Mohawk teachers had gone to school with Kimberly, and she says they complained to her that Jacob was getting away with violating the classroom dress code, which barred students from posing a distraction. When Aaron was eventually suspended for bullying Jacob, his teammates clapped for him when he returned to school. For Kimberly and Tom, this was proof that Jacob was exaggerating to manipulate his way out of getting in trouble himself.

"It's a tight-knit school," Tom said. "I find it hard to believe, if a kid was really getting picked on, that the other kids wouldn't have stood up for him."

Aaron and his parents were careful to say that Aaron didn't have a problem with Jacob because he was gay. It was Jacob's insistent, in-your-face self-expression that pushed Aaron over the brink and made him feel like he had to assert his own masculinity. "Look, you don't go to school with a bunch of farmer kids in the country, put makeup on, and expect to have nothing happen to you," Aaron said. He sighed. "Just act like normal people."

Robbie met again with Rinaldo in November of Jacob's eighth-grade year to try to work out a plan for protecting his son. He didn't want to see Jacob get hurt, or lash out in response to a provocation and get punished. The principal agreed to let Jacob use his cell phone during school to call home if he needed help, and he designated a conference room next to his office as a "safe room" where Jacob could go if he felt threatened. But Rinaldo didn't tell his staff about these accommodations, and teachers immediately took away Jacob's phone and didn't let him go to the safe room.

"I didn't notify the staff well enough, and that's one of the big regrets I have," Rinaldo told me. "In hindsight, I wish I'd sat around the table with all of Jacob's teachers to discuss a plan. I should have put it out to them."

Still, for a time, things calmed down for Jacob. He had a few weeks of relative peace. The punch he had thrown at Aaron seemed to do some good. "Everyone cooled it with him after that," Alyssa said. "Once you get into a fight in school, people know to back off."

But it didn't last. In December, Jacob started dating a boy at Mohawk for the first time. They weren't obvious about it, but they didn't go around denying it, either, and the relationship caused ripples of disapproval. A group of boys pushed Jacob on the school stairs, nearly causing him to fall over the railing. This time Jacob knew who pushed him, and he told the principal. Rinaldo called in the boys and gave them detention. Jacob's family protested that detention wasn't a sufficient consequence for pushing him down the stairs. "The principal said Jacob was going through a sexual identity crisis because he was wearing eyeliner. I couldn't understand that. Why was it a *crisis*?" Tiffany said. "It didn't seem to matter what we said. Those kids pushed Jacob down the stairs, and the principal just gave them detention. I'm not saying kick the kids out of school forever, but get something done."

A grim pattern emerged. Jacob would get hassled. (Two jeers he remembers from technology class: "Lose the makeup, lift weights, lose the faggot voice, and start liking girls," and "You're a disgrace to the human race. Do the world a favor and die because no one would miss you.") Then he'd tell his father, who'd come to school, demand Rinaldo take action, and see no results. Jacob would get hassled again, and the cycle would repeat itself.

Jacob and Robbie remembered a meeting in March in which Rinaldo said, "I'm not here to cater to homosexuals." This is the most contested fact in the story, because Rinaldo adamantly denies making the remark. "Never, ever, ever would I say that," he told me. "Did I make mistakes? Absolutely. But I would never, ever demean someone like that."

Jacob and Robbie, however, are steadfast about this. "He said that *in front* of me," Jacob said. "I'm like, 'If it's bullying, it doesn't matter who you are. The school has to fix it.' He said, 'I will in my own time. I have other things to worry about.'"

Whatever Rinaldo said at that meeting, school was becoming unbearable for Jacob. Some days he made himself throw up so he could stay home. Other days Robbie would drop him off and Jacob would walk into the front door of the school, down the main hallway, and out the back exit. His grades plummeted.

In June, a few weeks before the end of the year, Jacob's already tenuous situation at school completely fell apart. It started with a prank. A girl in Ilion whom Jacob had just met started texting with him. She sent him a photo of herself and asked him to send one back. He did, texting a picture of himself sitting outside his mother's house wearing sunglasses. Pretending to be Jacob, the girl then sent his photo, along with a sex-filled text, to an eleventh grader at Mohawk named Danny—a seventeen-year-old who was "all muscle and in anger management and on probation," Jacob told me. Danny didn't recognize the cell phone number, so he assumed it was Jacob's. He charged up to Jacob in the school auditorium and snarled at him to stop the texting. Jacob protested that he hadn't sent Danny a message, but Danny didn't believe him. A week or two later, Jacob and Penny were walking into the school for an evening concert when Danny came up to them and called Jacob a "fucking faggot." Jacob's mother chased Danny away. Jacob wasn't sure which was more embarrassing: having his mother overhear Danny call him a faggot or standing there while she ran after him.

Jacob went back to school spooked, looking for Danny around every corner. A few days later, he had a substitute teacher for

Spanish—a class he took with Aaron. The sub lost control, and the class turned into "an animal house," as one school official later wrote. In the free-for-all, Aaron started taunting Jacob and the male friend he sat next to about being a couple. Jacob denied it and called Aaron a scumbag. Aaron says Jacob also threatened to kill his family, including his little sister. Nobody else in the class heard that. But ten or twelve students heard what Aaron said next: he threatened to string Jacob's "faggot ass" up the school flagpole.

Jacob says that under the desk, where no one else could see it, Aaron flashed a pocketknife and threatened to stab him. "I'd never seen him more serious in my life," Jacob told me. He ran out of class and called his father. When Robbie didn't answer, Jacob thought about how Tiffany had been telling him to leave school if it ever seemed like he was in danger. He walked into the hallway, down the stairs, and out the front door. Cynthia Stocker, director of student services, saw Jacob cross the parking lot and asked where he was going. The nurse was sending him home, he lied, and kept walking.

Stocker called Robbie a few minutes later to ask what was going on. Robbie raced home, talked to Jacob, and heard about the flagpole threat. He called Stocker and reported it. Four days later, Stocker wrote a memo for Jacob's file that included her interviews with all twelve students in the class. The ten students who'd heard Aaron threaten Jacob also said Aaron had started the fight, though they hadn't seen him with a knife. Aaron admitted to calling Jacob a faggot and to saying he was going to hang him from the flagpole—he stuck to his story that he was retaliating against Jacob's threat to kill his family even though no one in the class backed him up. "When Jacob said that about how he'd kill my family and my sister, I blacked out," he told me. "I said all kinds of stuff. I couldn't help it. But I didn't have a knife."

Rinaldo didn't believe his story that the flagpole threat was retaliation. "By then, Aaron had been accused of saying so much about

Jacob," he said. Rinaldo suspended Aaron for five days, the maximum punishment he could mete out on his own. The principal also recommended a hearing with the superintendent to determine whether Aaron deserved a longer punishment. Robbie, meanwhile, went to school once again to talk to Rinaldo about how he could protect Jacob for the last two weeks of the year. Rinaldo said he couldn't guarantee Jacob's safety and predicted the harassment would carry over into ninth grade. He suggested that home schooling might be a safer option. Robbie and the principal agreed that Jacob would miss the rest of the school year; he'd come back only to take his final exams.

"I have been speaking with Mr. Rinaldo on a regular basis all year and he hasn't done anything to protect Jacob," Robbie wrote in a final letter to the school in June. "I don't know what else I can do to protect my son."

As I talked to teachers, administrators, and other students about Jacob's struggles at Mohawk, I kept hearing the name of a student who'd graduated the year before Jacob arrived—Aric Barnett. Aric, I was told, had been the first male student to come out at Mohawk. He'd done it differently than Jacob, because he wasn't the type to wear purple nail polish or write in-your-face MySpace messages; he'd done it the no-drama way. Some people in Mohawk invoked Aric as a more successful example of how to be a gay student, as someone who'd figured out how to be himself without provoking the students around him. It was a narrative that, by implication, cast Jacob as the source of his own troubles.

There were a couple of problems with this version of events, though. For one thing, it assumed there was one way to be out in middle or high school, and that was to be unobtrusive. For another, it glossed over a crucial part of Aric's story: Aric didn't think of his time at Mohawk as a success at all. To him, high school stood for rejection. That wasn't because Aric had been bullied. It was because the Mohawk administration and school board repeatedly blocked his efforts to create an officially sanctioned haven for LGBT students.

Aric got called "fag" and "queer" and "pussy" on a daily basis in high school, and finally decided to do something about it in his junior year by starting a Gay-Straight Alliance (GSA). Gay student organizations got going in American high schools in the 1980s, in California and Massachusetts, and the idea was to bring students together to fight homophobia. In the decades since, more than four thousand schools across the country have opened GSA chapters, forming a kind of national network (though they are still far more common in high schools than in middle schools). Much good has come of this movement: a GSA is one of the strongest bulwarks a school can erect against anti-gay harassment. Specifically, studies show that LGBT students at schools with these groups tend to experience less victimization, skip school less often, and feel a greater sense of belonging.

Aric knew this—he'd done his research. He got to work putting up posters in the Mohawk hallways announcing the formation of the GSA. The initial response wasn't encouraging: the posters soon had swastikas and the word *fag* scrawled on them. But Aric stuck with his plan, and a small circle of supporters—the single Mohawk student who was out as a lesbian, and a dozen others who had gay uncles or siblings—joined him. At first some didn't want to be seen going to meetings, so Aric chose a classroom at the end of a hallway and covered up the window in the door. He called his group the Mohawk Gay-Straight Alliance.

As the GSA members got more comfortable, they gradually began going public with a couple of school-wide events. About twenty-five students participated in the Day of Silence, a national event in April in which students take a vow of silence to protest anti-gay violence and discrimination. To Aric's relief, nearly all the teachers respected their refusal to speak in class. Next the group screened the documentary *The Laramie Project,* about the torture and killing of Matthew Shepard. Between fifteen and twenty students attended, as well as a few teachers, one of whom came up to Aric afterward, crying. She said she hated to admit it, but she could see her husband in the boys who had dragged Matthew to his death.

Aric could tell, though, that he didn't have the full support of Mohawk's administration. Before the movie showing, he was ordered to put up a sign stating that it wasn't a school-sponsored event. When the faculty advisor for the yearbook encouraged Aric's group to submit a picture, Mohawk superintendent Joyce Caputo nixed it, saying that the GSA couldn't be included because it wasn't an official student club. The faculty advisor told me she couldn't remember another time the superintendent had interfered with the yearbook.

Aric came back to school the following fall, his senior year, determined to make the GSA official. "I knew it would be hard," he said. "But we'd spent a year on it. And I thought, 'Wait a sec, there's a Bible study group holding a prayer circle around the flagpole every morning. If they can do that, we shouldn't have to hide.' I knew things wouldn't really change for me, but I thought we could help the people who came after us. I said, 'We're going to do it. We are not asking for funding, but we want to be part of the school.' "

Aric submitted a request to Caputo, in writing, asking the school to recognize the GSA as an official school club. The superintendent told him she couldn't grant approval herself; he would have to go before the school board. To gain support, Aric circulated a petition to the student body. He didn't ask his classmates to support gay rights. He asked them to support the idea that he and the other students in the GSA should be able to do their thing. "We said, 'Look, you don't have to join any group you don't want to join,' " he told me. " 'This is about whether we should be able to have this group at all.' " He won the signatures of 70 percent of the student body.

Aric handed in his application, with the petition, and was asked to make his pitch formally to the school board. He planned it carefully. "I wrote out my remarks," he said. "I put in the regulations in the student handbook about how every student has a right to a fair and equal education, plus all the anti-bullying stuff they have in there. I put in statistics about how LGBT youth who are bullied are at more risk of suicide. I printed out a copy for each person on the board and extras for the audience."

Caputo called Aric out of class two weeks later to tell him the board had rejected the application. Aric appealed, this time with a petition signed by 85 percent of the students and almost every teacher and staff member—janitors and lunch ladies as well as the union representative for the faculty—and again the school board said no. Under federal law, Mohawk had to let student groups meet on campus, but the law didn't require all groups to be recognized as school-sponsored clubs. "The district believes that all of our clubs have a curricular alignment," the board president told the local newspaper, even as Caputo refused to explain how the district defined a club. As part of the decision, the board stripped the GSA of the Mohawk logo, an Indian silhouette. On his group's website, Aric had replaced the figure's black hair with a rainbow. He was forced to take down the image. "The message was, 'You can meet here after hours, because we have to let you, but you're not a member of the community, you can't use our name,'" Aric said.

Without official recognition, the Mohawk GSA died after Aric graduated. And with it, his hope of helping the kids who came after him—kids like Jacob. Aric is now in his twenties and lives in California; he doesn't like to dwell on high school. But every year, when the youth group he helps lead does a session for students about how to form a GSA, he tells his cautionary tale about how his own effort to start one got blocked. "When that happens, it makes you less comfortable being yourself," he said. "Sometimes I'm talking to people in authority, and I think about the Mohawk superintendent and I wonder, will they be like her? It stays with you, for sure, the feeling that people won't accept you, that you'll have to fight. I learned a lot. At the same time, it was things I shouldn't have had to learn. And I absolutely think that if the school had supported me, things would have been different for Jacob, because the GSA could have built on the small changes we'd started."

I asked Jacob if he agreed—would a Gay-Straight Alliance on campus have helped him? He cocked his head. "It's so far from the way things were," he said. "It's kind of hard for me to imagine."

Jacob eventually found an outlet outside school, in the form of an LGBT teen support group in Utica, a larger town fifteen miles away. The group leader urged kids to be themselves but also to be realistic about the consequences. "Never lie to yourself about what could happen," she would say, counseling students to have a contingency plan in place when they came out to their parents, in case they got kicked out of the house. Over the course of the spring, the leader told Jacob he was being courageous, but she also warned him that his flamboyance was putting him at risk. Jacob could see that, but he refused to change. Instead, after he stopped going to school in June, he started wondering if he'd be better off not going back. When he got his report card and found out he'd failed math, science, and social studies, it felt like an admonishment.

Robbie couldn't imagine another year like the one he and his son had just been through, so grueling and conflict-ridden. "I was getting desperate but I didn't know what to do," he told me. "I didn't want to draw a lot of attention to Jacob. I was worried about making things worse." He talked about his fears with the group leader in Utica, and she suggested an option of last resort: calling a lawyer. She put Robbie in touch with the New York Civil Liberties Union. On the day Jacob left school after Aaron's threat, Robbie talked for the first time to Naomi Shatz, an NYCLU staff attorney. He asked her whether Jacob had any legal rights—did the law protect his son from being bullied at school because he was gay? It was a question about a newly developing area of the law, one that hadn't been tested in the New York courts. Shatz told Robbie that she hoped the answer would be yes, but she couldn't be sure.

Shatz drove up to meet Jacob and his parents the following week. She didn't know what to expect: at fourteen, Jacob was young to be a plaintiff in a high-profile lawsuit, the youngest person she'd worked with.

Jacob wasn't certain the meeting was a good idea. Maybe he'd be better off transferring to Ilion than trying to keep fighting in Mohawk. He had more friends there. He'd be rid of Aaron and the other kids he didn't like and who didn't like him. He'd get away from Principal Rinaldo and Superintendent Caputo. Like Monique, he wanted to start over.

But Jacob thought about what he'd been through, and the train wreck of his school year, and like Aric Barnett, he wondered if he could salvage something from it that could help the kids who came next. He decided to hear the lawyer out.

Chapter 3

Flannery

THE FIRST TIME FLANNERY MULLINS SAW PHOEBE PRINCE, THEY were the only students in an empty school. It was August 2009, a week or two before classes began again for the seven hundred students of South Hadley High, in western Massachusetts. Phoebe, who had just moved to town from Ireland, was stopping in to register for ninth grade. Flannery, who was about to start her sophomore year, heard the lilt of Phoebe's accent and thought, *Oh, cool, an Irish girl.* That was it—just a silly, glancing impression, with no inkling of the anguish that was to come.

Flannery looked the part of the iconic popular girl, with her long blond hair, porcelain skin, and blue eyes. In junior high she played lacrosse, but in high school she decided she didn't like the clubby, self-satisfied vibe on the team and switched to riding horses in equestrian competitions outside school, a choice that set her apart. Flannery's family didn't quite fit South Hadley's conventions, either. Her mother, Jen, had left her husband when Flannery was a toddler and moved from New York to South Hadley. After Massachusetts gave its legal blessing to gay marriage in 2004, Jen married a woman who happened to have the same first name, and among friends and family they became, inevitably, "the Jens."

Phoebe grew up in a seaside hamlet in County Clare, Ireland. Her father, Jeremy Prince, was a British-born writer who'd gone into advertising and then opened a plant nursery in his adopted Irish home. Her mother, Anne O'Brien, a Massachusetts native, was a teacher. In seventh grade, Phoebe's parents sent her to a boarding school called Villiers, an hour or so from home, but pulled her out in the middle of the following year when Phoebe ran into trouble, with other girls, over boys she was dating. "Phoebe said she couldn't take the other girls at her every night," her mother would later say. So Phoebe transferred to the local school where Anne taught, but that didn't go well, either—Phoebe was soon enmeshed in more drama over a boy. "It got so bad that Phoebe went through three or four months where none of the girls would talk to her," her mother said. "She went from being a straight-A student to nearly failing everything."

The following summer, Anne moved to South Hadley with fourteen-year-old Phoebe and her eleven-year-old sister. A year away from Ireland, Anne thought, might give her daughter a fresh start. Phoebe's father, Jeremy, stayed behind.

South Hadley is a middle-class town of seventeen thousand in the part of Massachusetts called, usually without irony, the "Happy Valley." Residents tend to own their own businesses or work as nurses or teachers or cops. The town has a median income of about $77,000 and is 94 percent white. There is a small Irish population, but Phoebe was enough of a rarity that, at first, many students referred to her as "the Irish girl." Standing out didn't hold Phoebe back socially, though. On a school form at the end of September, she described herself as "happy & garrulous." To many of the kids her age, as well as to her mother, it seemed she was settling right in—thriving, even. "She was really easy to make friends with, very sociable," one ninth-grade boy told me. "She hung out with whoever she wanted right away." Phoebe also got back into stride academically. "I had my old Phoebe back," Anne said. "She was talking and participating and writing. She was excited that in this country you could talk and express yourself in class."

Phoebe was pretty as well as bright, with high cheekbones, long brown hair, and a smile that could be sunny or sultry. It didn't take long for the boys to notice her—first the ones in her class, and then the juniors and seniors. By November, Phoebe's Latin teacher had noticed a shift in Phoebe's approach to her schoolwork and to making friends. "Phoebe started out the fall as one of my best students in terms of her grades, participation, and the fact that she always wanted to answer all of the questions," she said. "But she did want to fit in. She started connecting with good-looking, popular kids that were dumb. Those kids talked all through class and had no respect for the teacher. Phoebe started ignoring the kids that weren't as physically attractive. She didn't do homework anymore. She dressed more adult-like, with short skirts and low-cut shirts." In class she sat with a senior, a boy named James, who talked about doing drugs with her.

Flannery saw Phoebe at a weekend party or two, with James and other seniors, and she noticed that Phoebe was generating buzz. "There are lots of new and pretty girls in ninth grade, so you're one of the pack unless you put yourself out there," Flannery said. "Phoebe got attention—positive, negative, all kinds." She was the ninth-grade girl who was most sought after by the older boys who fit South Hadley's standard definition of popular—which is to say that they played sports, dated other athletes, and dressed well. Flannery didn't much care what those boys, and the junior and senior girls they hung out with, thought of Phoebe or anything else, because they weren't her crowd. No one was. "I never had issues with kids in high school because I didn't have a lot of friends," she said. "I didn't have cliques. No one had anything good or bad to say about me. I'd do my work and be like 'Peace out, bye, I don't care about this place.' "

One of the senior boys paying attention to Phoebe was Sean Mulveyhill, the school's football star. Sean had a long-running romantic relationship with a junior named Kayla Narey who played field hockey. Most of the time Sean and Kayla were dating, meaning they'd agree not to see other people, but once in a while they'd stop being an official couple, even though they still talked. In November they were in one of those lulls, and Sean started giving Phoebe rides to and from school. The relationship quickly gained intensity. Phoebe started telling Sean things about her past in Ireland that, until now, she'd kept secret. She confided a history of depression and of cutting herself. "I really got to know Phoebe for what a great person she was," Sean said. "I also learned what a sad person she was. I saw some of the scars."

Phoebe had started cutting herself in eighth grade, when the other girls at Villiers turned on her. Cutting is an increasingly common form of self-harm linked with depression, as well as borderline personality disorder. "We're hesitant to make that diagnosis in teenagers, though, because their personalities are still developing, and borderline personality disorder is a long-term pattern of behavior," research psychologist Colleen Jacobson told me. "But what's very clear at all ages is the link between cutting and depression." Teenagers typically say that they cut to regulate their emotions and get attention. "Cutting was a release," a sixteen-year-old from Michigan named Britt explained on a parenting website. "It was a way to make the outside match the inside. Cutting brought the focus of the suffering to the surface. . . .

Cutting was a way to say 'Hello, I'm still here,' even when I didn't feel alive. It was a way to stop myself from going completely numb."

Some researchers think the behavior can also be a way to "practice" suicide. It's not clear how common that is. Still, cutting overlaps with thinking about suicide and attempting it, and doctors treat it as a warning sign. "Kids who cut have a higher rate of attempting suicide, and attempting more means succeeding more," Jacobson said.

When Phoebe came home from Villiers, she stopped cutting for a while, but after another round of problems with the girls at the local school, she started up again. In May, a few months before she moved to South Hadley, she began taking Prozac, and Anne renewed Phoebe's prescription when she brought her daughter to the United States that summer. She also took Phoebe to be evaluated at a hospital in Northampton, Massachusetts, where a doctor prescribed Seroquel, a drug used to treat mood and sleep disorders.

When she enrolled Phoebe at South Hadley High, Anne told the school about her daughter's history of depression and said she'd been bullied by other girls in Ireland. At the time, Anne was concerned about explaining why Phoebe's poor grades from the previous year didn't reflect her true abilities. Phoebe's aunt, who lived in the nearby city of Springfield, asked staff members at the school to keep an eye on her niece. The director of guidance mentioned Phoebe's history to the principal, and one of the school counselors made sure to introduce herself. In those fall months, leading up to Thanksgiving, Anne didn't ask for more from the school.

Phoebe's mother was confident enough in her daughter's well-being to leave her alone on Saturday nights, when Anne would visit her sister in Springfield and stay over. The idea, she said, was to give Phoebe space. In an email to a friend in Ireland in the beginning of November, Phoebe struck a blithe note about the arrangement. "Dude, me and my mom have this sweet deal," she wrote. "She's got to give me a free house once a week so I don't get sick of her and run away."

But if that sounds confident and brash, the freedom may have been too much for Phoebe. In the same early November email, she told her friend that "a few seniors came over and brought weed and beer and vodka . . . ah man you'd love my gravity bong!! . . . they had so much weed and we rolled blunts and man they put some coke in one of the blunts . . . aww . . . it was like better than sex!!" Two weeks later, when the partying repeated itself, Phoebe's report to her Irish friend started on the same giddy note, but ended tinged with misgivings. "I had a party last night because my mom went away and . . . we were in the room with gravity bong . . . and this fucking gorgeous strawberry vodka . . . so much it can't be good for me . . . I was in the emergency room Friday night because I don't want to take my pills anymore." These emails are mostly just teen-speak confirmation of Phoebe's troubles. When I asked Jacobson about them, she pointed out that "the combination of major depression and alcohol and drug use leaves people at a significantly heightened risk for suicidal behavior."

On another Sunday, Anne came home to find her daughter in bed with Sean, sleeping. Both teenagers were clothed. "She told me up and down that nothing happened," Anne said. "She told me that Sean was gay and trying to come out." In retrospect, Anne knew that her daughter wasn't telling the truth: in fact, Phoebe and Sean weren't formally dating, but they were having sex.

Finally, Phoebe had a Saturday night party, with alcohol, pot, and hash, to which the police were called. Anne found out from a neighbor, and she stopped leaving Phoebe home alone.

In school, Phoebe was talking about how much she missed her home in County Clare and her father, Jeremy. "She wanted to go home to Ireland, she always wanted to go home, she expressed that to me several times," her Latin teacher said. Phoebe mentioned her father often. In an essay she wrote for English class in October, she reminisced about her old home life:

I get into my pink fluffy onesie [and] my feet tingle as they rub off the soft cushioned fabric. I head downstairs into the kitchen. The walls our [sic] heath green with various paintings of vegetables. I live in an old country house with a barn door and all the furnishings to boot. My father's sitting at the dining table reading a thriller type novel as per usual with a half glass full of white wine next to him. The fire is roaring and the smell of hydrangeas wafts through the air. I curl up on a chair adjacent from my father making sure to be cosily tucked in near the fire. He puts down his book and says, "Now what is on your mind tonight my dear?" From there on we start a heated debate about almost anything. Our conversations range from sex, drugs and rock and roll to matters of great importance such as ancient religions, politics and criminal justice. No subject is off limits with me and my father.

Jeremy, too, treasured the relationship. "Phoebe talked to me about everything," he told me. "Sex and drugs and everything under the sun." Reading her words, it's hard not to think about how far away her father was when Phoebe started falling through the cracks.

As Phoebe spent more time with Sean, she talked about them being together for real: she wanted to be his girlfriend, the way Kayla had been. This wasn't what Sean had in mind. "It was complicated," he said. "Kayla and I were talking, but we weren't dating. I also was not dating Phoebe, but we were friends and we were having sex. Kayla knew that I was hanging around with Phoebe, but didn't know that I was having sex with her."

In mid-November, Sean decided that all the deception was too much to handle, and broke off his physical relationship with Phoebe. On the Friday after Thanksgiving, Phoebe called him and said she was having a bad day. She asked him to come over. Sean drove up and they went into the garage to talk. "She told me that she had cut herself," Sean said. "She showed me one of her arms. She was cut from wrist to elbow on the inside of her arm. The cut did not look that deep, but she had just done it. It was still bleeding. I kept asking her why she did it, and she kept telling me she didn't want to know why."

Cutting can come from different impulses at different times. One possibility is that when it brings temporary relief, it can be on the opposite side of the spectrum from the permanence of death—and in this guise, it can actually represent the antithesis of suicide. Phoebe hinted at this in an essay she wrote that fall, about a book she'd read called *Cutting: Understanding and Overcoming Self-Mutilation.* "From a personal point of view," she wrote, "I can see that Levenkron does truly understand the concept of self mutilation and how it's not about suicide in most cases it's about trying to transfer the pain from emotional to physical pain which is a lot easier to deal with for most adolescents who most likely don't even understand how they're feeling." No teacher seems to have asked Phoebe why she chose to read this book, nor to have probed more deeply into what she'd written.

But if cutting offers a respite of sorts in the short term, it often makes teenagers who do it feel worse about themselves in the long run—that's why it's a warning sign for suicide. The self-loathing can morph into a longing for self-annihilation. Phoebe wrote about this, too, in a poem:

Breathe
Crimson regret pours
Out along with all
Pain and feeling

Phoebe went to her room after Sean drove away on that day after Thanksgiving, and when she came out, she told her mother she'd swallowed all the pills in her bottle of Seroquel. Anne rushed her to the hospital, talking to Phoebe as she drove to keep her awake. Phoebe went into organ failure and was hospitalized for a week.

A suicide attempt like this isn't an empty gesture. It's a flashing red light, a sign of real danger. Alarmed, Anne told the South Hadley guidance department what had happened, and consulted with a therapist before sending her daughter back to school. When Phoebe didn't come back the week after Thanksgiving, rumors started to swirl: she'd gone to a mental hospital; she'd gone to live with her aunt; she'd gone home to Ireland. By the time she returned in the second week of December, Sean and Kayla were back together. They were public about being a couple, hanging out together in school, going to parties. Kayla knew Sean had been giving Phoebe rides and hanging out with her in November, but he didn't volunteer that they'd had sex, and she didn't ask.

When Sean and Kayla got back together, Phoebe started spending more time with James, the senior who talked in Latin class about doing drugs. Other senior boys, too, expressed interest in her—asking if they could take her out or give her rides—but Phoebe wasn't ready to move on from Sean. One day at school, she went up to Kayla, whom she hadn't spoken to before, and asked if they could talk for a minute. They sat down on a bench together. Phoebe told Kayla that she'd had sex with Sean, and wanted to apologize for it. Since Kayla had chosen not to know, the revelation hit her hard, in a way that Phoebe may or may not have expected. It didn't much matter, in the moment, that Sean and Kayla hadn't been officially dating at the time; they had a history, and they'd been spending time together. Kayla had expectations about what that meant—and those expectations didn't include hearing from Phoebe that she had a claim on Sean, too.

At this point, though, Kayla didn't blame Phoebe. She blamed Sean. "I thought it was brave of Phoebe to tell me that, seeing that she was new to the school and a freshman," she said. "I told Sean that later. I told him that I had more respect for her than for him." Kayla got up from the bench and sent Sean a text breaking up with him.

A few minutes later, Phoebe came up to Sean in the hallway and tried to talk to him, but Sean didn't want to. "I was mad at Phoebe," he said. "I took it as Phoebe was trying to mess up my relationship with Kayla. Phoebe wouldn't get out of my way, so I stopped, turned around, and went the other way."

Sean eventually succeeded in convincing Kayla to give him another chance. But to make it work, he had to prove himself. To show his allegiance to Kayla, he had to cut Phoebe off.

Phoebe didn't confide anything about this to her mother. In counseling sessions, she and Anne spent much of the time fighting. Like a lot of teenagers, Phoebe accused her mother of not understanding her, and like a lot of parents, Anne yelled at her daughter for not coming home when she said she would. Mother and daughter divided, too, over why Phoebe was hurting herself, with the cutting and the November suicide attempt. Anne told the counselor her daughter was acting out because of "issues with her boyfriends," while Phoebe said she was upset that her parents might get a divorce and because she felt her mother misunderstood her.

As a way of dealing, Phoebe turned to other boys. They tried to help her; the problem was, they didn't know how. She sent a senior named Chris despairing text messages about her fallout with Sean. "She told me that he chose Kayla over her. Phoebe was devastated when that happened," he said. Chris tried to comfort her on his own rather than telling an adult. It became a pattern: Phoebe would confide in an older boy, who would listen but keep her emotional distress to himself. Around this time Phoebe showed James that she was cutting herself. "She lifted up her hoodie and showed cuts on her chest above her bra and all the way down to her hips," he said. "I really didn't look too long. I found it to be very painful. This was someone I cared about and she was harming herself." When Phoebe asked him what she should do, James was at a loss. "I told her to use Neosporin, but I wasn't too sure," he said.

Christmas break brought a brief respite. Phoebe's father, Jeremy, came to visit, and Phoebe was full of hope—that he and her mother would reconcile, that he would stay and live with them, that her family would be reunited. Jeremy remembers their time together as peaceful. He made snowmen with his daughters, and Phoebe modeled her new dress for the cotillion, the upcoming school dance. She asked Jeremy to help her redo the basement, where she wanted to move her bedroom.

The image of Phoebe as depressed and self-destructive is "a picture I don't recognize," Jeremy told me. Differing from the doctors, Jeremy wasn't convinced that Phoebe's overdose in November qualified as a serious suicide attempt. "Taking an excess of pills," he said, was "open to interpretation." And at this point, Phoebe didn't seem vulnerable to him. "She hadn't had any Seroquel for over a month. She was seeing a therapist who gave us a written report that she wasn't at risk of suicide, and she was okay to go back to school."

But in the middle of the vacation, Jeremy abruptly flew back to Ireland, and Phoebe was distraught. The separation from him would continue, and fairly or not, Phoebe blamed her mother and turned again to older boys. In the week after Christmas, Phoebe went over to the home of a senior who had his bedroom set up as a makeshift tattoo parlor. While he inked a Celtic cross into Phoebe's lower back, she talked with a friend of his who'd come over to smoke some pot and hang out that afternoon: another South Hadley senior, eighteen-year-old Austin Renaud.

Austin wasn't a football player like Sean, or much of a jock, and he and Phoebe had never really talked before. Now she found that Austin was a sympathetic listener who could especially relate to the turmoil she was going through with her parents. Earlier in high school, Austin's father had died suddenly, and his mother had remarried; he spent the next couple of years angry, struggling in school. But as a senior, Austin had settled down. He was on track to graduate if he passed his spring classes and went to summer school. The adults at school credited his turnaround to his relationship with a girl Austin had pursued a year and a half earlier, and had been going out with ever since—Flannery.

There are a few romances in high school that everyone treats as real—lasting, loving, committed—and Austin and Flannery's was one of those. All the kids knew they were together and could see that Austin was better off for it. Flannery, who'd never had a boyfriend before, knew how needy Austin was, and she responded to his sadness with a mix of concern and affection. "We were very close," she said. "I really do think that we loved each other." Adults at the school could sense this, too. "Flannery mattered a great deal to Austin," one of them told me. "He was an angry kid for a long time, but he had come a long way. This thing with Phoebe appeared to throw him."

The "thing with Phoebe" was a physical relationship and an instant emotional connection—Austin, over that Christmas break, showed he could handle Phoebe's confidences. "We would talk on the phone and she would tell me her problems," he said. "Phoebe told me that she missed her father and that her parents made her move here and that she didn't want to come. She said that not a lot of people liked her. She never singled anyone out. She told me that it was a little harsh because of the personal problems she was dealing with at home."

Austin and Flannery had a fight just before he and Phoebe met up in his friend's bedroom/tattoo parlor, and for the next few days he didn't see Flannery at all. He also didn't tell her that he'd started hanging out with Phoebe. "On the day before we went back to school, he came over and I thought we were together, like always," Flannery said. "Then we got back to school and all of a sudden he didn't want to look at me. He wasn't talking to me. I was walking with him in the hall, asking what's going on, and Phoebe came up. He tried to avoid her, and she was like, 'Austin?' and put her hand on his arm. I looked at him and said, 'How does she know your name?'"

Austin told Flannery it was no big deal, he'd just met Phoebe when she'd come by his friend's house to get a tattoo, but the next day, a ninth-grade girl who was supposed to be Phoebe's best friend stopped Flannery to tell her to watch out. "She said, 'Phoebe is trying to get with Austin, and she's saying that he likes her back.'" Phoebe wanted to be Austin's girlfriend, not his hookup. And she was telling her friends that she was confident Austin wanted this, too, and that he would break up with Flannery to go out with her.

"We'd been together for a year and a half and it was extremely hurtful," Flannery said. "I thought, 'Holy shit, I can't believe he'd do that to me. Who is this girl?' My stomach just dropped. You have to understand: we were really close. I didn't get it. I kept asking myself, 'What is happening?'"

That night, at home in her room, Flannery vented some of her anger on Facebook. In response to a post from a friend about an equestrian event they'd recently gone to, Flannery replied, "Hahaha best night of my life :) ya we kick it with the true irish not the gross slutter poser ones :)." When another girl asked if *she* counted as true Irish, Flannery answered, "Yes I love you . . . I think you no who im talking about :)." She was talking about Phoebe. A couple of girls replied with a chorus of "hahas."

Flannery's anger also spilled over at school. She talked about Austin's betrayal with a girl in her chemistry class named Sharon Chanon Velazquez, who expressed outrage: what was this Phoebe girl thinking, first making a play for Sean, and now for Austin? Sharon had once been burned by a boy who'd cheated on her, so she knew how it felt. She decided to enforce the high school code, as she saw it, by standing with the girlfriends—Flannery and Kayla—against the interloper. She would call Phoebe out. On January 6, she went up to Phoebe in the school's crowded cafeteria and loudly called her a whore; she also warned her to "stay away from people's men."

Slut shaming, as it's called, is coarse, retrograde, the opposite of feminist. Calling a girl a slut warns her that there's a line: she can be sexual, but not *too* sexual. "If you're in a relationship with a guy for a long time, and you do stuff with him, it's not that big a deal," one fifteen-year-old told me. "It's the girls who do stuff with a bunch of guys they're not close with who get called sluts." If that sounds ill-defined—how many guys, and what does "not close with" mean?—that's because you often don't know where the slut line is until you've crossed it, as the sociologist Kathleen Bogle points out in her book *Hooking Up*. Often girls get called sluts for being *perceived* as being too sexually active even if they think they've played it safe. Either way, the reputational damage can lead to other kinds of harm. In a survey by the American Association of University Women, students reported that girls who stand out as "too sexual" are at greater risk for sexual harassment, which the AAUW has linked to a host of bad outcomes, including impaired concentration, reduced emotional well-being, difficulty studying, and missed school. James Gruber, a sociologist at the University of Michigan, has compared the responses students give in surveys about sexual harassment to the responses they give in surveys about bullying, and found that for girls, the most upsetting way to be targeted is to be the focus of a sexual rumor, which often includes being called a slut. "Sexual imagery and language is the most potent, period," Gruber told me. "It ramps up everything for girls in a way that's the most hurtful."

Slut shaming (or slut bashing) isn't easy to talk about, either. "Kids who are bullied in this way can't go to adults for help the same way kids being bullied for more 'favorable' behavior (like being smart or nerdy) can," a blogger on *The Frisky* wrote in telling her own slut-shaming story. "I faked sick, unable to face the abuse. But when my mom asked me what was wrong, I couldn't bring myself to tell her. How could I explain it?"

As Sharon's outburst toward Phoebe shows, girls often serve as their own slut police. Tina Fey captured this deftly, and devastatingly, in her movie *Mean Girls*. After a burn book filled with anonymous insults gets into the wrong hands, makes the rounds of the school, and causes chaos, Fey's nerdy teacher character herds the girls in the junior class into the gym. She asks them to close their eyes and raise their hands if they've ever been talked about behind their backs. All hands go up. Fey asks the girls if they've ever talked about someone else behind *her* back. The hands go up again. "You all have got to stop calling each other sluts and whores," Fey exhorts the students. "It just makes it okay for guys to call you sluts and whores."

Sharon continued her attack after lunch, walking into Phoebe's Latin class before the bell rang and calling her a whore again. The other students hadn't filed in yet, but the teacher, who was sitting across the room at her desk and hadn't heard what Sharon said, could see that Phoebe was upset. "Phoebe came over and was kind of weeping," the teacher said. "I held out my arms and she just walked into them and I hugged her. Then when the boys walked in, Phoebe gathered herself and begged me not to say anything." The teacher told Phoebe that bullying wasn't okay and that she had to report it, and told the assistant principal what had happened. He'd already heard about the slut shaming at lunch, and he called Sharon to his office and gave her a two-day suspension.

When Flannery heard about Sharon's outburst, it didn't feel to her like vindication. She was still furious with Austin and with Phoebe. The next day, January 7, Flannery vented to a classmate about Phoebe in gym class, saying, "Someone ought to kick her ass." Phoebe wasn't in the class, but the teacher sensed a fight was brewing and tipped off the assistant principal. He summoned both girls and gave Flannery a verbal warning—she'd never been suspended before, so that seemed sufficient to him—and counseled Phoebe and Flannery to stay away from each other. Flannery didn't speak to Phoebe after that.

Kayla, however, had decided Phoebe was out of control. She and Flannery weren't friends, but she saw Phoebe's behavior with the boys as unacceptable. It was the infamous high school double standard, easy to condemn in theory but hard to resist in practice: boys who have sex with different people are players, while girls who do that are sluts. Kayla and her friends talked about Phoebe that way, and on Facebook, Kayla wrote something to the effect of: "Know what I hate? Irish sluts."

Phoebe didn't have her own Facebook account, so she didn't find Kayla's post herself. But James saw it, and he showed Phoebe on the afternoon of January 12, when he was hanging out at her house after school. With Phoebe beside him, James responded to Kayla: "You shouldn't say things like that," he wrote. "You don't know her."

Meanwhile, Austin persuaded Flannery to talk to him on January 13. She raged about his betrayal, he swore he was sorry, and they talked about getting back together. Afterward, Austin texted Phoebe to say he wanted to be with Flannery. Her message back alarmed him; he thought she was threatening suicide. Austin immediately wrote back: "Your crazy stop acting that way" and "You can't just give up! Relax . . . take it slow. be a cool girl! You know you are."

The next morning, Phoebe went to see the school nurse about a burn on her upper chest, visible above her shirt. When the nurse asked how the mark had gotten there, Phoebe said she'd been smoking pot and dropped a hot pipe on her chest. The nurse didn't think Phoebe's story matched the burn, which was eight centimeters long and crescent-shaped. She called in Sally Watson-Menkel, a licensed social worker, and asked her to take a look.

Watson-Menkel had been in regular contact with Phoebe and her mother since the middle of November. She knew about Phoebe's overdose, and since then she'd made an effort to check in every few weeks, though Phoebe had consistently put her off. Now in the nurse's office, with Watson-Menkel asking about the burn, Phoebe stuck to her story about the pipe. She was worried about how she would cover the mark for the cotillion, which was two days away. Watson-Menkel told Phoebe they needed to call her mother. Phoebe resisted, saying that if her mother knew she'd been smoking pot, she might not let her go to Ireland in the spring. But Watson-Menkel couldn't just let this go.

On the phone with her mother, Phoebe was distant, matter-of-fact. Anne asked whom Phoebe had been smoking with, but her daughter wouldn't say. Phoebe asked if they could talk about it when she got home, and her mother agreed. But Phoebe's day was about to go horribly wrong, and she and her mother would never speak again.

Phoebe went to the library during lunch and sat with Chris, one of the seniors she frequently texted with, so he could help her with her math homework. At another table nearby were Sean and Kayla, sitting with a girl named Ashley, who had a difficult family life and a reputation for lashing out at other kids. She'd been suspended three times as a junior, for truancy and smoking. Ashley and Sean weren't in the same social circle, but he was a popular kid who'd been kind to her. In the library, Ashley swooped in to play the role of slut-shaming enforcer: she would show that she had Sean's back. Shouting over to Phoebe's table, she called Phoebe a whore—an insult she'd hurled at other girls in the past—and also yelled, "Close your legs" and "I hate stupid sluts." Sean and Kayla laughed. Phoebe kept talking to Chris, seemingly unaffected, he said. But when the bell rang, Ashley walked by their table and loudly repeated that she hated sluts, and Phoebe definitely heard her. She turned to Chris and told him that she hated "fucking girls."

Phoebe had to face Sean, Kayla, and Ashley again at the end of the school day, when she passed them on her way to the parking lot. Sean said, "Here she comes," and Ashley called Phoebe a whore again; when Phoebe didn't stop, she yelled, "I'm fucking *talking* to you."

Phoebe made a peace sign and kept walking. She had her iPod earbuds in, and some of the kids who saw her thought maybe she hadn't heard. But she had. Sean and Kayla walked by Phoebe crying on their way to Kayla's car. A few minutes later, Ashley drove by in a friend's car, rolled down the window, called Phoebe a whore, and threw an empty soda can at her.

Phoebe texted Chris at 2:23 p.m., the first in a series of increasingly desperate messages. "I cant do it anymre im literally hme cryn, my scar on my chest is potentially permanent, my bodies fukd up wht mre du they want frm me? Du I hav to fukn od!"

Chris wrote back: "No no phoebe ill legit kill mysf too I can['t] live knowing one of my friends died, and the girl who said it is a fat whore anyways so it doesn't mean shit."

The texts continued in brokenhearted bursts:

Phoebe at 2:28 (talking about Sean and Ashley): Why wud he stop her? he hates me, and what hurts the most he of all ppl shud kno I cant deal with this shitt

Phoebe at 2:32: It wud be easier if he or any of them handed me a fukn noose.

Chris at 2:34: Phoebe of course it would b easy for u but my life would be destroyed

Phoebe at 2:35: Na man i think sean condoning this iz one v the final nails in my offin I cnt take much mre.

Chris at 2:39: No no I talked to him he said hell try to talk to her and ill talk to her too phoebe and trust I'm good with words shell stop

Phoebe at 2:39: He wny do shit he thinkz worse of me then any of those girlz.

Chris at 2:42: Who cares what other people think phoebe I know you're a good person

Chris at 2:45: Phoebe

Phoebe at 2:48: To quote Taquore, men are cruel, man is

> *kind. One person cant help me, im a lost cuase. Even ppl I*
> *once cared for hate me, sean z a perfect example.*
> *Chris at 2:51: Honestly phoebe no one is making u do this*
> *and if u are for my sanity please don't please*

Phoebe stopped answering. At home in her bedroom, she plugged in her cell phone to recharge it, as if she hadn't entirely absorbed what she was about to do. In her closet, she found a black scarf woven with multicolored thread her younger sister had given her.

Sometime before 4:30 p.m., Phoebe used the scarf to hang herself from a beam in the stairwell of her house. Her younger sister found her, tried and failed to undo the knots around her neck, and, hysterical, called 911. Later the police searched Phoebe's room and found several drawings. One shows a person with a noose around her neck. In a note, pinned to the figure's chest, Phoebe asked for forgiveness.

Almost every detail here about Phoebe's life and death can be found in the police investigation that followed her suicide. The police, in conducting their investigation, talked to Phoebe's family and friends, South Hadley High administrators and staff, and dozens of students. They also collected medical records and the notes from counseling sessions Phoebe and her mother had from November to January. The investigation runs to hundreds of pages, and it tells a tragic story, filled with warning signs, missed opportunities, and flashes of cruelty. What the documents don't tell is a simple story. Many factors contributed to Phoebe's suicide. Yet prosecutors decided to reduce all the complexity to one clean narrative: Phoebe Prince was bullied to death.

This was sensational stuff, media candy. In screaming headlines and TV segments, the conflicts Phoebe had been embroiled in were rendered as a one-way set of attacks by a vicious pack against one innocent victim. The notion of a "bullycide" took hold, and it didn't matter how much complexity it obscured. "Students harassed Prince through texting and Facebook, so much so that she took her own life," *Good Morning America* reported eleven days after Phoebe's death. A former prosecutor called for making bullying a crime, arguing that "cover-ups are why kids like Phoebe Prince end up dead." Online commenters ran wild with the call for retribution. "I think the names, home addresses, current photos, license plate numbers, routes to school and any possible means of identifying them should be published in every newspaper and posted on billboards all over town, so that those little bitches can find out what it REALLY means to live in fear all the time," one person anonymously wrote.

This is the dangerous side of the newfound focus on bullying: when the word becomes a weapon and we think we know who the bullies are, the drive to condemn and punish them spins out of control.

The story of how this happened in South Hadley started with a swirl of rumors, and also a display of insensitivity by school officials. While some students held a candlelight vigil the day after Phoebe's death, on the following night the high school principal, Dan Smith, made the big mistake of going ahead with the cotillion as planned. Phoebe's parents were understandably stung by the decision. And their resentment deepened when they heard that kids at the dance had boasted about playing dumb to the police and that before her death, girls had told Phoebe they hoped she'd "go kill herself" and then, after her death, had written "She deserved it" and "Mission accomplished" on Facebook. Smith made things worse with a rambling letter to parents in which he accused unnamed students of making "mean-spirited comments" about Phoebe in school and online, and by saying that Phoebe had "several public disagreements" with other students about "relationship/dating issues." What did that mean? Who was responsible for what? Smith didn't say, opening the door to endless speculation.

Some details from the day of Phoebe's death—that she'd been called a slut and a whore in school—soon began to surface. Along with this part of the story came the accusation that no one had reached out to help her, that the school had failed her. A small but vociferous group of local critics became outraged that no students or staff had been publicly reprimanded, or seemed to be facing discipline, for the role they'd played. One critic, Darby O'Brien (no relation), ran his own PR firm and had a history of championing underdog causes. O'Brien decided that South Hadley's principal, Smith, and the district superintendent, Gus Sayer, were covering up, shielding popular students and their well-placed families at the expense of a powerless immigrant girl. The bullies who'd tormented Phoebe were getting away with it because she didn't have connections. So O'Brien would use his connections for her. He called an old friend of his, Kevin Cullen, a *Boston Globe* columnist, and fed him the materials for a column that appeared on January 24.

Under the headline "Untouchable Mean Girls," Cullen wrote that a group of bullies "followed Phoebe around, calling her a slut. When they wanted to be more specific, they called her an Irish slut. The name-calling, the stalking, the intimidation was relentless." After her suicide, Cullen said, "they went on Facebook and mocked her in death." How could it be, he asked, that "the Mean Girls who tortured Phoebe remain in school, defiant, unscathed"? Alongside Cullen's scorching prose, the *Globe* ran an appealing family photo of Phoebe. With her long brown hair held back on one side by a barrette, a smudge of gray eyeliner, and a sparkly smile, Phoebe looked like a girl anyone would want to befriend, or date, or mother.

And now she was dead, because of her schoolmates' cruelty.

Cullen's column, with its mix of facts and innuendo, was the media equivalent of a lit match. Superintendent Sayer threw gasoline on the fire by sounding lawyerly rather than clearly explaining how the school was handling its investigation into Phoebe's death. "All students who engage in any bullying activities—and there are a wide variety of things that fall into that category—are subject to the disciplinary code, which includes suspension," Sayer said, his eyes darting away from the camera on local television. Behind the scenes, the school suspended Ashley, Sean, and Kayla, who soon withdrew from South Hadley High pending resolution of their cases. Confidentiality laws bar school officials from discussing individual students' disciplinary records, and for weeks Sayer wouldn't even confirm or deny whether anyone had been punished at all. The superintendent left an information vacuum in the crucial days after Phoebe's death that suggested the school had done little or nothing in response. "The punishments have been vague, secretive and too little too late," one South Hadley parent complained.

The Internet can't abide such a vacuum, and anonymous commenters rushed to fill it. On YouTube, Craigslist, and especially a Facebook page called "REMOVAL OF THE SOUTH HADLEY GIRLS WHO BULLIED PHOEBE PRINCE!" commenters posted names and photos of kids reported to have bullied Phoebe. "Sorry but if Phoebe's name is everywhere . . . then why aren't their names???" one poster wrote. "I don't even know these girls and they should be removed, hell, they should get charged for all of this 100%," another added. "Where are these little bitches and their parents???" a third asked. The invective extended to a woman in town who happened to have the same last name as Kayla. She went to the police when her name and address were posted along with a map to her home and threats including "Does anybody know about amputation, how to do it?" and "Is anybody on the ground in South Hadley to go to the house?"

School officials and the local elected school committee dug in to deny responsibility, and also continued to alienate the Prince family. Strikingly, no one from the district's leadership attended a benefit to raise money for a memorial fund in Phoebe's name. (Smith claimed that Phoebe's family, through their lawyer, asked the school not to post information about the benefit, and so he thought they didn't want any school involvement.) When critics asked whether any of them had ever called the Prince family to offer condolences, the members of the school committee refused to answer.

Darby O'Brien was far more deft at handling the media attention. *People* magazine sent a reporter to South Hadley, and O'Brien got in touch with Jeremy Prince to suggest he give the magazine a series of personal photos of Phoebe. Let the world see what her family had lost: Phoebe, at turns soulful and vibrant, posing in a witch's hat, opening Christmas presents. *People* ran the photos with two cover stories in quick succession, titled "Why Was Phoebe Prince Bullied?" and "Bullied to Death?"

As the rage continued to spread, O'Brien began calling publicly for the resignations of the principal and superintendent. Parents lined up at the microphone at a school committee meeting at the end of January to blast the district and tell their own stories of bullying at South Hadley High—an hours-long litany of grievances, past and present. One father said his daughter, now a junior, had been bullied since eighth grade. Another described how he'd "spent from about third grade on in absolute misery and terror." Addressing Sayer, one parent's voice rose to a shout. "Wouldn't we all agree that you have *failed*?"

I first heard about the trouble in South Hadley at the end of January—about Phoebe's death and the messy, vitriolic aftermath. I found Cullen's column, along with a mountain of anguished and outraged comments and social media posts, and it all made South Hadley High sound like an out-of-control, slut-shaming *Lord of the Flies* nightmare—a high school where popular kids could choose a weak girl to terrorize and ruin at will, and even as she sobbed in the hallway, no one—no teacher, no fellow student—would go to her aid. How exactly did that happen? Where had they—we—gone wrong? I have three younger sisters, and Phoebe's photo reminded me of them. I'd just started writing my series on online bullying for Slate, and I'd been looking for a story to dig deep on. Here was one, exploding seventy-five miles from my house.

My first phone call was to Darby O'Brien. He told me he expected a big protest against Sayer and Smith at the next school committee meeting in February, so I drove up for it. Inside the entrance to the school, a couple of parents and students sat at a table advertising the memorial fund benefit for Phoebe. Some of the people streaming in the door stopped to sign up, but most of them looked away and kept walking. A few people pointedly ignored them while passing out "I Support Dan Smith" stickers. O'Brien stood nearby with a knot of fellow critics, their hopes of a protest fading.

When Smith rose to speak, the applause built to three-quarters of a standing ovation. He choked up as he addressed the crowd. "What's been happening has to stop in our community," he said, pausing to blow his nose. "I'm really hopeful for our kids—for their good—which so many of you are here about. It's time to move on."

When the speech was over, the Smith haters left. Other parents and students broke into small groups to discuss an agenda for an anti-bullying task force. I went to the library and listened to a frank discussion among three dozen parents, and a few students, about the pitfalls of raising a child in the era of smart phones. It had moments of both humor and pathos. The parents wanted guidance—and they wanted it forced upon them. "We have to take a two-hour class now for our kids to get a driver's license," said one mother. "Isn't there a way to do that for how kids use the Internet—mandate it so that we have to take a class with them? I had to have my daughter show me how to get into Facebook." Another mother asked if the school could prevent students from using their cell phones during school by turning the campus into a dead zone. A girl with blond hair piped up: "No one gets service if they have T-Mobile. If you want to block your kid's access, get him that." The room broke into laughter.

I went to South Hadley every week or so throughout that winter, spring, and summer. I talked to kids in journalism class, at band and theater rehearsal, in the school parking lot, and at a local coffee shop. I talked to kids from a variety of grades and social groups. I wanted to know what it was like to go to South Hadley High if you were a theater geek or a hockey player, a stoner or a good girl, a disaffected gay kid or the transgender student body president who strongly supported the school administration. For a while, like every other out-of-town reporter who swooped in to pry and gawk, I took it as a given that South Hadley High was a dysfunctional, frightening place, even if it looked like every other public high school I'd ever been to, with its bland linoleum hallways and student artwork hanging in the library. I also assumed that with the departure of the terrorizers—Ashley, Sean, and Kayla—the rest of the student body was heaving a collective sigh of relief.

I'd gone looking for black-hearted monsters, but found only shades of gray. Nobody seemed to feel safer and happier with the three seniors who'd been cruel to Phoebe gone. Ashley, it was true, had a reputation for being rude. "She's not very nice," one sixteen-year-old told me. "After I started going out with a boy who a friend of hers liked, she'd walk by me and say 'nasty girl' or 'slut,' loud enough so I could hear it." But other kids allowed that she came from a rough family and that they felt sorry for her. Sean and Kayla, meanwhile, were generally well liked. They could be a little full of themselves, maybe, but they weren't mean. "We miss the kids who left," the sixteen-year-old said.

It wasn't that South Hadley students didn't see bullying as a problem. They did. In 2005, the last time the student body was surveyed, 30 percent reported they'd been bullied in the last year, a higher rate than the state average of 24 percent. "How long can the school department ignore the increasing rate of bullying before reality sets in?" two students asked that year in an editorial in the school newspaper. "How many more harassed kids will it take, how many more enraged parents, how many cases of depression, and how many attempted suicides?"

Now those questions seemed all too prescient. But the notion that Phoebe had been the victim of a pattern of one-way bullying, as opposed to an active participant in "girl drama," as the kids put it, didn't make sense to the students I talked to. While they didn't want to sound like they were blaming the victim, they tried to explain that Phoebe had gotten into separate conflicts with different kids. "I'm upset and angry that bullying wasn't taken more seriously here before this," said one fifteen-year-old who'd been taunted for being a "poseur" by a group of girls in middle school. But Phoebe's death "has been turned into this Lifetime movie plot. It's so unlike what actually happened." The students didn't exactly condone slut shaming, but they saw it as a fact of life. "I don't want to be mean because something terrible happened, but if you come to a new school and sleep around, you're going to get backlash," one sixteen-year-old told me. A seventeen-year-old girl added, "It was just high school drama, but they did it to the wrong person." It didn't seem fair to the other students to pin the blame for Phoebe's suicide on Ashley or Sharon or Kayla, or even on Sean. They'd behaved badly, for sure, and it was easy to condemn them in retrospect. But how could they have foreseen the impact their actions would have?

As an administrator told me: "In the end you can call it bullying. But to the other kids, for almost all of her time at school, Phoebe was the one with the power." It reminded me of Monique, and how Gianna had gotten carried away in her cruelty. Gianna had thought she was fighting with a girl who could take it. Social power is so fluid among teenagers. In South Hadley, no one realized that Phoebe had lost hers, and was terribly vulnerable inside, until it was too late.

As the police interviewed a parade of students and staff after Phoebe's death, and a few kids were identified on the Internet as her tormentors, strange unmarked packages and hate mail started arriving at Flannery's house, and reporters showed up uninvited. Jen quit her job to stay home with her daughter, who she worried might fall apart or come to harm. She and her wife, a criminal defense lawyer, had already told Flannery not to talk to the police without a lawyer, even though that's what most of the kids were doing. With the firestorm of attention, why trust the cops?

Other kids, meanwhile, were struggling with what I came to think of as bystander guilt. Why hadn't anyone reported Ashley for calling Phoebe a whore in the library or outside the auditorium? How many people had heard her? You could look at the research about how few kids intervene when they see other kids being cruel—the studies that say bullying takes place in front of an audience in nearly nine out of ten cases, yet kids who witness it defend the victim less than 20 percent of the time—and still feel like there was no good answer to these questions. At the time, most kids took for granted that it was best to stay out of Phoebe's drama. In retrospect, that was a "moral failure of, like, the community," as one girl put it to me.

How do you end the tacit acceptance, or at least allowance, of a damaging behavior such as slut shaming? It takes a village, or in South Hadley's case, a town. A school has to commit to changing a bad norm and then get traction not just with staff and students but also with their families and the larger community. "When I talk to parents, I say, 'Imagine you're home, and your mother shows up for Thanksgiving dinner,'" said Elizabeth Englander, the Massachusetts research psychologist, who watched the aftermath of Phoebe's death unfold with dismay. "You call your twelve-year-old and tell her to give her grandma a kiss. She makes a gross-out face and rolls her eyes. You're mortified. You take her by the ear and drag her into the kitchen and say, 'That was *awful*. If you ever want to see your laptop and cell phone again, you're going to tell her you are sorry right now.' That's what we call communicating a norm—making it very clear what the behavioral standards are."

Sayer and Smith had actually taken a stab at bullying prevention a few months before Phoebe's suicide, but it was glancing and hadn't led to the sustained effort Englander urges. South Hadley spent $9,000 for one day of staff training, at the outset of Phoebe's ninth-grade year, with Barbara Coloroso, author of a best-selling self-help book about bullying. Coloroso spoke to the teachers for six or seven hours, and some of them complained afterward about the passive format and the buzzword-laden presentation. She also gave a session for parents, at which attendance was low. This is the kind of one-off gesture toward changing a school culture that drives experts such as Englander crazy. It didn't have any real effect.

After Phoebe's death, Coloroso attacked South Hadley for failing to carry out her prescriptions. Whether or not she had actually given the school the guidance it needed, surely a concerted campaign to stop the targeting of girls as sluts would have benefited the school and its students. Amid all the finger-pointing over bullying prevention, however, a key point got lost: Phoebe's death was preceded by the reddest red flag for suicide. That problem is depression.

Again and again, in study after study of teenagers (and adults), it is depression that predicts whether someone will try to kill herself. Since bullying can contribute to making teens depressed, it's a risk factor. But it's not the only factor, or even necessarily the main one. The causes of suicide are almost always complex, and preventing it involves much more than preventing bullying. To reduce Phoebe's death to a "bullycide," as the media did, was myth making. It wasn't a benign error, either. "That jump to causality is so easy and heart wrenching and sensational," Columbia University psychiatrist Madelyn Gould told me. "But it's also irresponsible. Suicide, in general, is never caused by one thing. The impression we're giving to parents and schools, and kids themselves, is that anyone who is bullied is at a heightened risk of killing themselves, without taking into account the other facts in their lives that have made them vulnerable."

That crucial nuance was nowhere to be found in the media frenzy that followed Phoebe's death. Instead, the coverage amped up the sensational accusations that South Hadley students encouraged Phoebe to go ahead and kill herself, and then went online afterward to celebrate. I looked everywhere for those posts and I couldn't find them. It was true that a few commenters had written cruel things on a Facebook memorial page for Phoebe, but there was no evidence they were from South Hadley. I did find a *Boston Herald* article quoting an anonymous local source about the "she deserved it" and "mission accomplished" posts, in repetition of the rumors all over the Internet, and then the migration of this gossip to national television, where it was treated as unimpeachable fact. Of course, the likely untruth of these particular rumors didn't excuse the ugly things Ashley *had* said to Phoebe, with Sean and Kayla egging her on, or that Sharon had shouted in the cafeteria a week earlier. But the "mission accomplished" allegations gave the story its salacious, viral, made-for-morning-TV zing. The media and the online commenters turned Phoebe's suicide and its aftermath into the paradigmatic parable of teenage evil.

And then prosecutors stepped in.

At the end of March, the district attorney for northwestern Massachusetts, Elizabeth Scheibel, announced that she was filing charges against six teenagers in connection with Phoebe's death. Scheibel had grown up in South Hadley and gone to high school with Dan Smith. At the press conference, she detailed the harassment Phoebe experienced in the library, at dismissal, and on her way home on January 14. Then she went further, describing the day as "the culmination of a nearly three-month campaign of verbally assaultive behavior and threats of physical harm toward Phoebe, on school grounds, by several South Hadley high school students." She said that the misconduct "far exceeded the limits of normal teenage relationship-related quarrels," calling it "torturous" and "relentless."

For this reason, Scheibel implied, she'd taken the unusual—maybe even unprecedented—step of bringing serious criminal charges for nonviolent bullying. I wasn't sure what to think. I hadn't talked to a single teenager in South Hadley who described an orchestrated, relentless three-month campaign against Phoebe.

Standing there at the podium, the DA reeled off the charges. Six kids faced a total of twenty counts. Sean: statutory rape, violation of civil rights with bodily injury, criminal harassment, and disturbance of a school assembly. Kayla: violation of civil rights with bodily injury, criminal harassment, and disturbance of a school assembly. Ashley: violation of civil rights with bodily injury, criminal harassment, disturbance of a school assembly, and assault with a dangerous weapon. Flannery and Sharon: violation of civil rights with bodily injury, stalking, criminal harassment, and disturbance of a school assembly. Austin: statutory rape.

When the press conference was over, I went online and looked up the Massachusetts criminal code. Stalking and harassment were straightforward, each carrying a maximum two-and-a-half-year sentence. Disturbing a school assembly meant disrupting any gathering in school, as Ashley and Sharon had apparently done by yelling at Phoebe. Assault with a deadly weapon referred to Ashley throwing the empty can at Phoebe. Sean and Austin were charged with statutory rape for allegedly having sex with Phoebe. The sex, which Austin denied, could be consensual and still criminal, because Sean was seventeen, Austin was eighteen, and Phoebe was fifteen. The sentence for this old common-law crime was indefinite. A conviction or guilty plea would mean the boys would have to register as sex offenders.

The charge of civil rights violation that the four girls and Sean faced turned out to be the heaviest artillery. Previously the statute had been used to prosecute racist group violence. Scheibel made a new argument: Phoebe's civil rights had been violated because she'd been called "Irish slut" and because the bullying interfered with her right to an education. The "bodily injury" in the indictments was Phoebe's death. By bringing this charge, the district attorney was directly blaming five teenagers for another teenager's decision to commit suicide—and if it stuck, each of them could go to prison for ten years.

Principal Smith called Flannery's mother an hour before the DA's press conference to say that he was sorry, but she had to come get her daughter, as students under indictment weren't allowed to stay on the grounds of South Hadley High. Jen drove over in a downpour, numb with shock, her mind racing as she tried to absorb the gravity of what Scheibel's decision meant for her family. She found Flannery in Smith's office. He was reassuring her that he didn't think she had anything to fear. "He said, 'We talked to the DA and we told them you had nothing to do with it,'" Flannery remembered. "But then he asked me if Austin was in school. I said no. He said, 'Well, his name is going to be mentioned, too, for statutory rape.' I said, 'Are you joking?'"

Watching the press conference on TV with her mother, Flannery still felt like it wasn't real. "There's Betsy Scheibel talking about three *months* of bullying," she told me. "I was confused. I didn't understand how she was putting this twist on it. Because to my eyes, that was not at all how it went. It was literally two girls fighting—you know, equal conflict."

Flannery paused. "I was always confident that what I did was normal, normal high school stuff. I held on to that. But now I knew it didn't matter. Nobody would believe me anymore."

Part II

Escalation

Chapter 4

Monique

MONIQUE, HER MOTHER, ALYCIA, AND HER GRANDMOTHER Alexa drove across Middletown in the family Jeep on a February night in 2011, headed for a meeting at the city's Board of Education. Two weeks had passed since Alycia had pulled her daughter out of Woodrow Wilson Middle School, and now she wanted the school board and the people of Middletown to hear directly from Monique about the bullying and its impact. Alycia had picked out Monique's outfit—black pants and a white long-sleeved shirt with a flower—and Alexa had written a statement for her to read out loud. Monique was nervous: she'd never done anything like this before. When she walked in, she saw that the room was packed with dozens of teachers and parents.

Alexa and Alycia shepherded Monique to a seat between them in the second row. After the Pledge of Allegiance, the chairman of the school board opened the session to public comments. Alexa went up to the podium and spoke, and then Monique joined her. In a low voice, she read her speech, which she'd printed longhand on a page torn from a notebook:

> *My name is Monique McClain. I am the one being bullied.*
> *My grandmother says it's better to fight with words than*
> *with your fists.*
> *She's been fighting for me a long time. But I don't think it's*
> *really working.*

Monique's voice broke, and Alycia got up to put an arm around her shoulder. "You can do this," Alexa whispered in her granddaughter's ear. Teary-eyed, Monique kept going:

> *I used to love to go to school. But it's too dangerous now.*
> *Someone is going to get hurt.*
> *Please let me have a tutor. I know I'll miss all my teachers.*
> *But at least I'll be safe. . . . Thank you.*

When Monique sat down, Alycia added a few words of her own. She said her daughter felt isolated and depressed and wanted to be in school—somewhere other than Woodrow Wilson. Alycia had asked the district to transfer Monique to a nearby magnet school called Thomas Edison, but the superintendent, Michael Frechette, had said that wasn't an option. Because she feared for her daughter's safety at Woodrow Wilson, Alycia said, she'd decided to ask the district to provide home tutoring, the only other alternative she could think of.

In support of her request, Alycia handed each school board member a packet of documents, including a letter from a therapist who'd been seeing Monique since November. The therapist wrote that Monique presented with "difficulty focusing, increased isolation, and anxiety in the school environment." Monique's academic work was suffering because she couldn't concentrate, and the therapist was recommending an "alternate placement for Monique's schooling." The packet also included a list of eighteen kids whom the McClains called bullies. The list started with Cheyenne and Destiny and moved on to Gianna ("instigating people to fight, dirty looks, throwing food and pouring syrup . . . Sent hostile and vulgar text during Christmas vacation"), Aminah ("throwing food"), Jasmine ("tripped Monique causing bloody scrapes and bruises"), and Davina ("gets in face, name-calling, follows Monique, skips classes to fight"). The McClains didn't read the list out loud or release it to the press, but they wanted the school board to know which kids were involved.

When the meeting broke up, a local blogger and critic of the school board named Ed McKeon asked principal Charles Marqua what he was doing to help Monique. Marqua said he was following Middletown's bullying prevention policy, but conceded that "it just does not work in every instance." The problem, he said, was that different students had been accused of harassing Monique over the fall and winter, and the school had to address each incident separately. "They complain," he said of Alycia and Alexa, "and we address the complaints."

McKeon posted Marqua's response on his blog, along with Gianna's MySpace message. Thirty comments came in, most of them in support of Monique. "Where are these bullies' parents?" one commenter wrote. "The language is totally unacceptable and the threats are outrageous!" The local NBC evening news picked up on Monique's speech to the school board and did a story about her. So did the *Middletown Press,* with the headline "Bullying Nightmare: Middletown Teen 'Used to Love to Go to School,'" and a photo showing Monique, backlit and somber, staring out her apartment window.

Alexa and Alycia felt vindicated: surely now the school district would be forced to educate Monique somewhere—anywhere—other than Woodrow Wilson.

But if Superintendent Frechette felt pressure to respond to the McClains' plea for help, he didn't show it. Frechette had come to Middletown several years earlier with a mandate to address declining test scores, and he took pride in the headway he'd made district-wide. Scores at the middle school and high school still fell below the state average, but they were inching up every year, and Middletown had reduced the achievement gap between white and minority students.

In the rough realm of local politics, though, Frechette was having a particularly bruising year. He'd had a blowout with Mayor Sebastian Giuliano that culminated in a spectacular standoff with the police, who occupied the school district building and locked it down for more than a week because of unproven accusations of document shredding there. Frechette and the school board also clashed with the cops after an officer assigned to the high school Tasered a student in the cafeteria in front of hundreds of kids and teachers. The officer said the student he shot had resisted arrest for stealing a Jamaican beef patty. Rattled by this use of force, the school board asked the police to leave their posts in the Middletown schools, fueling the feud with the mayor, an ally of the acting police chief.

The feud was very much alive when Alexa went to see Mayor Giuliano four months before the February school board meeting. At this point, Destiny and Cheyenne were harassing Monique, Alycia was losing faith in the school officials, and Alexa was casting about for some way to help her family. She kept hoping that if she could just find the right person, someone in power, he would come through for her granddaughter. She'd never spoken to Giuliano before, but she walked into his office and he made time to talk to her, listening sympathetically. When she asked what she should do, Giuliano urged Alexa to speak out publicly. That was how Alexa and Alycia wound up at their first Board of Education meeting in October. Speaking for the family,

Alexa described the taunts of "biter" and "snitch," the ganging up on Monique, her growing dread of school. "She used to have a sparkle, but now she doesn't," Alexa said. "Please help Monique."

Alexa had every right to say her piece. But as Giuliano surely could have anticipated, Frechette didn't appreciate the public scolding, which led to a local newspaper story in which he stressed, again, that the district had a "strict" anti-bullying policy. Now, four months later at the February board meeting, with Monique out of school, Frechette sat impassively. Monique's troubles at Woodrow Wilson may have started in the small private world of thirteen-year-old girls, but now they had moved far beyond that, into a charged adult arena. And this made Monique's problems much harder to solve.

The publicity didn't win the McClains any fans on the staff at Woodrow Wilson, either. Alycia and Alexa hired a lawyer who drummed up more coverage, planting stories in the local papers and blogs in an effort to force the school board to find a new school for Monique or supply a tutor. School officials resented all of it. "The whole thing seems very staged," Principal Marqua told me. "It's a media show."

Meanwhile, the weeks ticked by with Monique out of school. A local mental health group tried to negotiate an end to the standoff, but nothing came of it. At the Board of Education meeting in March, a chorus of McClains took turns at the podium. Alexa said her granddaughter was being "psychologically abused by the apathy of the board," and Monique's father, who'd driven down from the town of New Britain, expressed his "disgust" with the way the situation was being handled. He was followed by Monique's uncle and then by her grandfather, who told the school board, "If you can't handle it, I will volunteer my time." Johnny Callas, the coach for the boxing program Monique had joined in the fall, also spoke up for her. Callas was a social worker and ombudsman at the Department of Children and Families in Connecticut. "I'm appealing to you, as parents and professionals, and most of all as human beings, to do the right thing on behalf of this innocent kid," he said. "Send her back to a different school."

After sitting through the barrage of criticism and entreaties, Frechette called to the podium Middletown's supervisor of special education, who flashed through a series of PowerPoint slides detailing school policies on bullying. She stressed that the district was trying to address kids' "mean behaviors" by comprehensively "improving school climate." School staff usually "intervened effectively" when kids were mean to each other, she said; she even claimed, oddly, that most victims ended up befriending their former bullies. Prompted by a Board of Education member for the number of verified bullying reports each year, Otis replied that there had been five in 2007–8, one in 2008–9, and two in 2009–10. The board chairman paused to let the numbers sink in. "Things are in fact improving?" he asked. The special ed supervisor said yes. "Could we do better?" the board chairman asked rhetorically, then continued, "We probably could—we're trying to do better. But we live in a world where violence in the home is acceptable and that has a connection to this. I wish I had a magic wand to end this, but we're not going to do it in one day. We're doing as much if not more than other districts, and I just needed to speak so everyone knows that within the bounds of the law, we're doing everything we can."

The next day, a police officer came to see Monique's grandfather and asked him to go to the Middletown police station to answer questions, because the school board had felt threatened by his remark at the meeting: "If you can't handle it, I will volunteer my time." Alexa insisted on going with him. When they arrived, she says, the investigating officer told them he'd reviewed the video of the meeting, saw nothing wrong, and apologized for wasting their time. To the McClains, the summons seemed like one more petty abuse of power—a veiled message about the cost of speaking out.

———

Most of the kids I talked to at Woodrow Wilson thought Monique and her family were right to press the school to do more about bullying—including Aminah, Gianna, and Jasmine. "My personal opinion is that her mom is right," Aminah said. "This school tries to make a big deal about bullying, but when people are really getting bullied, they're just like—" and she opened her hands and raised her shoulders to mime an adult's empty shrug.

Melissa Robinson, the Youth Services Bureau social worker, worried about how combative the school climate had become. Relationships among students, especially for the status-seeking girls, were frayed by rivalry after rivalry. "Let's Start Drama" simmered with nasty gossip, and Robinson tracked it with increasing dismay. The girls caught up in the rumor-mongering struck her as untethered, in school and at home. Robinson and her boss, Justin Carbonella, had gotten a small grant a few months earlier from the state Department of Health to start an after-school program with a bullying prevention curriculum. Robinson asked students to volunteer and also recruited kids she thought would benefit. Jasmine and Aminah both joined. In all, about a dozen kids signed up, including a few assigned to the group as a form of discipline.

In the beginning of March, I went to see the class in action, watching as the kids streamed into a first-floor English classroom at 2:45 on a Tuesday afternoon. They ran the spectrum from well-behaved high achievers to loudmouthed troublemakers. Eight girls and a boy headed for the desk piled with Doritos, potato chips, and Capri Sun drinks. Robinson got up to close the door, and another girl with glasses, a blue Adidas sweatshirt, and cornrows bounded in, out of breath. Without meaning to, she made it clear what Robinson was up against.

"I'm late because two kids were about to fight," the girl explained. "So I had to yell 'Fight, fight.'"

Robinson raised her eyebrows. "And you don't see a problem with that?"

The girl looked at her blankly. "What?" she said, grabbing a bag of Doritos and taking a seat.

Robinson shook her head and picked up her notebook. The grant required her to use a curriculum that was several years old, made no mention of the Internet, and seemed designed for younger kids. Robinson made the best of it. One of her main goals was to get the kids to think about how they might be egging on fighting and bullying, even if they weren't instigators themselves. Robinson read a statement from the curriculum aloud: "Watching a fight and doing nothing is *supporting* a fight." She asked the kids to line up on one side if they agreed and on the other side if they disagreed. With some jostling, the kids split into roughly equal groups.

"Okay, if someone yells 'Fight, fight,' will that make people here more likely to fight?" Robinson asked. The kids nodded. "Right," she agreed. "We've talked about being a bystander. Look, I know that sometimes there's nothing you can do to stop the fighting, but do you think that's true the *majority* of the time?"

"If you jumped in to stop it, you'd get hit," the girl who'd rushed in late said. "You might try to stop it, but if you're there, the teacher will think you're in it, too."

"Do you know what a *culture* is?" Robinson asked. "A way that people think, right?" Sending the kids back to their seats, she sat down on a desk to face them. "It sounds to me like the culture of the students here—tell me if I'm wrong—is that you don't get involved when you see a fight breaking out. When you're a bystander, you don't take action."

"Well, if a fight has nothing to do with you, then you don't get into it," the girl with the cornrows said. Other kids nodded.

"What about bullying?" Robinson asked.

"You don't get into that, either," the girl answered. "Maybe you don't know that's what it is when you see something happen. Or maybe you don't want people coming down on you."

Robinson told the kids about the research showing that bullying involved an audience of peers in nearly nine of ten cases—yet the by-standers defended the victim less than 20 percent of the time. When they just stood around or laughed, the bullying tended to be pro-longed. "What if the bystanders stood up more often?" Robinson asked the class. "What if you did, when you saw a fight or you saw someone making fun of someone else whose feelings were getting hurt? Do you think that would matter?"

It's a tantalizing and frequently asked question, and for good rea-son. Some studies have shown that most kids who are bystanders don't like bullying and would like to step in, if they only knew how. And they can have an impact: when bystanders *do* stand up for vic-tims, they stop bullies in their tracks as often as half the time. "Stu-dents tend to look to each other for cues about what to do when they see bullying," Susan Swearer told me. "I like to tell this story from a group of fourth graders I worked with in a rural community. A boy moved in and started bullying other kids on the playground, as part of trying to figure out his place in this new environment. When the other kids told me about this, I asked them what happened. They said, 'We just told him, "You can't do that here." ' So I asked, 'Then what?' They looked at me like I was an idiot and said, 'He stopped.' "

Yet it's much easier to talk about bystander heroes than it is to play the part. Think about how reluctant adults are to intervene in a conflict. Often we're not sure whether we'll be hailed or jeered, or even hurt. I blundered into testing this on the subway one day in Washington, D.C., not long ago, when I saw four teenagers yelling at an older man. I didn't know what or who had started the fight. Other people in the car, who'd gotten on before I had and presumably had a better handle on the situation, looked away from the conflict and kept quiet. At first I followed their cue, but then the hectoring got more vi-cious, and I thought, *Wait, I'm writing a book about bullying! By-standers are supposed to speak up!* So I told the teenagers to stop, to leave the old man alone. At which point they turned their wrath on me, following me out of the subway car and up the escalator, yelling "bitch" and worse all the way. As my face got hot with embarrassment and I started to sweat, I wondered if everyone around me was thinking that I'd done something to deserve the curses raining down. Maybe, I thought, I should have stayed out of it.

Some prevention efforts (including Dan Olweus' program and another one called Steps to Respect, which has shown it can improve bystander behavior among participating students) try to ease up on kids by offering the option of supporting victims *after* the fact. In other words, you don't necessarily have to take the risk of confronting a bully to give comfort to a target. You can choose the lesser risk of standing by the victim in a more behind-the-scenes sort of way, and while you won't get the hero award, you'll still be helping. In one important survey, high school students who'd been bullied were asked to describe the best thing another student had done to help them, and victims consistently mentioned peers who'd called them at home or spent time with them after they'd been mocked. One thirteen-year-old wrote of a friend who didn't desert her, "It made me feel more confident that I would be able to keep being myself and not let this ruin my life." This made me feel a little better about my own lack of heroism in eighth grade, when I didn't stand up for my friend Allie in the lunchroom that day.

I was left with a question, though: what makes kids more or less willing to stand by someone who's being attacked? Only in the last few years have researchers begun to answer that question. They've found that defending victims is linked to showing greater empathy, as you might expect. But it also has a lot to do with who your friends are, at least for boys.

That finding comes from an intriguing study by Dorothy Espelage, the research psychologist at the University of Illinois. In 2011, she created a map of the social networks in the sixth and seventh grades of an Illinois school. Espelage found that the boys who were in friendship groups with higher levels of bullying were less willing to intervene, even if they weren't bullies themselves. The upshot: prevention efforts won't work well if they ignore the level of bullying within different social groups. "It's blind adult hope to think that kids will just stand up for each other," she told me. "You can try to instill in kids a sense of personal responsibility to help victims, but they'll still look to what their peers are doing and ask, 'Will they still be my friends?'"

Espelage's findings highlighted the importance of social context on a micro level—the feedback among friends. She also made the point that the best interveners are often the kids with high social capital, because of the outsized influence they can have. This reminded me of crucial support Monique got while she was out of school—from her boxing team.

Johnny Callas started teaching kids to box in 1988, as his championship career as an amateur featherweight was winding down. "We started out of an old housing project, Charter Oaks, in Hartford," he told me. "We built a gym there. Amateur boxing was the hook. Once the kid was involved, we'd try to surround the family with wraparound services. We had Big Brother and Big Sister, and Trinity College put together a tutorial homework program. The college students were coming to the projects to tutor and mentor three times a week. We wanted it to be a model nationally." While he trained his kids and oversaw his tutors, Callas earned a social work degree and went to work for Connecticut's Department of Children and Families, where he investigated allegations of abuse and neglect. "I was the guy who would knock on the front door," he said.

In the name of urban renewal, a 1990s federal grant demolished the housing project—and the gym along with it—and a promise from Hartford's mayor to give Charter Oaks another gym never came through. Callas' program went on a long hiatus. "I try to block that out, those years," he said. Then in 2008, a for-profit health club on the outskirts of Middletown called the Lion's Den asked Callas to run its youth development boxing program. Callas agreed on the condition that he could bring in high-risk poor kids along with the middle-class paying ones. He got the club's approval and city funding for scholarships. "That meant we could have an array of kids," he told me. "Every color, males and females, eight to twenty-one, every sexual orientation and background. We got huge—we had almost seventy-five kids."

When Monique signed up and Alycia told Callas about her daughter's problems at school, he got in touch with assistant principal Diane Niles at Woodrow Wilson. Callas urged Niles to do more to help Monique but came away frustrated. As fall turned to winter, he grew increasingly worried about how quiet, almost vacant, Monique seemed. When she missed two weeks of practice in late December, around the time Gianna sent the mean MySpace message, Callas called Alycia to find out what was wrong. She told him Monique felt too bad about herself to box. In response, Callas called his team together to figure out how to bring her back into the fold. "I wanted us to rally around her," he said.

It's a gamble to talk to a group of kids about one child's personal problems. It means trusting teenagers to be sensitive and discreet, something that teachers and administrators are often reluctant to do. But Callas was an independent operator and he thought his team could handle it. They appreciated his trust. "We were about to work out one day, and Coach started talking to us about how Monique was being bullied," said Juliebeth, the wiry, vivacious state boxing champion for girls under eighty-five pounds. "We really got into it. We talked almost the whole practice. We even went on someone's iPhone and Googled the stuff in the news about Monique. We said, 'We should really call her.' So I did."

Juliebeth was in Monique's class at Woodrow Wilson, and in sixth grade, she'd had a run-in with a girl who was friends with Aminah and Gianna. Juliebeth knew from that experience what Monique was up against and how it felt to be in her position. "I used to be friends with that girl, then she said I tried to steal her best friend,"

Juliebeth said. "She said stuff to me all the time on the bus. It got so bad I couldn't take the bus anymore. My mom was afraid something would happen. So she drove me to school every day last year. She tried to talk to her mom a few times, but her mom didn't care. My mom asked the school if I could take the bus from somewhere else. They said no."

Juliebeth's troubles had faded when the girl moved and started riding a different bus. Her success at boxing helped, too; she felt good about herself for it, and kids at school were impressed. By Espelage's lights, Juliebeth had the makings of a defender: she sympathized with Monique, she had the social capital to help, and Callas had made her feel like she'd be doing it for the team.

Juliebeth called Monique that night and told her she was missed at boxing. "She said the only place she felt like she could be herself was at the gym, because no one criticized her here," Juliebeth said. "Monique talked more then than I'd heard her talk before. I told her we wanted her to come back."

It was a small gesture—one phone call—but Monique came back at the next practice and stayed for good. She was chatting with four other girls on the steps to one of the boxing rings when I showed up to watch practice one day in April. A boy walked over, and Monique asked to see his iPod Touch. One of the girls asked if she could try on Monique's boxing gloves. She turned out to be Brianna, Destiny's cousin. Without saying anything, Monique handed over her glove, and Brianna tried it on, gave it back, and smiled.

Juliebeth wasn't just nice to Monique at the gym. She also invited Monique over to her house on the weekend. One of the seventh-grade girls who'd ganged up on Monique lived next door, and when she saw Monique go inside, she called Juliebeth to ask what Monique was doing there. Juliebeth told her they were watching a movie, then hung up, unfazed. "I said, 'She came over—so what?'" she told me.

Juliebeth defended Monique in front of the wider audience of Facebook, too. An exchange on the site from that spring:

Seventh grader: Monique takes boxing at the Lions Den?
Juliebeth: yeahhhh
Seventh grader: Fuck That, i'm not boxing there . . . My
  mom was gonna sign me up. Hell NOO
Juliebeth: why dont u like her ?
Seventh grader: Because she tlked so much shit about
  everybody . . . Including ME! She tlked shit about YOU too
  before. She twofaced & fake!
Juliebeth: ohhhh shes my friend.

Another small yet profound gesture. "I didn't really think about it," Juliebeth said. "That's how I felt, so I just said it."

If Monique's story were a movie, it would end with a knockout. She'd train with Callas, steadily gaining strength and skills and confidence, and then she'd deck Gianna, her tormentor, while Juliebeth and the rest of the team cheered her on. *The Karate Kid*, with girls.

Except that Gianna doesn't box, and Coach Callas would be fired (and maybe sued) if he encouraged Monique to hit a girl outside the ring. These days, the answer to bullying is always supposed to be nonviolent, especially in schools. "They never once mention that if the bully doesn't stop, we recommend you take a self-defense class," a police officer named Oscar Bocanegra pointed out to me at a three-day training for the Olweus prevention program. It seemed to him that, according to the Olweus method, dealing with bullying "is all about a lengthy process with a lot of meetings."

He wasn't sure this would fly in his hometown in south Texas, where some schools had to cope with gangs and crime. Over lunch, Bocanegra told me, a little wistfully, about a California program called Gracie Bullyproof, created by the family of a legendary grandmaster of the martial art Brazilian jiu-jitsu, which teaches—as the master's twenty-seven-year-old grandson, Rener Gracie, put it—that if you tell a bully to stop and he won't listen, "you take both of your hands and push him as hard as you can in the chest. You blast him. Knock him off his feet." Bocanegra didn't see why that response was officially off-limits. "I guess I'm old-school, but when I was growing up, bullying just happened and you dealt with it by hitting back," he said. "Why don't we still tell kids that?"

Oscar Bocanegra speaks for a lot of people in asking that question. Never mind that parents know they aren't supposed to advocate violence, and kids who hit back know they can expect to get into trouble—a lot of us want kids who are getting picked on to turn the tables, and when they do, we revel in the sweetness of the revenge; that's just human nature. *The Karate Kid* is close to thirty years old, but the feelings of righteous indignation and retribution the movie conveys remain fresh. (The same is true of George McFly rising up to flatten his tormentor Biff in *Back to the Future*.) In a one-way conflict between a violent kid and a peaceable one, we can't help hoping the bully will get his comeuppance in the end. It's a way to cheer aggression and feel moral about it.

Witness the reaction to a forty-second video called "Casey the Punisher," which became an Internet sensation a few weeks before I visited Monique's boxing practice. In footage shot from a phone, a short, thin boy steps up to a taller, heavy one in a schoolyard and punches him in the face. The bigger boy takes the punch, once, twice, as two girls stand by, laughing. It's clear this has happened before. The small boy dances around the big one, taunting him. The big boy takes it for a few more seconds. And then he grabs his tormentor in a bear hug, raises him above his head, and body-slams him onto the cement. The small boy gets up slowly and limps away.

The larger boy, Casey, turned out to be a fifteen-year-old from Sydney, Australia, and within days, he had several Facebook pages with hundreds of thousands of fans and his own South Korean anime video—full-fledged cult hero status. "I will be doing presentations on bullying at schools in Australia and hopefully I can make it to the USA afterwards," Casey wrote on his Facebook page. In a TV interview, he said he'd been bullied about his weight for years. "I didn't realize how much trouble he was actually in until I had seen that video," his father said. "And he said, 'Well, that goes on every day, Dad.' And I thought to myself, you poor little bloke, you know?" Ritchard, the twelve-year-old boy who'd punched Casey, turned out to be not seriously injured. He made a bid for sympathy on TV, saying he'd also been a victim of bullying in the past. But Ritchard didn't help himself by claiming that Casey had started the fight; he was soon buried in a heap of Internet sludge. Commenters denounced the school, too, for suspending both boys to enforce its zero-tolerance policy on violence.

An argument could be made, though, that Casey's school was actually protecting kids like him: research shows that victims who strike back against bullies often prolong or worsen their social woes. Engaging the bully on his own terms can encourage him—he's dragged you into the mud with him—and victims who do this sometimes have "extreme reactions due to an elevated state of arousal," in the jargon of one study. In English, they lose control and fly off the handle.

Also, there's a reason Casey is the exception rather than the rule: most targets aren't twice the size of their tormentors. The fact is, bullies often have a physical advantage, and fighting them just leads to getting beaten up. "My problem is that I retaliate," one perceptive seventh-grade boy who felt targeted by a few other boys told me. "It's just, the kids know me. I try to ignore them but I've retaliated so often before that by now they know that if they just keep going, I'll do something back. I've had my backpack jacked up and also thrown in the creek and one time I took a rock to the head. It keeps going and going."

I got this, and I've never suggested punching a bully in the nose to the kids I talk to, or to my two sons. But some part of me still couldn't help wondering whether, now that Monique knew how to box, she'd be better off going back to school and aiming one good jab at the next kid who bothered her, just to show she'd learned to defend herself. I called Callas to ask if it had ever secretly crossed his mind, too. "I've got to tell you, I'd love to just go over to that school some day and roll through everyone in the parking lot," he said. "So would the kids on my team. Of course we'd never do it. That's the antithesis of our whole program. We are teaching kids self-esteem and humility. But do I think Monique should strongly consider standing up for herself next time someone bullies her? Yes, I do." Callas paused. "Do I think she shouldn't *have* to do that, and that the real problem is that all the systems have failed her? Yes, I think that, too."

Alycia felt the same way. Sitting on the bunk bed in Monique's bedroom one day a few feet from her daughter, she previewed the advice she planned to give Monique when she went back to school. "Just make sure to try to be friends with everyone," Alycia said. "But you know, if you ever come across this situation again, you're going to defend yourself. You're going to knock their damn head off." Monique bit her thumbnail. Alycia looked away. "I understand she's not a fighter outside the ring, but we're not going through this again. I told Monique, if you get suspended or arrested for fighting back, we'll deal with it. If anyone gets in your face, you get them out of your face."

Monique cut in without looking at her mother. "I don't fight," she said.

I thought back to something Juliebeth had told me: "My mom thinks Monique should just punch them in the face. She is really against this whole bullying thing and she just feels like that's how you stop it. I'm like, 'Mom, you have to understand: she's *scared*.'"

Boxing or no boxing, Monique just had a gentle, passive way of being in the world. She wasn't going to do a turn as Monique the Punisher. She was more like Ferdinand the Bull, in the old children's story, who refuses to fight the matador and wants only to sit under the cork tree and smell the flowers. The story mocks aggression rather than praising it. We love Ferdinand the Bull even though he never strikes back or toughens up. Maybe that was what Monique needed to hear, too.

Back in the land of the adults, the fighting escalated. With Monique still at home instead of at school, Frechette's office reported her as truant to the Connecticut Department of Children and Families. "It's like they're the bullies now," Alycia fired back at the district in a local news story about the truancy complaint. She filed her own complaint with DCF. Both sides accused the other of "educational neglect."

From the end of January through March, Monique's teachers had been giving her a weekly packet of assignments so she could keep up with her classwork. Alycia picked them up from the front office on Mondays and returned them, completed, on Fridays. But when Alycia came in one Monday in mid-March, she was told there would be no more packets; the district's position was that Alycia had to send her daughter back to Woodrow Wilson or fill out the paperwork to home-school her. There were no other choices.

The McClains' lawyer responded to this ultimatum with a stunt engineered for maximum press coverage. She hired a state marshal to go to Woodrow Wilson to ask for Monique's coursework—alerting the media first, of course, so reporters from the *Middletown Press* and NBC local news were there to catch the marshal walking away empty-handed. If the lawyer thought she could force Frechette to cave with such tactics, however, she'd misjudged him. He didn't budge.

Desperate, Alexa sent a Hail Mary email to the commissioner of the Department of Children and Families, cc'ing Mayor Giuliano, the governor's office, and the commissioner of the state Department of Education, which had refused to get involved. "HOW DO WE PREPARE Monique to FINISH 7th grade on her own with no help from the District (WWMS)????????" she wrote. "WHERE DO WE GET the preparation work so that we will be able to show that she will be qualified to enter the 8th grade???????? WE ARE NOT HOMESCHOOLERS!"

The only response she got back was a suggestion to call the state's consultant on bullying and character education. Alexa had already done that, to no avail.

The McClains cobbled together the bits of help they could find. A local nonprofit found a Wesleyan student who volunteered to tutor Monique two or three times a week. Monique participated in a state-wide Kid's Court competition, winning second place for her age group for an essay about Rosa Parks and fighting for your rights. Best of all, Johnny Callas scored an introduction for her to a top middleweight boxer, Sergio Martinez, who then dedicated his spring championship fight at Connecticut's Foxwoods casino to Monique. He gave her and Alycia and Alexa VIP tickets, and HBO flew them to California to appear in a promotional spot that linked Monique's problems with bullying to Martinez's experience of violence growing up in Argentina. "He has made me feel like that's my second family, because he took the time to meet me and know what I went through," Monique said shyly for the cameras. Back at home, she covered the walls of her bedroom with Sergio souvenirs: a hat with a glitter band, posters of his bouts, and a pair of boxing gloves he'd signed.

But on the many days between the flashes of activity, Monique was bored and restless. She knew she was missing out and she needed to go back to school. Her mother and grandmother knew it, too. More than anything else, Monique wanted to feel normal again. She wanted the drama to be over.

At Woodrow Wilson, the seventh-grade girls weren't talking about Monique anymore. It was the adults who were stuck. Speaking to me on background, school officials made it clear they felt the McClains were asking—and not nicely—for special treatment for a student who had no good reason not to go back to Woodrow Wilson. After sitting through another round of testimony from the McClains and their supporters in April (during which Monique's tutor said Wesleyan students were "all ashamed of the Board of Education"), the school board, instead of softening its stance toward the McClains, discussed changing its bylaws to restrict public comments. "Everyone has to understand that this is *not* the public's meeting," one board member said, looking pointedly at Alycia and Alexa. "It's *our* meeting."

When the parents of affluent kids feel disappointed by a school, they can pay to switch to another one. Alycia didn't have the money for that. She thought about uprooting herself and her four-year-old son, as well as Monique, but she'd been in Middletown for a decade. She had a job. She had friends and family. She didn't want to move away from them and start over again. She didn't feel she should have to.

In investigating the dueling complaints that Alycia and the Middletown schools brought against each other, the Department of Children and Families found neither side officially at fault. Behind the scenes, the agency's legal director tried to help Monique. The clearest way to do that, she told the McClains, was through special education: if Monique qualified for special ed, Middletown would have no choice but to find an alternative placement for her. The problem was that Monique wasn't a good match for special ed. The psychologist who assessed her found no evidence of any disability, and tests showed her performing at grade level. The psychologist suggested that when she returned to school, Monique would need help negotiating the "aggressive/confrontational hassle associated with school relationships," but that wasn't enough to make her eligible for any special services.

At this point, the DCF legal director told the McClains there was little more she could do. She didn't have the authority to order Frechette to find another school for Monique, and Alycia had unknowingly missed the deadline to apply for a place in a magnet school for Monique for the following fall.

Alycia knew plenty of people thought she was being stubborn and should just send her daughter back to Woodrow Wilson, but she couldn't bring herself to trust Frechette and Marqua and the other officials who she felt had failed Monique. She would hear about outpourings of sympathy for victims of bullying who'd committed suicide, children whom it was too late to help, and wonder why Monique's plight prompted no sense of urgency. "It's like there's the school and the Board of Education, and our kids are in their hands, and they can get away with treating them however they want. If they decide they don't have your back, that's just how it is," Alycia said. "Then when a child takes her own life, that's when everyone wants to talk about doing something about bullying. But why does it have to come to that?"

At Woodrow Wilson, Principal Charles Marqua had become a detached and defeated presence. He no longer made eye contact or said hello when he walked the halls. One day Aminah and Gianna sassed him; Marqua snapped at the girls and then retreated, leaving them to roll their eyes as he walked away. When I sat down with him before the end of the school year, Marqua had nothing good to say about his teaching staff ("This is a traditional group of employees with strong entrenched attitudes") or the student body ("These kids have great difficulty understanding appropriate attitudes and respect").

However beleaguered he was, he was trying to make Woodrow Wilson a better place. He tried a variety of initiatives to improve the school climate and strengthen connections between students and staff, but changing the culture of a school requires strong leadership. A principal has to inspire. Marqua had good ideas on paper, but it was hard for him to make them work in practice.

Take, for example, the system of rewards Marqua was trying to institute for students, part of an approach called Positive Behavioral and Intervention Supports. PBIS has a strong track record for improving student behavior at schools that execute it faithfully, and I'll explore it much more extensively in Chapter 8. Middletown hadn't adopted PBIS exactly, but Marqua was trying to implement one part of it by instructing teachers to hand out Pride Cards as a token of praise. The idea was to focus attention on the small things students did well, as opposed to their misdeeds. "Teachers give the Pride Cards to students who do the right thing," he said. Marqua had also started a Pride Patrol made up of students. "They're trained to know what to do to help in bullying situations. They're often the popular kids who are good role models, and they wear colored lanyards so the other kids know who they are. We have sixty students trained and now we're working on the next forty."

I asked Gianna, Aminah, and Jasmine about Pride Cards and Pride Patrol, and at first they didn't know what I was talking about. This was not a good sign. The whole idea behind PBIS is that the rewards are embedded into the day-to-day life of the school and reinforced constantly. "Oh, those things," Jasmine finally said about the cards after some prodding. "Only one teacher gave them out. I think she stopped like two months ago." About Pride Patrol, Aminah added, "It's pointless. Some of the kids in it are bullies themselves, and the teacher in charge knows that. So all they can do is write someone's name down and give it to him."

Marqua had told me that as a result of his initiatives, the rate of suspensions had declined 30 percent from the previous year. "Serious problems have gone way down," he said. In fact, while out-of-school suspensions had indeed dropped significantly, the number of in-school suspensions was up. Combined, suspensions at Woodrow Wilson had actually risen slightly year to year (from 295 to 306). It was hard to tell why the switch from one type of suspension to another mattered much.

I kept going to Robinson's after-school leadership group, hoping to see signs of a shift among the kids in it. But by the end of the spring, I had to conclude that despite her efforts, the culture of Woodrow Wilson exerted too much counterforce for most of the students to resist. They had the problem Dorothy Espelage had identified in her study about why bystanders are unlikely to intervene: the dozen Middletown kids were being asked to take a stand against bullying while the rest of the school went unchanged.

The best thing the leadership group could offer was the chance for the kids to talk about their dilemma. Robinson couldn't come to the group's final meeting, so Justin Carbonella, director of the Youth Services Bureau and a smart Middletown native, filled in. He wanted the students to reflect on what they'd learned over the last ten weeks. He asked them to describe the kind of reputation they wanted to cultivate now, in middle school, and the kind they thought they should have in the future, as adults.

"Everyone wants a reputation for being a hard-core mofo," said a girl named Ashlynn, who was friends with Jasmine. "For being bad. You don't want anyone to think you're a softie."

"That's exactly the problem," Carbonella said. "Okay, think for a minute. Which reputation leads to being more successful *later* in life?"

Ashlynn didn't hesitate. "Being hard-core," she said. "If people know you're hard-core, they won't mess with you. If you're a softie, they'll go after you."

"Let's fast-forward twenty years," Carbonella said. "You're working at a business—like, for example, Aetna."

"Aetna?" a girl asked.

"It's an insurance company that used to be in Middletown," Carbonella explained. "Do you think people there say, 'He's a softie, let's jump on him'? You said that now you want to be known as hard-core. I get that—it makes sense. But my question is, in twenty years, will that *still* be true?"

Aminah jumped in. "You really don't care what other people think at that point," she said.

"You can be a softie, then?" Carbonella asked. Some kids nodded. Others shook their heads. "So how come we celebrate one thing at your age, but you need to be something else when you get older? How do we change? *Can* we?"

"Well, even now, you're not a hard-core mofo all the time," Ashlynn said. "Because when you're with your friends, you can be a softie, if you have true friends who are actually there for you."

"You can be both," Aminah agreed.

"I *am* both," Jasmine, a strong student, said. "In class, when I'm not with my compadres, I'm a soft little girl. In class, you want to get your work done and get a good grade. But in the hall, you don't get a grade. You have to walk with confidence, like you don't care what other people say. In the hallways, I'm a hard mofo."

Jasmine and Aminah had learned how to strike this pose, but they also looked forward to dropping it—if they could.

Marqua resigned when school ended in June. He blamed his long commute; members of his staff thought he was just a bad fit. Asked about Monique on his way out, Marqua told a local reporter that he was sorry she'd had to experience bullying, but that he considered the large number of snow days he'd dealt with to be a more pressing challenge. His departure didn't make much difference to Alycia, who still refused to send Monique back to Woodrow Wilson in the fall. School started again in September with Monique at home; for weeks, it wasn't even clear she'd been promoted to eighth grade.

When I went to see Superintendent Frechette that fall, he didn't want to talk about Monique. He wanted to stay positive. He was friendly and charming. He reminisced about throwing snowballs at the home of Joe Lieberman, who'd gone on to become Connecticut's longtime senator. He urged me to visit the elementary schools in Middletown, where he said students were thriving and the rewards the district had introduced for good behavior were working. Without criticizing Marqua, he said that Woodrow Wilson's new principal was already changing the tone of the school.

Frechette made a persuasive case that his job, and the job of his administrators and teachers, had become harder over the years as the student population had grown needier. "The behaviors we're seeing, you wouldn't have seen ten or fifteen years ago," he said. "We're taking on the social and emotional education of students in a way we never used to have to do. We're also adding school-based health care centers. We're working with the hospitals because we can't do it ourselves. The mental health component is very important but our teachers and administrators aren't trained in that. You see it walking through our doors every day. You throw in the stress of trying to close the achievement gap, and it's always that you have less funding to do more."

In a district overflowing with need, why should Frechette do something special for Monique?

I was not an overtaxed superintendent, however, and it was hard for me to watch Monique languish at home that fall, listless and at loose ends. I could see that the McClains had alienated the school district by pressing their case so publicly. I could see why Frechette, in a tough job and accustomed to playing hardball, didn't want to bend the rules for a girl whose family had crossed him. But people who deserve help sometimes make mistakes in the way they ask for it, and whatever had gone wrong, Monique wasn't to blame. She'd become the kid at the center of an adult power struggle. Also, how much was she asking for, really? Students transfer from one school to another all the time. How hard could it be to give her a chance to start over?

I started talking about her story to people I knew. Alexa and Alycia had tried hard to make connections for Monique. Figuring that there's nothing fair about who knows whom in life, I decided to use mine. This isn't the traditional role of a journalist, but it felt like the right thing to do. A friend recommended a veteran education lawyer named John Flanders who had a low-key, problem-solving style and knew some of the school officials in Middletown. In November I put Alycia in touch with him, and he started to make headway. It seemed there might be a spot open at Thomas Edison, the magnet school nearby that Alycia had requested from the start.

I also talked to Stefan Pryor, a guy I knew from law school

who—no kidding—was about to become the new Connecticut commissioner of education. Over a cheeseburger and a Diet Coke, Stefan listened to my tale about Monique, asked good questions, and promised to follow up. A week or so later, a member of Stefan's staff called Alycia, and a few days after that, Flanders got a message: yes, there was a slot for Monique at Thomas Edison. Did she want it?

"Monique is going back to school!" Alycia shouted to me on the phone a few minutes later, and for the first time in the year I'd known her, I heard her laugh. Monique started at Thomas Edison later that week.

The morning of her first day of school, Alycia asked Monique if she wanted to ride the bus home, expecting her to say no. Monique said yes. When she got on, a girl sitting next to her quizzed her: Was she the one who'd been in the news about bullying? Did she know Gianna and Aminah and Jasmine? What did she think of them? "Mom, I felt it in my stomach—'Oh no, here we go again,'" Monique told Alycia when she got home that afternoon. But instead of taunting or turning away, the girl told Monique that while those girls were her friends, it didn't matter, and she and Monique could be friends, too. "She asked me to sit with her and we talked the whole way, and I have people to sit with at lunch tomorrow," Monique reported to her mother.

Alycia threw a surprise party for Monique at the end of January, almost a year to the day since she left Woodrow Wilson. When Monique walked into the rec room of the family's apartment building— her mother had told her to wear red for a kids' concert her brother was playing in—she saw about seventy people standing in a sea of red, white, and black streamers and helium balloons. Alycia had persuaded local restaurants to donate chicken cacciatore, ziti, and barbeque chicken. There were two cakes: a small one with a pair of red-icing boxing gloves in a circle of letters spelling out "Hit Me with Your Best Shot," and a big one with two screened-on pictures of Monique, one on her first day of seventh grade with the telltale hairstyle, and the second with her hair in a ponytail, smiling on her first day at Thomas Edison. Alycia snapped photos of Monique with the mayor, John Flanders, Matt Donohue (her Wesleyan tutor), and of course Johnny Callas. Alexa made a speech thanking each of them, which made Callas cry. Best of all, five friends from Thomas Edison came to the party. On a poster board for Monique everyone was asked to sign, one of the girls wrote, "Hey Monique, who knew I could make a new best friend so fast. You sure know how to make an entrance lol. Love you chica."

To my disappointment, I didn't go to the party—months earlier, my old friend Allie had planned a baby shower for that day, and I couldn't miss it. A few days later, I drove to Middletown to hear about the festivities and see for myself how Monique was doing. She met me outside her apartment building, on her way home from school. I asked how she was, and a huge grin split her face. "I'm doing awesome," she said.

We went inside, where Monique showed me the new laptop she'd been assigned when she started school. "Tell Emily why she should give you high fives," Alycia prompted.

"I got all A's on my quizzes so far, in Spanish, math, and social studies," Monique said. "I got a hundred on my language arts essay. I love all my teachers. They have to walk us to class—we get in a line and they come with us. It's good, no problems. Every Thursday, we have this program on bullying called Second Step"—more about this in Chapter 7—"where they talk about bullying incidents and what you could do, and we act out the situation with a partner. The whole school does it, in our homerooms."

It was all so sunny and normal, and so different from every other visit I'd made to that apartment. I marveled about that to Callas the next day. "I know exactly what you're talking about," he said. "The first day she came to the gym after she started school, she was like a different kid, with this whole happy, confident aura I'd never seen before."

Monique had saved her small birthday cake to eat with me. Alycia took it out and set it on the kitchen table. Monique and I admired the fancy icing, with the red boxing gloves, and then she cut each of us a piece.

Chapter 5

Jacob

ON HIS WAY TO FAILING THREE CLASSES, JACOB MISSED FORTY days of school. To pass eighth grade, he would have to go to summer school. In one sense, this wasn't so bad: the kids in the summer program came from a bunch of surrounding towns, and they didn't give Jacob a hard time the way some of the kids at Mohawk had. On the other hand, Jacob had been too distracted and rattled to focus on his studies all year, and now he had a lot of catching up to do. He wasn't feeling great about himself, either.

Naomi Shatz, the NYCLU lawyer who'd agreed to take Jacob's case, sent a letter to the school district at the beginning of July asking for counseling and a summer-school tutor. She also pushed the district and Jacob's family to look beyond the summer: what, she asked, could everyone do to make sure Jacob's ninth-grade year went better than his last one? Posing that question, Shatz and two NYCLU colleagues, Corey Stoughton and Matt Faiella, drove up to Mohawk in July for a meeting with all the key players: Jacob and Robbie, Superintendent Caputo, and Eric Wilson, the district's lawyer.

It was a frosty affair. The two sides faced each other across a long table. Shatz and Stoughton asked the district what they planned to do for Jacob in the fall, and that put the Mohawk officials on the defensive. These were lawyers, from New York City—what did they know about education, or this school and its community? The meeting grew heated enough to scare Jacob a little. The school officials kept insisting that there was nothing wrong with their treatment of gay kids. Other Mohawk students, they said, had come out without incident. They'd done their best to help Jacob succeed at school as well, trying to respond to Robbie's complaints. The problem was the attention Jacob had sought, and how he'd handled himself.

"The superintendent had this way of making me feel like if I had a gay child, it was my fault, and to try to accomplish anything for that child—to stick up for him—it was like I was doing something wrong," Robbie said. "She made me feel ashamed."

Wilson later told me, "I think the issue is, it's never a one-way street. The kid coming out has a responsibility to do that in a way that is equally mature as the response they anticipate getting. To the extent that the child isn't ready to project their sexuality in a responsible way, the peers may not respond appropriately, either."

Mohawk officials also presented their version of the history of the Gay-Straight Alliance Aric Barnett had tried to start. Caputo said the GSA died a natural death when Aric graduated, and while the district wasn't hostile to a new GSA, Mohawk was cutting clubs and extracurricular activities for financial reasons. "We were trying to save

money, and at that point, there was no demonstrated student interest," Wilson said.

Having made no headway, the NYCLU lawyers asked for a few
small specific accommodations for Jacob, including changes to his
schedule, so that he wouldn't have classes with Aaron, and a chaper-
one to walk him from class to class. They also wanted Jacob to have
permission to go to a "safe room" at the school if he needed to get
away from the other kids, and to carry his cell phone so he could call
home. These interventions hadn't worked well the previous spring,
but they were worth trying again, Jacob's parents felt. Shatz and her
colleagues also made a couple of other proposals for school-wide re-
forms: district-wide staff training about student-on-student harassment and the addition of material on sexual orientation and gender
identity to the curriculum. These strategies have been shown to help
gay students. The Mohawk officials said they would consider the accommodations for Jacob but weren't interested in implementing the
school-wide measures—they saw no need for them. Wilson, the district's lawyer, leaned across the table.

"Go ahead," he said. "Sue us."

What *were* Jacob's legal options? Ever since they'd met Jacob and
Robbie and heard the story of Jacob's struggle to get help from his
school, Shatz and her colleagues had been trying to figure that out.
The short answer was that Jacob's case wasn't a slam dunk. But from
the point of view of the NYCLU, it was certainly worth bringing.

To understand the obstacles, let's start with this question: why
can't *any* bullied student simply sue a school that fails to protect him
from his fellow students? That turns out to be a question the legal
profession began contemplating almost a century ago. Back in 1936,
the American Law Institute, in an authoritative treatise, discussed a
"duty to anticipate danger" on the part of one person who has custody

of another. The treatise explicitly ascribed this duty to a sheriff who knows that his prisoner may be threatened by mob violence, and to a schoolmaster "who knows that a group of older boys are in the habit of bullying the younger pupils to an extent likely to do them actual harm." A schoolmaster (or principal) who knows of this habitual misbehavior is required to intervene when he sees the bullying *and* to be "reasonably vigilant in his supervision of his pupils" so he can anticipate when the misconduct is about to happen.

The duty to anticipate danger could have given rise to a lot of lawsuits over bullying, but in a reflection of the reigning indifference to the problem at the time, it turned into the legal road not taken. Courts didn't enforce this duty on schools, largely because they were reluctant to interfere with the decision making of principals, leaving bullied students with a far narrower path to court. Today, students have to argue that the mistreatment they've suffered in school is a form of discrimination. In other words, bullying has to be framed as a loss of equal rights. Recourse begins with the most foundational American law of all—the Constitution. Specifically, the Fourteenth Amendment, which protects us from being discriminated against on the basis of race, sex, national origin, or religion.

The first gay student to invoke this protection, in an unsung case brought in 1993, was a seventeen-year-old from Wisconsin named Jamie Nabozny. Jamie was a soft-spoken A student from Ashland, Wisconsin, who'd overcome hardship: when he was young, his home life was chaotic and both of his parents struggled with alcoholism, though by the time he finished elementary school, they'd worked hard to stop drinking and stay employed. When he was around eleven, Jamie went for a ride in a Cadillac with his uncle, who was gay, and when he returned, Jamie told his grandmother that he was gay, too. She tried to persuade him otherwise. "She said, 'You don't have to be gay to have a Cadillac,'" Jamie told me. "But she didn't change my mind."

Jamie's troubles, like Jacob's, started in seventh grade, at Ashland

Middle School. He was a nerdy kid with no interest in dating girls, and a group of boys started calling him "faggot" and "queer," pushing and tripping him in the hallways and knocking his books out of his hands. Jamie didn't tell them he was gay, but he didn't deny it, either, and when a counselor asked him directly, he said yes. Jamie talked to the principal, Mary Podlesny, who said she would address the harassment. But when she spoke to the boys involved, they gave Jamie a hard time for telling her and the situation worsened. Jamie left toward the end of the year, finishing seventh grade at a Catholic school. But in eighth grade, his parents could no longer afford the tuition, and he went back to Ashland. The abuse started right up again.

Part of the way through that year, three boys cornered Jamie in a school bathroom and shoved him against a wall. One of them, Don Grande, was the brother of a boy named Roy who frequently picked on Jamie. Feeling hounded and unprotected, Jamie left school, went home, and told his parents what had happened. They asked for a meeting with Podlesny, the boys who had ganged up on Jamie, and their parents. Mary Grande came with her son Don. With everyone in the room, Podlesny asked the three boys if they'd called Jamie names or shoved him in the bathroom. They denied it. The principal turned to Jamie's parents. "She looked at them," Jamie remembered, "and said, 'Mr. and Mrs. Nabozny, I can't make the entire school different for your son. He has to expect trouble if he insists on acting this way.' "

That night, Jamie swallowed a bottle of pills and was admitted to a psychiatric unit. He would be hospitalized four more times for attempting suicide in middle school and high school.

One afternoon in science class a few months later, the teacher, who was a substitute, put Jamie and Roy Grande at the same table and then left the room for a few minutes. Roy and another boy grabbed Jamie, calling him a faggot and throwing him to the ground. Two of them straddled his back and mock-raped him while the rest of the class watched. Jamie ran, sobbing, to Podlesny's office, and she scolded him for barging in without an appointment. She also said that if he was going to be openly gay, he had to expect these things to happen. Jamie walked out of the school and refused to go back. None of the students involved in the mock rape was punished.

In ninth grade, things didn't get any easier for Jamie. Early in his freshman year at Ashland High, one student shoved him into a urinal while another one peed on him. Kids went after him on the bus, tripping him and spitting on him. A teacher, who let Jamie eat lunch in her classroom, reported the harassment to administrators, who blamed Jamie for hitting on members of the hockey team. After another suicide attempt and hospital stay, Jamie ran away. When his parents tracked him down, two hundred miles away in a Minneapolis youth shelter, he told them he loved them but that he couldn't go back to Ashland High. His mother promised to home-school him. But later his parents decided they couldn't afford the tutoring involved and sent him back to Ashland High. Trouble on the bus started up again in tenth grade, and Jamie began walking two and a half miles to school.

The next year got scarily violent. A pack of boys surrounded Jamie in the library in the beginning of eleventh grade, pushing him to the floor and kicking him repeatedly in the stomach. Jamie ended up in the hospital for several days; he was bleeding internally and needed abdominal surgery. A couple of months later, he ran away to Minneapolis again with $100 in cash. He found his way to a gay and lesbian community organization, which helped him find a foster home with a gay deacon—and also connected him with a lawyer, so he could sue the Ashland schools.

Jamie's case was a long shot. The suit made two claims, based on the Fourteenth Amendment's provision for "equal rights under the law," which no one had ever brought before in a case about an LGBT student. The first was that the schools hadn't taken the necessary action to help Jamie because he was gay. The second was that by punishing students for harassing girls, but not for the same-sex harassment Jamie experienced, the schools discriminated against him because he was a boy.

The federal district court judge assigned to the case summarily dismissed Jamie's claims before trial. "There is absolutely nothing in the record to indicate that plaintiff was treated differently because of his gender," the judge wrote, ignoring the separate and real question of whether Jamie had been discriminated against because he was gay. A year later, in 1996, three judges for the U.S. Court of Appeals for the Seventh Circuit reversed the lower court ruling. The Seventh Circuit said Jamie had presented evidence to show he'd been treated differently because of his perceived homosexuality *and* because of his sex. Focusing on Jamie's contention about the mock rape and the principal's response that "boys will be boys," the judges said they found her alleged remark "somewhat astonishing." They continued, "We find it impossible to believe that a female lodging a similar complaint would have received the same response."

Jamie's lawyers, at the gay rights group Lambda Legal, quickly began preparing for trial. To win, they would have to show that the Ashland schools were not just negligent but "deliberately indifferent" to Jamie's mistreatment. This meant proving that officials knew of bullying that was severe and pervasive. The Lambda lawyers tracked down Roy Grande, one of Jamie's chief tormentors, who was now in prison for assault. They wanted Roy to testify about the mock rape and the name-calling, and to tell the jury that he'd been punished for calling his girlfriend a bitch but not for anything he'd said or done to Jamie—which would help prove that the school had treated Jamie differently because of his sex. But Roy was noncommittal. When the lawyers talked to his mother, Mary, she denied that her son had done anything wrong and said she knew nothing about any seventh-grade meeting at which Podlesny brushed off Jamie and his parents.

Mary Grande called Jamie's mother shortly before the trial. She said she'd been diagnosed with cancer, and she'd been thinking about what Roy had done. She would tell the truth on the stand, she promised, and she'd make sure that Roy would, too.

On the opening day of trial, Roy Grande entered the courtroom, wearing his orange prison jumpsuit. In front of the jury, he admitted that he had tripped, punched, and kicked Jamie. "Do you recall that he was harassed in the boys' room?" Jamie's lawyer asked. "And everywhere else, yeah, I do," Roy answered. About the mock rape, Roy said he and his friend grabbed Jamie while the other students watched and laughed. "I put my hands on his rear end," Roy admitted. No, he'd never been punished for anything he'd done to Jamie, but, yes, he'd gotten suspended for calling his girlfriend a bitch. This evidence helped Jamie by showing that the school district took harassment of a female student more seriously than harassment of a gay male student.

Mary Grande took the stand next. She testified that she'd gone to the seventh-grade meeting with Jamie, his parents, and her son Don, and she'd heard Podlesny say that if Jamie didn't want to be called names or harassed, he "shouldn't go around the way he was going around expressing his sexual preference." Mary continued, "Mrs. Podlesny said that he should not, you know, keep doing what he was doing." It was a coup for Jamie and his lawyers: confirmation of Podlesny's bias and indifference, from a witness who had no reason to be on Jamie's side.

When Podlesny took the stand, she said she'd never known Jamie was gay and that she had no memory of ever speaking to him or to his parents. "I do not recall ever meeting them," Podlesny told the jury. Asked about the harassment Jamie experienced, she said she'd learned of it only when he filed suit.

"Are you saying that no one while you were serving as the Ashland principal brought to your attention the fact that Jamie Nabozny was experiencing physical assaults and degrading name-calling in the hallways at school?" Jamie's lawyer asked.

"I don't recall," Podlesny answered.

The high school principal, William Davis, issued similar blanket denials. "I don't remember anything about Jamie Nabozny when he was in school," Davis testified.

It took the jury less than four hours to rule in Jamie's favor. For the first time, a gay student had succeeded in holding the school where he'd been tormented accountable. Before the phase of the trial that would have determined Jamie's award for damages, the school district settled for $900,000, plus $62,000 for medical expenses.

In the days after Jamie's victory, Lambda fielded calls from school districts across the country, asking how they could protect themselves from liability. Suddenly school officials had an urgent reason to care about the welfare of gay students.

Jamie's suit turned the Constitution into a shield for kids who had never been able to say before that they had a *right* to be safe from harassment and abuse in school. A second path to court soon followed: Title IX of the federal Civil Rights Act. Best known for providing equal access to sports programs, Title IX also protects students more broadly against sex discrimination. In 1999, the Supreme Court said a fifth grader named LaShonda Davis could bring a Title IX suit against her school for failing to protect her from months of harassment by a boy who rubbed up against her in the hallways and tried to touch her chest and genitals in class while saying, "I want to get in bed with you" and "I want to feel your boobs." *Davis v. Monroe County Board of Education,* as the case is called, was a landmark victory for feminists because it extended to schools the rules about sexual harassment that applied in the workplace. From now on, Justice Sandra Day O'Connor wrote for the court, a school could be held liable for showing "deliberate indifference" to harassment that "is so severe, pervasive, and objectively offensive" that it deprives victims of access to education.

The U.S. Department of Education made it clear that a gay student could also seek the protection of Title IX for harassment, making it easier for more students like Jamie to have their day in court. One was a girl in California who'd found notes in her locker saying, "Die dyke bitch." When they were followed by a picture of a bound and gagged woman with her throat slashed, the girl went to the assistant principal—who told her to return to class. Another was a gay student in Nevada whom other students surrounded in the school parking lot, lassoed around the neck, and threatened to drag behind a truck. His school, the student said, had ignored earlier pleas he'd made for help, and that day, after he'd broken free, he was sent home on the bus with some of his attackers. Thanks to Title IX and the law of equal protection, he settled for $450,000, and the girl in California shared a damage award of $1.1 million with a few other gay students.

Kids who were harassed for being perceived as gay, even though they weren't, also successfully brought sex discrimination claims. Dylan Theno was called "pussy," "flamer," and "faggot" after he quit the football team at his Kansas school in seventh grade. A boy who'd told Dylan to shove a banana "up his ass" even talked a teacher into calling him "banana boy." As Dylan testified, "I guess because, you know, my hair [was different] and I did Tae Kwon Do and I wore earrings, to them I was kind of a girly girl." At trial, the school's psychiatric expert said Dylan had "invited chiding by his outlandish personal style." The jury awarded him $250,000.

Reading through these rulings, Naomi Shatz felt pretty good about taking Jacob's case to court. He'd been bullied not only because he was gay but also, like Jamie and Dylan, because he was seen as effeminate—not a typical boy. That could count as sex discrimination. And she could argue that Mohawk's lack of coordinated response to Robbie's complaints about the bullying added up to deliberate indifference. Also, in New York, it was against the law to discriminate against a public school student on the basis of sexual orientation. Jacob could sue based on the Constitution, Title IX, and state law—and his suit could break new ground because it would be the first of its kind in New York.

Over the summer, Jacob warmed to the idea of going to court. He still worried about what it would mean to be known as the kid who sued the Mohawk schools, but the NYCLU lawyers were taking him seriously in a way no one but his family had before. They were giving him a way to make the nightmare of his middle school years mean something. He decided to take the chance.

Just before the start of Jacob's ninth-grade year, the NYCLU filed his lawsuit. Jacob chose a picture to give the local newspaper that showed him with brown hair, not pink or purple, wearing a sweatshirt with peace symbols. The reaction to the suit was mixed. The local paper wrote an editorial chiding the school district, and supporters set up a Facebook fan page for Jacob. But some of his friends pulled away, and out in the world, Jacob thought he was getting hostile looks. Then the host of a morning radio show ripped into him, accusing Jacob and his family of bleeding money from the school district and of being in love with one of his bullies. Callers said Jacob had brought trouble on himself. "It was very difficult," Robbie said. "Jacob and me and my wife went to Walmart, and the pastor from our old church was there. He was the kind of guy you could talk to if you had a problem. So we walked up to him, and I explained the situation, and he said Jacob was going against nature. Then he started quoting the Bible and calling Jacob an abomination. By then there was a crowd of people standing there, and Jacob heard that, and he ran into the parking lot crying. And I'm thinking, how could I make such a mistake? It was like anyone I thought I could trust, it turned out I couldn't."

The lawyers asked the judge if they could quickly take the depositions of superintendent Joyce Caputo, former principal Edward Rinaldo, and Cynthia Stocker, who'd moved up to become principal, before the new school year began, to build their case that Mohawk hadn't done enough to help Jacob. The judge agreed, and he also gave the school district approval to depose Robbie and Jacob. On the morning the depositions were scheduled to begin, Eric Wilson, the district's lawyer, pulled the NYCLU attorneys aside. Mohawk was ready to talk, he said; what did the NYCLU want?

Surprised but gratified, Shatz and Stoughton huddled with Wilson for two hours to hammer out an agreement. Jacob would have a schedule free of classes with Aaron, a hall pass he could use whenever he needed, adult chaperones to walk him from class to class, permission to use a safe room and the teachers' bathroom, and permission to carry his cell phone. To the NYCLU lawyers, it seemed like a breakthrough. "For the first time it seemed like the school district was ready to acknowledge there was a problem," Stoughton said.

And yet the new school year still got off to a rocky start. Jacob told me how his chaperones sometimes stood by and watched him being harassed rather than stepping in to protect him. The other accommodations didn't seem to help much, either—without school-wide reform, the lawyers concluded, the individual measures could only be Band-Aids. In early October, Robbie reported in a letter to Mohawk that students were, once again, calling Jacob a faggot and throwing rocks at him. "This is my fourth attempt to fix these ongoing problems," Robbie wrote, referring to his efforts since September. "As far as I know nothing has been done."

Mohawk had, in fact, done one big thing—they'd suspended Aaron for six months. To Aaron's parents, Kimberly and Tom, this made no sense. Aaron had already served a five-day suspension the previous June for threatening to string Jacob up the school flagpole. He'd come back to school with everyone else in September. Now all of a sudden Mohawk officials were upping the punishment for Aaron's "verbal altercations" with Jacob to *six months*? Aaron would have to go to special "twilight classes" for two hours each afternoon. He'd miss the football and wrestling seasons.

Kimberly called the local paper to vent. "The district is throwing my son under the bus because they're facing a lawsuit," she told the reporter. "My son hasn't been perfect, but what fourteen-year-old has?"

For the NYCLU, this was all very awkward. The lawsuit was against Mohawk for failing to do enough to help Jacob, not against

Aaron. On principle, the NYCLU opposed long suspensions for kids, which a series of studies has linked to lower grades and graduation rates, as well as repeat offenses—it turns out there's no evidence to suggest that sending a troublemaking kid home will make him easier to reach, less angry, or more malleable. The NYCLU had no interest in pushing Aaron out of school. They wanted Mohawk to figure out how to *prevent* bullying, by making the school a welcoming, safe place for its gay students.

Aaron's parents hired their own lawyer, who fought to get him back in school. They also turned, publicly, on Jacob. Kimberly said that it was Aaron who'd been a victim—of sexual harassment—because Jacob had hit on him. "If my son had done that to a girl, it would have been *bad*," she told me later. "They said they wanted open-mindedness from us. But I told them, you don't have an open mind when a boy hits on a girl." Aaron, though, downplayed his mother's accusation when I asked him about it. "Every now and then he'd try to be funny, be like, 'You and me, we'd make a perfect couple,'" he said of Jacob. "He was kidding around, trying to get me to say something back."

Jacob denied all of this. "I never ever . . . noooo," he told me, waving his hands to push the idea away. "Me and Aaron were enemies, like the worst." In Jacob's school file, there is no evidence to back up Kimberly's harassment claim.

The lawyer Aaron's parents hired persuaded Mohawk to shorten his suspension, and he went back to school in late November, after missing two and a half months of classes. He and Jacob stayed away from each other, and in the end, they were only in school together for a handful of weeks. Jacob decided in the winter of ninth grade that he'd never feel comfortable at Mohawk, and he moved from his father's house to his mother's little cabin in the woods. Living at Penny's, thirty miles outside town, Jacob could switch to a new school.

———

Meanwhile, the action in Jacob's lawsuit moved from New York to Washington, D.C., where the case caught the eye of lawyers in the civil rights division of the U.S. Department of Justice. This instantly raised the stakes. The civil rights division has an illustrious history of fighting racial segregation in schools and protecting minorities' right to vote. Its stamp of approval meant that Jacob would be part of a larger civil rights battle, an effort to turn Jamie Nabozny's victory into the law of the land. The arrival of DOJ's lawyers would send a strong signal to Mohawk, too: Jamie's lawsuit mattered not just locally but nationally.

Whitney Pellegrino, a lawyer from DOJ, came to Mohawk that fall to do some investigating of her own. She left convinced that Jacob's story held up. The Obama administration's Justice Department had been looking for a case like this, one that could help expand the courts' view of the protection a student deserves when he or she is harassed for not acting like a typical boy or a typical girl. "With Jacob, the way the harassment took place was really tied to his sex and his gender," Pellegrino told me. "Obviously, he came out during the time it was going on, but he was called fag and queer before then, too, and it wasn't always about his sexuality. He was also targeted because he didn't act like a typical boy. It was the connection between how he didn't conform to gender stereotypes and the harassment— that's why this was a great case for us."

This wasn't a new idea for the Justice Department so much as a return, by a Democratic administration, to a decade-old one. Ten years earlier, when Bill Clinton was president, the department submitted a brief on behalf of a Kentucky student who was humiliated by graffiti, scrawled on a wall in his school parking lot, that included his name above a drawing of two boys touching each other sexually. Clinton's DOJ also entered a suit brought by a Missouri student who was harassed because other students thought he was effeminate, and who left his school as a result. But then George W. Bush got elected, and his Justice Department backed off: in eight years, it didn't intervene in a single civil rights action involving a student who was bullied because he or she didn't conform to gender stereotypes. Civil rights lawyers in DOJ now wanted to "reignite this area of law," Pellegrino told me. "Gender nonconformity can be easier for some parents to talk about than a teenager's homosexuality. It affects not just gay boys but boys who are called gay. Mohawk is one tiny district and Jacob is one kid who didn't look and act like other boys. But after we got involved, we got calls from all over the country asking about the case, from people describing a similar pattern in their school and saying they didn't know the federal government could do anything about it."

Pellegrino, along with other Justice Department lawyers, had recently worked with the Obama administration's Department of Education on a letter, sent to every school district in the country, laying out the responsibility to protect students from bullying that constituted illegal harassment. The letter laid out hypothetical scenarios that could expose a district to litigation or the loss of federal funding. One involved a gay student who dropped out of the drama club when he was called names, assaulted, and threatened because of his "effeminate mannerisms, nontraditional choice of extracurricular activities, apparel, and personal grooming choices." A school that reprimanded the bullies but didn't recognize the problem as sex discrimination would fail to meet its obligation to "eliminate the hostile environment" for the gay student, and so could be hit with a lawsuit, the letter warned.

When Pellegrino asked the judge in Jacob's case for permission to intervene on his behalf, she and her colleagues thrust the Justice Department into the heart of America's culture wars. "They are making up a legal violation where there hasn't been one," a conservative public interest lawyer named Roger Clegg told NPR when news broke of DOJ's involvement in the beginning of 2010. Clegg, who'd also worked at DOJ under President Reagan and the first President Bush, accused his Democratic successors of usurping the role of Congress to further a pro-gay agenda. "If the Civil Rights Division and the Obama administration want to propose that Title IX be amended to include sexual orientation, that's something they can do and that can be debated in Congress," he said. "But Congress has not passed a law that deals with discrimination on the basis of sexual orientation."

Clegg made sure to add that he condemned bullying. He parted company with the Obama administration's DOJ not over whether bullying was bad but over what to do about it. Christian conservatives make the same distinction when they oppose curricula about gay history or identity—the kind of additions that the NYCLU asked of Mohawk. "We need to protect all children from bullying," a Focus on the Family staffer told the *New York Times*. "But the advocacy groups are promoting homosexual lessons in the name of anti-bullying." Or as one pastor put it, "Of course we're all against bullying. But the Bible says very clearly that homosexuality is wrong, and Christians don't want the schools to teach subjects that are repulsive to their values."

There's a clear contradiction here. Study after study shows that the best way to prevent the harassment of gay students is to make it unacceptable. Schools can take various steps toward this goal: they can institute staff-wide training in how to respond to anti-gay taunting, a curriculum that includes gay and lesbian history, a Gay-Straight Alliance, and a policy that bars discrimination or bullying on the basis of sexual orientation or gender identity and expression. That's why the NYCLU made these demands of Mohawk: because they've been proved to work.

In fact, research shows that schools have to teach not just tolerance of an alternative lifestyle—the old code for keeping homosexuality at arm's length—but acceptance. They have to teach, early and often, that there is nothing *wrong* with the sexuality of gay students or with the lives they will lead. To truly take this on, schools have to get young kids to think about how family structure can vary and about the ways in which children themselves police gender boundaries—discouraging boys from playing with dolls, say, or girls from joining a football game at recess. The point isn't to push more boys to play with dolls or more girls to play football. It's to free the few who want to from peer condemnation.

These arguments have gained urgency in the wake of well-publicized suicides by gay students in recent years. The studies showing that a culture of nonacceptance can contribute to students' taking their own lives strengthens the rationale for putting books such as *Heather Has Two Mommies* or *My Princess Boy* on the kindergarten or first-grade bookshelf. The case is stronger now than it was twenty years ago, when the opening rounds of these culture wars were fought. The dilemma for schools is that the parents who don't want to read *My Princess Boy* to their kids at home probably don't want their kids reading it at school, either. Which means the most effective means of protecting gay kids at school runs into the wall of religious and moral objection to homosexuality.

Fueled by groups such as Focus on the Family, that collision has occurred at school boards, legislatures, and courts across the country. In Helena, Montana, parents and local pastors protested in 2010 when the schools started teaching first graders that "human beings can love people of the same gender," as the district's guidelines put it. After four months of fighting, the school board agreed to scrub this language, replacing it with a vaguer call for young children to "understand that family structures differ." In Michigan in 2011, the state senate tinkered with an anti-bullying bill—named Matt's Safe School Law, after Matt Epling, a ninth grader who committed suicide in 2002—that had been in the works for six years, by adding an exception to exempt kids who bully out of a sincerely held belief or moral conviction. The change was supposed to ensure that students could speak out against homosexuality in the name of religious freedom, but it was denounced by Matt Epling's father. "I think it fails the memory of Matt," he said. "We cannot go backward and say, in any way, shape or form, in a piece of legislation that it is okay under religious grounds to harass or harm your fellow student." In the end, Michigan's Republican governor signed a version of the law without the exception—but also without explicit protection against discrimination for gay or minority students. That kind of omission has become a favored tool of conservatives.

A few school districts in deeply conservative parts of the country have truly held out against teaching anything that could be interpreted as acceptance of homosexuality—even in the face of serious risk to students. The school board of the Anoka-Hennepin district, which serves thirty-nine thousand students north of Minneapolis, passed a Sexual Orientation Curriculum Policy in 2009 that on paper instructed teachers to "remain neutral" about sexual orientation, and in practice operated as a gag order. Teachers could not explain that being gay is not a choice, even if they were quoting the position of the American Psychological Association. When history teachers included gay rights in a unit about how the strategies of the black civil rights groups influenced subsequent movements, the district deleted the reference. For a staff diversity training session, the district rejected a book called *How Homophobia Hurts Children* because it did not "include an opposing viewpoint." The schools also struck LGBT support services, like a gay and lesbian helpline, from the list of health resources provided to students. Meanwhile, a conservative Christian parents' group called the Parents Action League pushed to teach gay students how to root out their homosexuality using the discredited practice of "reparative therapy."

With the Sexual Orientation Curriculum Policy in place, LGBT students reported being mocked, urinated on, and physically harmed by their classmates, and nine students—four of whom identified as gay, and some of whom had been bullied—took their own lives. The head of the Minnesota Family Council, the statewide sponsor of the Parents Action League, told the *Minnesota Independent* that the students had killed themselves because of "homosexual indoctrination" and their own "unhealthy lifestyle." In 2011, six students sued the school district; their lawyers from the Southern Poverty Law Center and the National Center for Lesbian Rights described an "epidemic of anti-gay and gender-based harassment within District schools" that was "rooted in and encouraged by official District-wide policies singling out and denigrating LGBT people." The Obama administration's Justice Department investigated, as it had in Jacob's case, and found that the harassment was severe and pervasive enough to be illegal, because it was creating a hostile environment for gay students.

At first the school board refused to budge. The superintendent angrily denied that the district had any special duty to protect LGBT students, dismissing the possibility of a link between the claims of harassment and the suicides. After months of negotiations with the plaintiffs' lawyers and the Justice Department, however, the school district folded. Anoka-Hennepin finally scrapped the curriculum policy about sexual orientation, replacing it with a new one that affirmed the "dignity and self-worth of all students," regardless of a list of traits including sex/gender and sexual orientation. The district also agreed to take steps such as conducting surveys about the rate of bullying, creating an anti-bullying committee of students, parents, and teachers, and training peer leaders. Anoka-Hennepin promised to hire a coordinator to make sure all of this actually happened, as well as a mental health consultant to review its approach to helping the targets of harassment. The district agreed to allow DOJ to monitor its efforts for five years, and to pay the students who sued a total settlement of $270,000.

A spokeswoman for the Parents Action League told the Minneapolis *Star Tribune* that the settlement was a "travesty," writing in an email that "making schools safe for 'gay' kids means indoctrinating impressionable, young minds with homosexual propaganda." This time, however, she was on her own. The superintendent greeted the settlement by saying publicly, "Our gay students deserve to feel safe and be safe, just like everyone else in our public schools." At a press conference, one of the students named in the lawsuit described the abuse he'd suffered in the past. Then he brightened. "I haven't had an experience in about a month and a half and that has never happened before," he said. "I've already seen change and I want these kids to know in the future they're going to be safe and they're going to have a great time in high school and I'm here for them if they need anything."

Jacob's lawsuit had a mixed ending. In the spring of 2010, after he left Mohawk, the district settled for $50,000, along with money for counseling and $25,000 to the NYCLU for attorneys' fees. Mohawk officials also agreed to bring in an outside expert to train staff on how to prevent harassment because of sex and sexual orientation and help write a plan for working with students. Superintendent Caputo had not, however, sounded a conciliatory note, as the superintendent in Anoka-Hennepin had. Emphasizing that the district had admitted to doing nothing wrong, she insisted that "the vast majority of the measures that the district has agreed to were already in place" and were not being taken simply "because the NYCLU has demanded them."

It was hard to see how that could be true, but when I met a year later with Caputo and principal Cynthia Stocker, they stuck to that line. "We do want you to know that the district denies *all* the factual allegations that would have amounted to discrimination," Caputo said of Jacob's lawsuit. "We feel we've been victimized by the circumstances and unfairly characterized as being homophobic when that was not how it was. This was a personal issue between two students. That's all."

It was Rinaldo, who'd left the school, who was willing to say Mohawk could have done better by Jacob. "There are things I would do differently, if I could," he told me three years after the lawsuit. "Looking back, one thing I appreciate is that Jacob had a loving father who tried to help him. I wish more kids had a parent like that, and I know I've learned something from what Jacob and his parents went through." He paused. "I'd like to be an advocate for kids like Jacob, kids in his situation."

Driving home from Mohawk after I left the school offices, I kept thinking about one of the last things the district's lawyer had said to me: "Look, this district found itself in the middle of a massive cultural change nationwide with regard to the expectations for how administrators and faculty deal with the social lives of students." About this he was right. The legal victories of Jamie Nabozny, the students in Anoka-Hennepin, and Jacob represent a huge shift over a short period of time. There was no such thing as a Gay-Straight Alliance when I was growing up. My gay teachers kept quiet about their sexuality. When a French teacher died of AIDS, no one spoke out loud about the disease. I remember a memorial assembly at which a gay colleague wept for him. I loved and admired the teacher who was crying, and I wanted to say something comforting, but I had only the vaguest understanding of why he was so upset or what had happened. Here we are, only one generation later, and some courts—and the federal government's lawyers—say that schools must embrace an entirely different set of norms. They have to make sure students understand that homosexuality isn't scary or immoral or taboo; it's part of our lives.

In reality, of course, judges and lawyers can effect change only on paper. In places like Mohawk, where gay rights are still sharply contested, it's not clear how lawsuits and laws translate into transforming a culture—if they make the hundreds of kids and adults who walk through the doors every morning more accepting of a kid like Jacob. In some schools, this is a period of uneasy transition, similar to what the South went through in the wake of *Brown v. Board of Education* in 1954. The Supreme Court ordered desegregation, finding that "separate but equal" was a myth, and that black children were hurt by the message they couldn't help receiving: that they were lesser. It was a ruling that laid claim to moral urgency. Yet, mindful of the limits of their power and of the order of magnitude of the social shift they were demanding, the justices gave American schools time to desegregate, asking only that they move toward this goal with "all deliberate speed." Yes, the Court was mistaken then to condone foot-dragging, but *some* patience is required in our era, too. "You're asking a school to do something differently than what's done at home and church," Whitney Pellegrino of the Justice Department told me. "It's a long process."

In Mohawk, Stocker and Caputo talked about how they wanted to lead the way in realizing the promise of a law New York had recently passed—the Dignity for All Students Act, which, among other things, added highlights of LGBT leadership throughout history to the character-building curriculum schools are supposed to offer. Not only that, but the district planned to roll out the school-wide bullying prevention program designed by Dan Olweus the following year. "It's of great academic benefit," Stocker said. "Think about it: if kids feel comfortable in a classroom, they'll ask more questions, because they're not going to feel they'll be made fun of if they don't know the answer. They'll be daring. They'll be fearless about their education."

Aaron, meanwhile, was back on steady footing as a ninth grader at Mohawk. After high school, he told me, he wanted to become an officer in the military. Looking back, Aaron wasn't repentant about how he'd treated Jacob. "I don't really regret anything," he said. "He just got away with it." Kimberly got on the phone, still full of anger toward Jacob, his parents, and the Mohawk schools, and I understood why Aaron wasn't ready to reconsider his own role. I could see, too, that his family felt steamrolled, and why that would be hard.

Jamie Nabozny draws a more inspiring conclusion from his lawsuit. At thirty-six, he credits his victory in court with nothing less than saving his life. "So many things could have happened to me that didn't—abusive relationships, drug and alcohol dependence," he told me. "I owe it to really good therapy and to the lawsuit, to being able to stand up and fight back." It hadn't been a straight line from victory to contentment, of course. For years Jamie distanced himself from the emotional weight of his past, refusing to grant interviews about the case as he concentrated on working his way up through the ranks at Wells Fargo in North Dakota. Then he decided to participate in filming a documentary about his case, called *Bullied,* which has become a staple of anti-bullying education across the country. (My son's class watched it in sixth grade.) After the film came out in 2010, Jamie started traveling to schools to speak about his experience. "The film helped me see myself not as the kid who got beat up, but who fought back and made a difference for lots of other kids." In his presentations to students, Jamie encourages the bystanders among them to defend their peers, and when he speaks to teachers and counselors, he emphasizes the importance of teaching empathy, of looking another person in the eye and thinking about who he is and how he feels. "No one ever hit me to my face," he tells his audiences. "They always came up from behind."

It's too soon to know whether Jacob will look back on his lawsuit with the same mixture of gratitude and pride. When he left Mohawk and moved in with his mother, the taunting followed him to his new rural high school. After a couple of months, Penny decided to home-school him. Jacob took most of his courses online and worked on getting his driver's license so that he could get a job as a waiter and see more of his boyfriend. "My life is good now," he said, giving me a peace sign.

The next time I talked to Jacob, he was back in school for the last semester of his senior year, so he could graduate with a regular diploma and then prepare for college. "I've been back for five days and I've been called a faggot twice," he told me. "That's not good, but it's a lot better than it was. There will be people who oppose you wherever you go." Jacob, it seemed, had learned the best lesson that adversity can teach: most of the bad stuff isn't bad enough to mow you down, not if you don't let it. He'd figured out how to turn his sense of self toward wearing nail polish *and* succeeding in school. "I'm strong-minded," he said. "My head is up high."

Chapter 6

Flannery

IN THE WAKE OF THE CRIMINAL CHARGES AGAINST FLANNERY
and the five other accused teenagers, South Hadley found itself
marked as the bullying capital of the world. As the media frenzy reig-
nited, the reporters who flocked back to town were primed to hear
one thing and one thing only: the accused bullies denounced. After
all, they were now to blame for Phoebe's death in the eyes of the law.
A local blog called *The Litterbox* exploded with calls for prison sen-
tences, the longer the better. In the wave of attention, any hope of an
honest discussion about grief and responsibility, in South Hadley or
anywhere else, was washed away.

"I felt horrible that Phoebe died," Flannery told me, yet she also rebelled against the shame the media coverage suggested she was supposed to feel. She didn't defend Sharon and Ashley for calling Phoebe out as a slut, or Sean for encouraging it, but she didn't think she had bullied Phoebe, and she definitely didn't think she'd done anything to cause her death. What she thought, though, didn't matter. "I'd turn on the TV and there was this story about a girl who lived in a house with a white picket fence," she said. "We were the mean popular girls who just attacked her, and we weren't mad at our boyfriends at all—we just took it all out on Phoebe. She was the angel and we were the devils. I knew there were layers and layers of this girl, but no one would discuss any of that because they didn't want to blame the victim."

Flannery hadn't spoken to Phoebe in the week before her death. In fact, aside from their brief meeting in the assistant principal's office, after Flannery vented in gym class about her anger over Austin, she'd hardly talked to Phoebe at all. But the TV shows and the tabloids didn't care about the varying degrees of culpability from Ashley to Kayla to Sharon to Flannery. The media lumped the kids together as the "South Hadley Six," using their old yearbook photos instead of mug shots.

During the two-and-a-half-month-long investigation, Flannery never apologized to Phoebe's family because she didn't know what exactly to apologize for, and because she was trying to lie low rather than bring a new spike of attention to herself. None of the kids had said they were sorry—a fact that only deepened the distress and anger of Phoebe's family. Once district attorney Elizabeth Scheibel announced the criminal charges in April, their lawyers advised them not to apologize, because they saw no way for the teenagers to take a share of responsibility without exposing themselves to legal risk. This is standard advice, but it made the kids seem heartless.

"If these charges hadn't been brought, it would have been a completely different situation," Flannery told me. "Maybe there would have been remorse. But they put me into a corner. I had to defend myself."

Scheibel had charged Flannery and Sharon, both sixteen, and Ashley, who was seventeen, as minors. But in an unusually aggressive move, the DA bypassed the privacy protections of juvenile court and made all six of the kids' names public. (Sean, Kayla, and Austin were indicted as adults.) And once they were named, the press had no compunction about hounding them. Reporters camped out on Flannery's lawn, making it almost impossible for her to go to work. One of her neighbors screamed "slut" and "whore" at her whenever she left the house, and started blogging about Flannery's movements. The household was under siege, and the stress strained the marriage of Flannery's mother, Jen. The public nature of the indictment "meant the end of our lives as we knew them," Jen told me. "People get indicted every day and you never hear about it, but Betsy Scheibel's mission was to smear these kids." Everywhere Flannery ventured where she met new people—parties, stores—she faced questions and denunciations, with people assuming her guilt and her responsibility for Phoebe's suicide. "It was like a runaway freight train," Jen said.

Flannery's lawyers tried to reassure her and her mother that the case against her was full of holes. For starters, the most serious felony charge—civil rights violation with bodily injury—required an act or threat of force, and Flannery's remark in gym class that "someone should kick [Phoebe's] ass" was a stretch. For another, the causal connection between anything Flannery had done and Phoebe's death was, to say the least, attenuated. Still, the lawyers cautioned Flannery against talking to Austin or seeing him. Isolated and living under a kind of media-imposed house arrest, Flannery was touchy and antsy. She felt as though her whole existence was about being under indictment—and it was impossible to imagine returning to normal.

Scheibel didn't charge any teachers or administrators at South Hadley High, but in her press conference, she made a point of mentioning the school, saying that some staff members had been alerted to Phoebe's harassment. "The actions, or inactions, of some adults at the school are troublesome," she said ominously. Later she added, "There was a denial of . . . not only wrongdoing, but I think any inaction that may have contributed to not protecting Phoebe. And let's face it, the school had a duty to protect her while she was in school."

Armed with Scheibel's critique at the press conference, Darby O'Brien, the PR pro who'd started the media ball rolling, took his case for Principal Smith's and Superintendent Sayer's resignations to the *Today* show and anywhere else that would have him, saying they couldn't be trusted with South Hadley's children. Sayer, who had no PR training, was defensive and unpersuasive in the national TV appearances he made in an effort to quell the rising outrage about the role of the schools. Responding to Scheibel's "troublesome" remark, Sayer told Matt Lauer of *Today,* "She'll have to explain what's troublesome. It is not—it's not troublesome to me."

Before the day was out, Scheibel had fired back a winning shot: "Mr. Sayer does not have access to some of our investigative materials; therefore, he can't have a basis for some of his comments."

Next Sayer tried pleading ignorance. "The kids have a way of communicating with each other without us knowing about it," he told the *Boston Globe.* "Everyone expects the schools to solve these problems, but we don't have magic-bullet solutions to how kids behave." To a stern and skeptical Anderson Cooper, Sayer made more excuses, saying that Smith and his staff did everything they could. If the school hadn't been able to help Phoebe, that was because she had never *asked* for help. "I deeply regret the fact that no one came forward to us and reported that this bullying was taking place," Sayer said.

It was a losing strategy. The editorial page of the *Boston Globe* jumped all over the superintendent: "Rather than declare 'we did everything we could,' as Sayer did, he should launch a new probe to determine what signals were missed and why. If teachers truly didn't know of the bullying until a week before the suicide, how might they have learned earlier? If some knew and failed to take sufficient action, what might have prompted them to do so?"

After months of reporting on this story and the events that led up to Phoebe's death, I was deeply interested in those questions, too. I could understand the grief and rage of Phoebe's parents, but I couldn't square the DA's statement that Phoebe was the victim of a three-month "campaign" of relentless bullying and civil rights violations with what I'd learned from talking to South Hadley students: that she'd tried to go out with Sean and Austin, and when that didn't work out, she had gotten caught up in conflict with them and their girlfriends, and other students peripherally. I worried I'd missed something.

And then I got a chance to look at hundreds of pages of court documents—the record that was the basis of Scheibel's decision to press charges against the South Hadley Six.

The materials, which Scheibel had submitted to the grand jury, included dozens of police interviews, as well as cell phone records, school reports, and other documents, and were given to me by someone whom I promised not to identify. Here, I thought, would be the key to understanding Scheibel's case. But when I finished reading, I felt more confused. The court documents *didn't* change everything I thought I'd learned. Instead, they confirmed it: the story of Phoebe Prince's suicide was a terrible tragedy, but it was a different and far more complicated story than the one the DA was telling publicly.

Regarding the bullying, the court documents added little to the facts that were already known—they described Sharon's outburst at Phoebe on January 6, Flannery's expression of anger in gym class on January 7, and Ashley's outbursts (with Sean and Kayla's encouragement) on January 14. Other scattered allegations of misconduct basically amounted to unreliable, often contradictory gossip. For example, four or five girls separately told the police they'd either seen Flannery go into a school bathroom at the same time as Phoebe one day in the first week of January or heard that had happened. A few of the girls said they'd heard reports that once inside, Flannery had called Phoebe a whore, or dirty. But the girl who was actually in the bathroom at the time said the two hadn't spoken to each other.

The main revelation in those hundreds of pages was the write-up of the police interview with Phoebe's mother, on January 20, six days after Phoebe's death, in which she made clear that her daughter's psychological struggles predated the bullying in January—and even the family's move to South Hadley. In Chapter 3, we talked about Anne O'Brien's account: she said that Phoebe clashed with girls at two schools in Ireland in eighth grade, and started cutting herself and taking antidepressants. After the move to South Hadley, Anne thought her daughter seemed better for a time, but then Phoebe slid into depression and tried to kill herself after Thanksgiving, when her relationship with Sean ended. I learned from other documents, later, about Phoebe's cascading fights with her mother and how crushed she had been when her parents didn't reconcile over Christmas. And on the day of Phoebe's suicide, a detective stated, "Anne O'Brien is concerned that she is to blame due to a conversation she had with Phoebe. When Phoebe had disclosed to her mother that she had smoked marijuana, her mother threatened to take away her trip to Ireland." The district attorney's documents also showed that Phoebe had gone off her medication after the November suicide attempt, six weeks before her death, and in those weeks she'd turned for help to older boys who were ill-equipped to provide it. James, one of the senior boys involved with Phoebe, summed up her underlying fragility for the police. "Honestly," he said, "I'm not surprised by the suicide. Phoebe had a lot of emotional problems."

For Sean, Kayla, and Ashley, the students who had been cruel to Phoebe on the day she died, the most damning documents in the file were Phoebe's cell phone records. In her texts that afternoon after school, an hour or two before her death, Phoebe was unquestionably full of pain about how Sean had encouraged Ashley to call her a whore in school. The timing suggested that the texts were a trigger: the day's events had surely contributed to tipping Phoebe into utter despair. But the texts implicated only Sean, Ashley, and perhaps Kayla, not Flannery, Sharon, or Austin. And read as a whole, the record made clear that when Phoebe fell apart, it was because of a cascade of troubles that were not all, or perhaps even mostly, of South Hadley's making.

Also in the court record were notes and drawings the police found in Phoebe's room. In one of them, she wrote "PEOPLE ALWAYS LIE," and underneath, *"mom? dad? me?"*

On another page, question marks and a drawing of an eye vied for space with the word "HELP," which was written in bubble letters. Phoebe had also written her name, in sharply angled 3-D, and the words "Mother looking at me tell me what do you see." Her parents as well as her failed relationship with Sean had been on her mind in the days and weeks before she died. This didn't mean Anne and Jeremy were to blame, of course, but it did further complicate the tidy narrative Scheibel's office had created to justify criminally blaming a group of bullies for Phoebe's death.

When I finished reading the file, I was crying for Phoebe, and I felt terrible for her family, but I could not understand the DA's decision to lay the burden of her suicide at the feet of six adolescents. Given the many factors that led to Phoebe's suicide, all the history, how could a prosecutor say that Flannery's or Sharon's or Austin's actions, or even Sean's or Ashley's or Kayla's, were the criminal *cause,* in the eyes of the law, of Phoebe's decision to kill herself?

I called Alan Dershowitz, a criminal law professor at Harvard, to ask what he thought of Scheibel's decision to press charges. "That's an old idea," he said. "In the early nineteenth century, there were prosecutions in which a woman was raped, and then killed herself, and the rapist was held responsible for her death. In the most famous one, a man named Stevenson who was a head of the Ku Klux Klan in the

Midwest in the 1920s kidnapped a woman named Madge Ober-holtzer. He took her on a long ride and raped her repeatedly, and afterward she took mercury tablets to kill herself. The court sent Stevenson to jail: the idea then was that a woman who was raped would have no choice but to kill herself because her life was ruined." But this is a notion the law has since repudiated. "Now we think of the decision to commit suicide as an intervening factor that is usually made of one's own free will."

In line with that thinking, the American Law Institute's Model Penal Code states that to win a conviction for "causing suicide as criminal homicide," the prosecution must show that the defendant purposely caused the suicide, by "force, duress or deception." Dershowitz said he'd never heard of a prosecutor criminally blaming anyone—much less a teenager—for a suicide by charging him with a civil rights violation with bodily injury. "That's a real stretch," he said. "People want to think that there's always legal accountability where there should be moral accountability. But in the criminal context, you should always err against overextending the law."

I wrestled with how much to publish from the court documents, with the question of how to give a full account of Phoebe's death without being exploitative. Normally a fifteen-year-old's history of depression and struggles with suicide would remain private, and I kept thinking about the pain of her family. I didn't want to add to that. But Scheibel had made Phoebe's history a public matter, and the narrative she'd crafted was misleading. She'd used it to go after six teenagers in the media and in court. If I had information that was relevant to the national conversation the DA had started, and that cast things in a different light, my editors and I decided that our job as journalists was to publish with sensitivity, not withhold. In July 2010, six months after Phoebe's death, I ran a story in Slate called "What Really Happened to Phoebe Prince?"

When I called Scheibel's office two days before the story ran to ask for comment, her deputy said she wouldn't discuss any specific evidence. A couple of hours later she called Slate's office in Washington, D.C., threatening to sue to block publication. We went ahead with the story.

Scheibel responded with a press release in which she said:

> Ms. Bazelon's article suggests that Phoebe's internal struggles alone caused her death and it is unfair to hold these defendants accountable for their behavior. As a matter of law, the existence of a victim's disability does not legally excuse a defendant's criminal actions. Under many statutory schemes it serves to aggravate the offense, rather than mitigate it.

I wrote back in Slate:

> I didn't say that Phoebe's internal struggles alone caused her death. I do think the six kids charged should be held accountable for their behavior—but through school discipline, not through the criminal justice system. . . .
>
> Scheibel is right that a victim's disability doesn't technically excuse a defendant's actions. That's the lawyerly response. But the issue here is prosecutorial discretion. It was Scheibel's decision to bring a 10-year maximum felony charge that blames the kids for Phoebe's death. This is an extremely unusual response to suicide and to bullying. . . .
>
> Like almost all of us, Phoebe wasn't entirely passive and she also wasn't merely a victim. She was a person who had social power some days and none others, and who seems to have suffered from a terrible mental illness that left her especially vulnerable. It's complicated, and if we want to really understand what happened to her, and to really unpack bul-

lying more generally, we need to make room for a more complex set of dynamics.

Then the law professors weighed in. "If you bully someone to death, that's murder. But if you bully someone, and then they kill themselves, and that's not something you anticipated, that's not a crime," said Joseph Kennedy, a criminal law professor at the University of North Carolina at Chapel Hill. "There's an understandable wish by prosecutors to respond to the moral outrage of society," said Orin Kerr, a law professor at George Washington University, "but the important thing is for the prosecution to follow the law." It's cause for concern, he continued, when it seems as if the government is "prosecuting people not for what they did, but for what the victim did in response."

This was the winning argument in a court of law, but in the court of public opinion, it lost in a landslide. I got more email and comments for my articles about Phoebe's death than for anything I'd ever written before. Some readers thanked me for telling a fuller story, but many, many more—"What is wrong is wrong and the children bullying her is wrong and should take whatever punishment they get," and "With people like emily bazelon and the six bullies, people like phoebe never stood a chance to live" and "SHAME ON YOU, Emily!!!!!!!"— accused me of blaming the victim. I'd tried hard not to do that, but I understood the anger. This story wasn't about the facts anymore, if it ever had been. Phoebe had become a symbol.

I wasn't arguing that Flannery and the other five teenagers hadn't done anything wrong. I was arguing that they didn't deserve to be criminally charged for their wrongdoing. What bothered me was that the adults involved were letting a bunch of teenagers take the fall for a girl's death. I wasn't interested in blaming the school, or Phoebe's parents, for her suicide, but I did wonder if there was something to be learned from the missed opportunities evident in the record. South Hadley High, for example, had a Student Assistance Team, which gave counselors, administrators, and the nurse a means of sharing information about students having academic, emotional, or behavioral problems, yet Phoebe hadn't come up at any meeting the team held in the fall or winter before her death. In retrospect, this seemed a glaring omission. Then there was the morning of Phoebe's death, when she'd gone to see the nurse about the burn on her chest. Given her depression and her recent suicide attempt, should the nurse or the guidance counselor have probed more deeply? Should the school have done more for Phoebe? Should someone have asked Anne O'Brien to pick her up on that awful last day?

Anne and Jeremy were asking those questions themselves. They filed a complaint against the South Hadley schools with the Massachusetts Commission Against Discrimination in July 2010, accusing the South Hadley schools of creating an "intimidating, hostile, and sexually offensive educational environment" for their daughter. When I talked to Jeremy Prince around the same time, he was understandably still angry. He had lost his daughter, after all. He said he wanted to forgive, but he needed an apology. "I'd dearly like to see admission of contrition, so that I could forgive," he said. "If they confessed to the court and said they were sorry, I'd appeal to the court for total leniency. You can go two ways: you can look to the court for revenge or you can look for leniency. The latter path is mine."

Some juvenile courts use a practice called restorative justice, which aims for apology and the taking of responsibility rather than punishment. The person who has caused harm must make amends. But no one in the DA's office, or anywhere in South Hadley, was talking about restorative justice. They were after retribution.

District Attorney Scheibel pursued the charges against Flannery and the other five teenagers with the zeal of a true believer, a woman who believed she was standing up for a persecuted girl whom everyone else had failed. With this case more than any other in her seventeen years in office, she made a name for herself—and generated glowing coverage. Scheibel didn't use the attention to fuel a bid for reelection. Instead, she endorsed a protégé she'd groomed to replace her, and made him the public spokesperson for questions relating to Phoebe's death. In September, however, Scheibel's candidate lost to a challenger who'd taken no position on the Phoebe-related charges during his campaign.

To no one's surprise, a few months after taking office the new district attorney was ready to make a deal. In the end, after all the tough talk and threats of prison, all the blistering TV interviews and the "Justice for Phoebe" bumper stickers, only one of the six teenagers, Sean, would be required to plead guilty to one charge—a misdemeanor count of harassment. Kayla would accept responsibility for harassing Phoebe, without a guilty plea, which meant that after she completed probation and community service, she would have a clean record. In light of the charges, Harvard law professor Alan Dershowitz told me, these were "amazing" plea bargains. "If the prosecutors come down so quickly from a charge like that to a plea like this," he said, "they're clearly playing games."

The deals had to be approved by a judge, so Sean and Kayla each had a public hearing in early May 2011, in a high-ceilinged courtroom in Northampton, a dozen miles from South Hadley High. Sean went first. He sat in the front of the courtroom facing the bench, his hair buzzed short, in a black suit. The benches behind him were packed with his family and the press. Judge Henry Kinder entered the room, and the audience rose.

The new assistant DA, a young man with a shaved head, recited facts that were mostly familiar by now: Sean had a brief relationship with Phoebe. He got upset with her because he thought "she caused friction between himself and Kayla." Sean came up to Phoebe at school and called her names. He also encouraged Kayla and Ashley to be mean to Phoebe. At lunch in the library, when Ashley called Phoebe a whore, Sean "was taking pleasure in it." At dismissal time, Sean prompted Ashley to taunt Phoebe again—and when she did, he and

Kayla laughed. When Ashley texted to say she'd made Phoebe cry by throwing the empty drink can at her on the way home from school, Sean responded with a cruel text that said, "Good job."

When the prosecutor finished, the judge asked the lawyers if they were ready to recommend a sentence. The assistant DA asked for probation, as the prosecution and the defense had agreed. "But first, I'd like to state for the court that this recommendation is one the Commonwealth proposes with the informed consent and support of Phoebe Prince's family," he said. "Before sentencing, we will hear from Phoebe's mother, Anne O'Brien."

Anne rose from her seat, on the opposite side of the courtroom from Sean's family, and walked to the podium. Phoebe's mother had not spoken publicly since her daughter's death. Now she would have her say, in a courtroom setting, in the form of what is called a victim impact statement. Anne did not have to stick to the facts the prosecution and the defense had agreed on. She could say what she wanted. She could forgive, or she could not.

She put on tortoiseshell glasses, and, voice shaking, read from prepared notes. "Phoebe Prince is my daughter," she said. "It is nearly impossible to measure the impact of Phoebe's death upon our lives. How do you measure a future loss?" She talked about all the things she would never again get to do with Phoebe—visit Irish castles, debate the motivations of a character in Evelyn Waugh's *A Handful of Dust,* play an early morning game of tennis. Abruptly, but how could it be otherwise, Anne moved to the aftermath of Phoebe's death. "As I said my final goodbye to Phoebe at the crematorium, I lifted her from the coffin and held her for the very last time. My little girl, once so full of life, was now so cold. I wept and asked her, 'What am I going to do?' There is a dead weight that now sits permanently in my chest. It's an unbearable pain and it will stay with me until my own death. I would not wish this kind of pain on any parent. It is torture."

Anne looked up from her notes. "Phoebe trusted Sean Mulveyhill to take care of her, guide her through the maze of South Hadley High

School," she said, looking not at Sean but at the judge. "I can only imagine the pain she felt at his unrelenting desire to harass and humiliate her. He then set upon her, with actions designed to humiliate her and destroy her spirit. . . . Her final text messages were about Sean and the girls that tormented her." Anne quoted from Phoebe's texts: " 'I think Sean condoning this is one of the final nails in my coffin. And I can't take much more. It would be easier if he or any one of them handed me a noose.' " Anne's voice broke as she asked, "Why could he never have stepped back to see the pain he was causing her? Where was his empathy?"

This was the price for Sean's lenient sentence: Anne's judgment, sanctioned by the weight and gravity of the law.

Judge Kinder thanked Phoebe's mother for speaking and said that she had acceded to the punishment he was about to impose. On that note of compassion for Phoebe's family, and also deference, the judge gave Sean probation—a sentence that seemed a mismatch for O'Brien's fury.

The painful ritual repeated itself minutes later with Kayla, who entered the courtroom after Sean left. She'd broken off contact with him since they'd left school, and she didn't want to see him. But now Kayla, too, was pulled back to the unhappy day, sixteen months earlier, when holding on to Sean had been paramount—a reason to stand by and laugh while Ashley, at his prodding, humiliated Phoebe. The prosecutor read the facts Kayla had admitted to a year and a half earlier, when the police first interviewed her: she'd written about hating Irish sluts on Facebook, and she'd laughed when Ashley taunted Phoebe.

Phoebe's mother rose again to speak, and again her words were vengeful as well as grief-stricken. "Phoebe found the courage and compassion to seek out Kayla Narey and apologize to her when she discovered Sean had lied to her. Kayla had the opportunity to be a true leader of her school community and put a stop to Phoebe's torment. Instead, she joined in, in subtle and cunning ways, too weak a character to match Phoebe's courage," Anne said. "Kayla Narey is not capable of compassion, even to those she is aware of who are suffering. Why did Kayla not find the courage and compassion to help Phoebe?"

When the barrage ended, Kayla stood and gave Phoebe's mother the apology that Jeremy had said was all the family wanted. "Your Honor, I would like to extend my heartfelt sorrow and apology to the Prince family, and more importantly, to Phoebe," Kayla said, her voice tremulous. "My parents instilled in me to be kind and considerate and generous to others. For most of my life, I have been able to fulfill that. Unfortunately, during a time in high school, my relationship with my boyfriend became the priority over my core values. My behavior in those days leading up to Phoebe's death was unacceptable." Kayla started to cry. "Phoebe, I wish we could go back to December tenth and eleventh, when you bravely apologized to me. We had respectful words to each other and though I wasn't happy, I was kind to you. It was my hurt, anger, and jealousy that later changed my behavior, after Christmas vacation. That's when I had the chance to be the person I was raised to be. I failed. That failure will always be with me." Kayla paused, weeping now. "I'm sorry, Phoebe. I'm sorry for the unkind words I said to others about you. I'm sorry about the unkind posting on my Facebook page. But mostly I am sorry for January fourteenth of 2010, in the library and in the hallway, when I laughed when someone else was shouting humiliating things at you. I am truly sorry, Phoebe, for my role in this tragedy. I am immensely ashamed of myself."

Kayla had taken responsibility for what she'd done, even though at the time she never could have imagined the disastrous outcome. Her lawyer, Michael Jennings, tried to point this out. "This young woman has been skewered across the globe for more than a year because people don't understand the context of what happened," he said. "She's here today for her one opportunity in the public square to admit to what she did, but I also want to say she shouldn't be held responsible for everything."

Jennings wasn't through. "I'm chilled by Mrs. O'Brien's statement," he continued. "No one can hear those words and not reach deeply into themselves. But Kayla Narey is also a wonderful girl. Most of her life has been perfect. Her behavior has been perfect. She's done all the right things. Until this."

The next day it was Flannery's turn. She appeared before a different judge, with Sharon and Ashley, at the smaller, humbler juvenile courthouse in Hadley, one town over. Flannery had struggled over whether to accept her plea deal. She thought about daring the prosecution to take her case to trial. "I thought, let them try," she said.

But that would have meant months, or even years, with serious criminal charges hanging over her head. Flannery had turned eighteen, and it was time to move on, to look ahead, to stop reliving the upheaval that split her life in two: before and after. She agreed to admit to what she'd said about Phoebe, about how "someone ought to kick her ass," the basis for the charge that she'd disturbed a school assembly, that is, her gym class. In a strained resolution of the civil rights charge, Flannery also took responsibility for Sharon's misconduct—calling Phoebe a whore at school—even though Sharon said from start to finish that she'd done this on her own. In exchange, Flannery would get probation and community service with the understanding Kayla had: once she completed her sentence, her record would be clean. Ashley and Sharon got the same kind of deal. Austin fared even better: the statutory rape charge against him was dropped.

At the hearing, Flannery wore a white oxford shirt, the collar crisp at the fold, and her blond hair coiled into a bun. The lawyers dispensed with the preliminaries, and Anne O'Brien rose to speak again. "Phoebe had as much right as Flannery Mullins to be in school," she said, reading from her notes. "She was an intelligent student with a promise of high achievement. She loved her accelerated English class and having her own blog to share her writing. Phoebe loved her history class. . . . She loved the challenge of her Latin class and was in awe of her teacher's intelligence. . . . Yet with Flannery Mullins' very numerous threats to beat her up, school for Phoebe became intolerable. In her words, it was not a place of solace and intellectual challenge, but simply a challenge to make it through each day without coming to harm."

Flannery was looking straight ahead, her features unmoving, betraying nothing. O'Brien kept going. "Flannery Mullins used her time in school to berate Phoebe in corridors and in the classroom. . . . When she was brought before school officials to address her actions, she took no ownership of them, and placed the blame on Phoebe. . . . She followed her into the bathrooms, the hallways and classrooms of the high school. Phoebe soldiered on, struggling to get through each day, hoping the next would be better. Phoebe drew a sketch on one of the folders I keep my school papers in, of a candle with a flame. And underneath she'd written, 'There is always a light.'" Anne's voice broke as she turned to look at Flannery. "Phoebe tried to be strong but sometimes people want nothing more than to break you."

Anne paused, but she wasn't finished.

"Phoebe ended her pain, brought about by the harassment of many, including Flannery Mullins, harassment that could easily have been stopped if any of those involved had ever reached inside themselves to find their own compassion. I have not yet buried Phoebe's ashes. I've been waiting for peace to do so. I know now today it may never come. So I will return home and bury my daughter. With her qualities of compassion, empathy, and zest for life, Phoebe gave me some of the happiest moments of my life. My pain is unbearable and it will stay with me until my own death and I would not wish this pain on any parent."

In this wrenching torrent, Anne had again claimed her right, as a mother in mourning, to go beyond the facts in the record. No one dared question her judgment in doing so.

But it was hard for Flannery to swallow her defiance. She knew Phoebe's mother had suffered, but she couldn't accept Anne's narrative of her daughter's death. "Everyone said I was heartless because I wasn't crying in court, but in my mind, I didn't do anything," she told me later. "Of course it's so sad Phoebe died, but her mother screaming at me, telling me it's my fault—I thought that was extremely immature. I know that's horrible to say."

I asked if she'd thought about changing her name or moving away from western Massachusetts, and Flannery shook her head. "I'm not ashamed," she said. "I have no problem defending myself. I don't want to be ashamed. I think it would be harder for me if I sat down and was like, 'I'll change my name, and I'll move, and no one will know me.' No. If you have a problem with me, you can tell me, and I can explain that it's not the truth. If people are ever going to digest the real story, they have to accept the fact that the picture of Phoebe that was painted isn't true." Flannery knew that the tragedy of Phoebe's suicide made that extremely difficult to do, but she was holding fiercely to her reality.

The relationship between bullying and suicide turns out to be complicated. It's true that there's an association between the two, for both girls and boys: studies show that kids who are bullied are also more likely to think about or try suicide. The link is especially strong for gay kids.

Whether bullying *predicts* suicide, however, is a separate inquiry. It's a chicken-and-egg question: are kids who are involved with bullying more likely to be suicidal in the first place, or does the experience of victimization place them more at risk? For kids who experience school-age bullying, the research is mixed. Finnish and Australian studies found that bullying didn't predict depression or attempted suicide once a child's prior mental health was taken into account—in other words, when children were bullied, they didn't become more likely than they otherwise would have been to develop, as teenagers, the symptoms of depression that are the biggest risk for suicide. On the other hand, a study of Norwegian eleven-year-olds by Dan Olweus, and another study of Korean seventh and eighth graders, found that bullying *did* predict depression and attempted suicide. Still another Finnish study of eight-year-olds who were bullied, and then followed up ten years later, showed the results varying by gender: among girls, frequent victimization was associated with later suicide attempts even when controlling for depression, whereas for boys the same was not true.

The upshot is that there is some reason to think that childhood bullying, on its own, elevates the risk of depression and suicide, but the picture isn't yet clear.

And it's even less clear for kids who are bullied in high school. In a recent study of whether bullying at this older age predicts suicide attempts—the only one of its kind I could find—Columbia psychiatrist Madelyn Gould and a team of researchers tracked three groups of teenagers. At an initial screening, the first group, which totaled 221 students, reported suicidal behavior or thinking, depression, or substance abuse. The second group, with ninety-six students, had the same psychological profile and *also* had been involved in bullying. The third group of 236 had been involved in bullying but were not depressed, suicidal, or substance abusers.

Four years later, Gould's team went back and interviewed the same teenagers. On average, the 236 young adults who'd experienced bullying but did not have the at-risk psychological profile were less likely to be suicidal than the young adults who did, whether they were bullied or not. "Involvement in bullying behavior (as a bully, a victim, or both) in the absence of other risks in high school did not predict later depression, suicidal ideation, or suicide attempts," Gould and her colleagues wrote.

Gould calls for more research, but she is adamant that it's wrong to attribute any one suicide entirely to bullying, as media accounts often do. "The problem with saying bullying caused a suicide is that it oversimplifies," she told me. "It implies that one person's death by suicide can be attributed to one event or factor, which is just not true." She sees these "bullycide" narratives as part of a longstanding misguided pattern. "We've singled out different scapegoats for suicide for decades," she said. "We blamed the mean teacher. Or the bad parents. Or Dungeons and Dragons, or working mothers, or divorce. Now it's bullies, and especially mean kids on the Internet. The thing is, there can be some truth to these explanations. When someone is vulnerable, and then they experience what we call a stressor event, and they are humiliated, that can be terrible for them. But it's crucial to remember that what we're also seeing as these narratives take shape is our underlying need to try to understand an event that family members and friends find so inexplicable."

It's imperative not to blame families for the current fixation on bullycide. This is something that Michele Dauber, a Stanford law professor whose daughter took her own life at twenty-five after a long struggle with depression, impressed upon me during a conversation over the course of several weeks. Dauber reminded me of an arresting image in the Harry Potter books: because they have seen death, Harry and a friend, Luna Lovegood, can see a winged, skeletal horse, called a Thestral, that's not visible to anyone else. This is Dauber's metaphor for being a parent who has lost a child. "I'm different from you," she told me. "Because I now understand that nothing is promised. Good things aren't a reward and bad things aren't a punishment. There is nothing we can do to avoid tragedy—sometimes it just comes, and when it does, the world is no longer a benign place full of excitement to look forward to, or even a place where we go to work and put food on the table, but a terrible, miserable slog in which one by one everyone we love goes away forever, unless we die first. That is what being the parent of a dead child is like. So how can we blame these poor people if they aren't seeing things the way we think they should?"

Parents who have lost their bearings so profoundly, because of the gravity of their loss, are particularly vulnerable to the media's and others' messages that bullying is the reason their beloved child is gone. "Nothing in the world makes sense," Dauber said. "Along comes someone to tell them that bullying is the cause, and that's a ready-made causal explanation that helps them to fill in the gaps in a world otherwise gone crazy. The parents want to believe this account. And it is often partially true anyway. Kids who are different or ill are often bullying targets, so the causal arrows are hard to work out, but it is undeniable that bullying is stressful and that stress exacerbates and causes depression, and that can make a child more likely, potentially, to take his or her own life. If parents don't immediately see the missed signals, or things that in hindsight *they* might have done differently to help their child, that should be forgiven. Be gentle with these families. They have a long road to walk."

At a bullying prevention training for educators and police that I attended in November 2011, several months after Flannery's hearing, a veteran instructor cautioned her audience against using the word *bullycide*. "With adults," she said, "we don't pick one problem—divorce, financial ruin—and say that's why someone attempted or completed a suicide. We don't say *divorcecide*. So why should we do that with a child's life—pick one fact and think it explains the whole?" She acknowledged, though, that the attention and awareness generated by the bullycide narratives—Phoebe Prince's perhaps chief among them—has had a beneficial effect, of "spurring the movement to bullying prevention more than anything else." The rate of teen suicide in the last two decades has dropped substantially. But that pattern of good news has been lost in the din of each individual tragedy. It's largely the stories of suicide that have driven states to pass the latest wave of anti-bullying laws. After Phoebe's death and the suicide of an eleven-year-old African American boy in the nearby city of Springfield, for example, Massachusetts mandated yearly training for teachers and staff on prevention and intervention, as well as instruction for students in every grade. Nine other states, like Alaska, Illinois, and Maine, require schools to report bullying to the police. In Missouri, school officials who fail to do so can be criminally prosecuted. States including North Carolina and Idaho have added provisions about bullying to their juvenile justice codes.

Massachusetts' new law is probably to the good. It has raised awareness and pushed principals and their staffs to take bullying seriously. The law has no funding behind it, but Massachusetts has the valuable homegrown resource of psychologist Elizabeth Englander, who (along with other faculty and a team of graduate and undergraduate students) offers staff trainings for teachers, consultations for schools, and leadership training programs and assemblies for students—almost none of which schools pay for. She and her staff use a "train the trainer" model, working with teachers who then bring what they've learned back to their schools, which is actually part of the Massachusetts law. "On the day the law passed, I got a lot of calls from legislators making sure I wasn't about to leave the state, to make sure they knew schools would have our help bearing the load," she said.

Englander is a resource that most other states don't have, and as a result, some schools have complained that anti-bullying laws are a financial burden. Following the suicide of a gay eighteen-year-old Rutgers freshman named Tyler Clementi, New Jersey passed an Anti-Bullying Bill of Rights with eighteen pages of specifications about the policies, procedures, and instruction every public school had to adopt. The law also mandated more staff training, imposed strict deadlines for dealing with reports of bullying, and required each district to appoint an anti-bullying coordinator. To evaluate compliance, the State Education Department started posting grades for each school on its website.

A few months after the law passed, the head of New Jersey's association of school administrators said publicly that the legislature had gone overboard. Pointing out that schools were given no money to put it into practice, one school district challenged the law as an "unfunded mandate," and a state council ruled it unconstitutional. Parents, too, wondered whether the legislation sought to control students, or protect them. A decade ago, some schools were ridiculed for banning games such as dodgeball, a form of free play that was suddenly frowned upon for being too aggressive. Now in New Jersey, schools were telling students that if one kid says to another, "You suck at tennis," and it's clear to both kids this is a joke, or if they have an underlying friendship that makes the remark harmless, they can still be disciplined if a third student overhears the comment and reports it as bullying. That kind of overkill alienates students. "The goal isn't to lay down the law and then adhere to it with mindless rigidity," Englander told me. "What we need is for educators to have the flexibility to take into account the impact that a behavior actually has. Otherwise, you're adding to the perception that adults just don't get it and can't really help."

The other problem with New Jersey's approach is that it invades the mental space students need to grow. "There's a part of growing up that's about being in the society of other kids when adults are not around and some of the rules are suspended," Englander continued. "It's a very necessary part of development. It's how children learn to cope with these social problems by themselves. They need the freedom and elbow room of not having adults come in and fix everything, so they'll learn to come up with their own solutions. And the odds are that the adults of today had far more time like that when they were growing up than today's kids do."

Flannery finished high school by taking night classes at a community college, glad to go for days without seeing anyone she knew from high school. She spoke up, though, when a teacher who didn't know her history brought up the South Hadley Six one day. "I told the class they didn't know the whole story and they probably never would," she said. To help pay her probation and school fees, she worked during the day at a real estate office in Holyoke. The town is only a few miles from South Hadley, but it's bigger, and for Flannery, it felt like free- dom. She hadn't told her mother yet, but she was looking for an apart- ment with a friend. She was nineteen and ready to be on her own.

By this point, Principal Dan Smith and Superintendent Gus Sayer had retired from the South Hadley school district, pensions intact. Elizabeth Scheibel had been named one of the Bostonians of the Year by the *Boston Globe,* for her role in the Prince case; when she stepped down a year after Phoebe's death, she said she had no regrets about prosecuting the six South Hadley students.

She appeared on CNN nearly a year later, long after all the crimi- nal cases had been resolved, with her deputy Elizabeth Dunphy Farris and Anne O'Brien. Piers Morgan, the interviewer, once again re- peated the likely falsehood that the "bullies" had posted "done" on Facebook after Phoebe's death and Anne said that they'd posted "she got what she deserved." Morgan called the teenagers' behavior "wicked" and "depraved." Anne said she wanted to clarify that prison terms were "never on the cards"—which was odd, given the many years of prison Flannery and the others had faced. If the DA's office never intended to ask for such a punishment, why had it brought such serious charges? Asked a related question, about why some of the kids had been prosecuted as adults, Farris said this "sent a message." She continued, "It needed to be put out in the public." O'Brien's and Far- ris' statements made it sound as if the DA had used the teenagers to make a point.

If the prosecutors emerged unscathed, the kids were struggling. At seventeen, Sharon was pregnant. Ashley and Austin had both been charged with drunk driving. Flannery was worried about Austin: his mother had told him he couldn't live at home anymore, so he was crashing with friends when he could. He'd stopped going to school, and his job at a packing plant meant he spent long days in a giant meat freezer. "There was no real closure for anyone," Flannery said. "Were we guilty? Or was the prosecution unfair? You couldn't really tell. So it's over but it's not really over."

Flannery's neighbor was still yelling "slut" and "whore" at her in public—in fact, she was facing a harassment charge. Flannery appreciated the irony of being on the other side of a criminal proceeding. "The DA's office calls and asks how they can help me," she said. But she was more interested in focusing on her future than her past. In another year, Flannery would graduate from community college with an associate's degree. She was thinking about where to finish her four-year degree. She wanted to study psychology.

Part III

Solutions

Chapter 7

Freedom

IN 1938, A SEVEN-YEAR-OLD BOY NAMED PETER PAUL HEINE-
mann boarded a small boat, bound for Sweden, with his family. The
Heinemanns, who were Jewish, were fleeing Nazi Germany. The family had hoped to get as far from Hitler as possible by going to New
Zealand, but after a year and a half of limbo in Holland, they learned
that Sweden was the only country that would take them. Everyone
was sick on the boat, and Peter Paul could tell that his father was
frightened—of the war, of exile to a foreign land, of what would happen to his family. The rough passage and his father's uncertainty

made him scared, too. A girl tried to speak to Peter Paul in Swedish, but he couldn't understand a word she said, leaving him even more bewildered. "It is a feeling so stupid and full of alarm," he wrote later of this moment. "You know you don't understand, but you can't even say so."

Things improved when Peter Paul's family reached Gothenberg, a city on Sweden's west coast where Volvo had opened its first factory in the 1920s. His father, who had practiced law in Germany, eventually started a plant nursery, and the family felt well treated. But Peter Paul never entirely got over the feeling of being different, apart. And those feelings flooded back to him thirty years later, when he saw his own son fall prey to small-town ignorance.

By then, Peter Paul had become a surgeon and married one of his medical school classmates. The couple lived in Orebro, a midsized city 125 miles from Stockholm, and one day in 1963, Heinemann's wife, who was by now a psychiatrist, called him at the hospital where he worked to tell him they were having a baby. Heinemann was thrilled about his wife's pregnancy—and then she said that no, she wasn't pregnant, but she'd just found out about a baby who needed a home, and decided they would adopt him. His name was David. He was the seven-month-old child of a very young mother who could not raise him, he was not eating well or thriving, and no one knew who his father was. David would arrive tomorrow! Oh, and he was black.

Black children weren't just unusual in Sweden at the time; they were unheard of. When Heinemann took David to the grocery store, people asked, "Can he withstand the climate? You are a missionary, I presume?" Heinemann came to think of this as "the decent people's indecent attitude." Even when they praised him for the noble deed of taking in a black child, Heinemann would seethe. "It is praise that doesn't comfort," he wrote. "It feels like a punch in the face. And one can't punch back. And the boy listens with big eyes and big ears that already have heard too much."

The most troubling comments, to Heinemann, came from other

children. As a small boy, his father said, David confronted packs of kids who called him "nigger." After being "exposed to the child mob," as Heinemann put it, his son "usually crawls up in bed, takes his sleeping-lamb, and falls asleep, leaving everything behind." For his father, the boy's pain was excruciating—and it brought back the darkest fears of his own childhood: "My father always had this feeling about people's vulnerability," David's younger sister, Kajsa, told me. "When he saw the children surrounding his son, he remembered Germany. It was like the first step to the much bigger terror of the Holocaust."

When I reached David over the phone while he was feeding his kids dinner one night, he told me, a little sheepishly, that he doesn't remember the jeers that so pained his father. Once he started school, he had a tight group of friends, and, in fact, his main memory of his childhood is acceptance, not rejection. "I'm celebrating my fiftieth birthday this summer, and I still see a few of my old friends weekly, and they say the same thing I remember: 'We never thought of you as being different,'" David said. "But before school, when I was younger, children must have said mean things, and my father, coming from Germany and his narrow escape from the Nazis, was very sensitive to that. Which is a good thing: if someone makes a racist remark to your kid, then as a parent you *should* react."

Peter Paul Heinemann's anguish was keener because no one outside his family seemed to share it. Teachers shrugged off the name-calling as inevitable, and Heinemann and his wife had nowhere to turn for advice: the topic of childhood cruelty was rarely even mentioned in the parenting books they read. No one, it seemed, was studying this problem or trying to address it. Yet Heinemann felt sure that he was confronting an unsettling truth: the hardest traumas are delivered by children.

Heinemann decided he had to do something. He'd started working as a doctor at a public school, and from his window he could see groups of children picking on other students who were different or who seemed weak. He wrote an article (published in 1969 in the small Swedish journal *Liberal Debatt*) that was a heartfelt call to arms.

Heinemann began by offering a theory to explain children's cruel behavior: he argued that children attack in packs, and he used the word *mobbing* for their behavior. Heinemann was borrowing the term from a growing body of science about the animal kingdom. In the mid-1960s, a well-known Austrian ethologist had coined the term *mobbing* to describe the collective assault of a flock of birds on a weak member of their own or another species. "Among people this behavior most closely resembles lynch mobs, pogroms and the like," Heinemann wrote. "What our culture and our society seem to have forgotten is that the human being starts mobbing already as a child." Mobbing, he wrote, "has ruined the entire lives of the more permanent victims in not a few cases." Heinemann listed the schoolyard taunts he remembered from his own youth—"tumble weed, bastard, four-eyes, limp-leg, carrot," along with "fatty, nerd, jerk, sissy"—and argued that these insults could have a crushing effect on children who were frequent targets. He called on Swedish schools to intervene as early and as often as possible. "I believe that children are the only ones who are susceptible to influence in a deeper form, the only ones who are still changeable human beings," he wrote. "I believe that antibullying indoctrination must start early on in childhood. . . . No day care or school should neglect this kind of education and upbringing."

Heinemann's plea, on behalf of his son and other children, resonated with a country that was struggling at the time to absorb a growing number of immigrants. And his theory of the mob captured the imagination of the nation's mental health professionals, who were just beginning to scrutinize the aggressive behavior of children, as opposed to adults. Sweden's counselors and psychologists made Heinemann's article the subject of their 1970 annual meeting, and the country's major newspapers interviewed Heinemann and wrote follow-up stories about the misery of other "mobbed" children.

No one read or debated Heinemann's ideas with more interest

than Dan Olweus, a thirty-eight-year-old Swede who had just finished his PhD in psychology. Olweus was one of the only people in Scandinavia who'd already begun to focus on the problem of childhood aggression—he'd written his doctoral thesis about the connection between personality and aggressive behavior among young boys. "I wanted to do research with social consequences," Olweus told me. "I had just completed my thesis when Heinemann put the concept of mobbing on the public agenda."

Olweus would go on to study children and teenagers from a new perspective, in the end launching a whole new field. What's more, he proved to be more than a researcher. Olweus answered Heinemann's call to help children like his son by prompting a nationwide campaign against bullying. It would begin in Norway, and eventually would make its way around the globe.

Dan Olweus was born in the small Swedish town of Kalmar in 1931. "It was a peaceful place," he told me. "We had blackout curtains during World War II, but the war did not really impact us." Olweus has only one recollection of serious bullying from his own childhood. "There was a boy who was new to town, and two other boys teased him mercilessly," he told me. "The bullying was also violent—they forced him to swallow worms. When I'm asked what stimulated my interest in bullying, people often expect to hear about some painful personal childhood experience. For me, however, the initial interest was mostly academic."

Reading Heinemann's much-talked-about work in 1969, Olweus was moved by the doctor's description of his son and his moral engagement, but skeptical of his theory of the child mob. Was it really true that children attacked in packs, like bird flocks? That question led Olweus to others: How did children themselves see aggression among them? Did the ones who became aggressors or victims typically share common characteristics? What about the school environment—how did it influence the level of aggressive behavior in the classroom and the playground?

Olweus spent the next three years surveying and studying one thousand Swedish boys, ages twelve to sixteen, about verbal and physical harassment in their schools. He talked to the boys, their parents, and their teachers, publishing the results of his research in his first book, which came out in Sweden in 1973. Olweus remained indebted to Heinemann for putting his finger on a problem that truly troubled the boys in his study, but he'd reached a fairly different conclusion about how the aggressors and the victims behaved. "Heinemann placed too much emphasis on large anonymous groups of children," Olweus told me. "He saw mobbing as crowd behavior, when actually this is very unusual. Typically, a small group of two or three students do most of the bullying in a class, and as many as 30 percent of bullied children report that they are mainly bullied by a single person."

Once he concluded that aggressive boys usually operated as lone alphas, or with a couple of henchmen, Olweus decided that *mobbing* wasn't the right word for their behavior. In the course of translating his book to English in 1978, Olweus came up with *bullying*. "It's a word you have in English that didn't quite have an equivalent in Swedish," he said. Olweus, of course, had picked a common word, a word that had been in use for centuries. Never before, however, had bullying been used this way in the academic lexicon.

Olweus gave bullying this status by coming up with a relatively narrow definition for it that, forty years later, remains standard among academics and educators. As I discussed in Chapter 1, bullying had to satisfy three criteria: it had to be verbal or physical abuse, it had to repeat over time, and it had to involve an imbalance of power—one child (the bully) lording it over another. All three of these factors had to be present. A onetime episode of meanness or violence by one stronger child against a weaker one, or repeated clashing between equals, could cause problems, but it wasn't bullying. And bullying according to his definition, Olweus believed, was the behavior with potentially devastating consequences for children. He called for combating it with an ambitious campaign involving not just the identified bullies and victims but the whole school.

That campaign, Olweus argued, should extend to every school. Where Heinemann thought that children in large schools with big classes were more prone to mob, Olweus found that the size of a school and the number of children in a class hardly mattered. Not only that, he challenged the common assumption that upper-class kids behaved better than lower-class ones, and that kids in big cities were more prone to systematic cruelty than kids in the country. Bullying, Olweus found, was an equal-opportunity problem.

He also went against the grain in finding that victims weren't usually marked as outsiders by their appearance, as Heinemann's adopted son had been. Instead, they tended to look and dress much like other boys. What they had in common, as a group, was that they were physically weaker and more prone to anxiety. Olweus was clear-eyed about the vulnerabilities many victims exhibited, calling *both* bullies and whipping boys "problem children" who "tend to arouse emotional reactions in the people around them." Nature versus nurture, individual psychology versus institutional environment—rather than raising one above the other, as many social scientists did, Olweus embraced both. This led him to recognize that asking schools to address bullying meant asking them to take on a problem that wasn't entirely of their own making. "It does not seem reasonable or fair to make the school and the school system responsible for the origin of whipping boy/bully problems," he wrote. "However, this does not rule out the view that it is a natural and essential part of a school's care for its students to try to limit or prevent these problems."

By the time Olweus issued this challenge in the 1970s, he had moved from Sweden to Norway, where he joined the University of Bergen as a psychology professor. It has been his home base ever since. "I hadn't planned to stay in Norway, but my wife and our two daughters liked it here," he told me. "You know, at that time Norway was like the little brother of Sweden. But then they found oil in Norway. We have a joke about how getting rich affected Norwegian self-esteem. A Swedish guy comes back from catching crayfish, and somebody asks, 'How was the fishing?' He says, 'Well, I've got a lot of ordinary crayfish and one Norwegian crayfish.' They say, 'How do you know it's Norwegian?' He says, 'Because that one is shouting all the time, "I'm a lobster, I'm a lobster!"' So you see, it was good timing for us to move there and live among the lobsters."

Times were prosperous, but there was darkness, too. In December 1982, three elementary school boys killed themselves in a single month in and around the town of Tromso, north of the Arctic Circle, where, on a clear night, the northern lights can frequently be seen flickering across the sky. The boys who committed suicide—all between the ages of ten and fourteen—attended different schools, but in all three cases, they'd been bullied before their deaths. One, for example, had been called a leper by classmates because of his measles scars. In the wake of the triple suicides, the consensus was that children were at risk of serious harm at each other's hands—and were suffering silently and alone.

As the country struggled to cope, Olweus fielded calls from reporters and government ministers, all looking for answers. He used this platform to renew his call for taking bullying seriously as a form of abuse, and for instituting a large-scale prevention program in schools. "We adults must make it absolutely clear we will not tolerate this," he said.

The Norwegian Ministry of Education was finally ready to listen. Olweus became a member of a small committee tasked with planning a school-based bullying prevention campaign. In that context, Olweus got government funding to conduct two large-scale studies. He started by surveying 130,000 students across the country about the frequency of bullying, and found that 15 percent of elementary and middle school kids, an alarming rate, were involved in bullying with some regularity, either as a bully, as a victim, or as both.

Olweus also conducted an intervention project with twenty-five hundred students in forty-two schools in fall 1983. The focus was on changing the culture of the school, and eventually the same would be true of Olweus' prevention efforts in the United States. Teachers and other adults should be involved in students' lives, set firm limits, mete out nonhostile punishments when rules were broken, and serve as both authoritative and positive role models. The program was designed to work at three interrelated levels: throughout the school (for example, with clear rules against bullying and improved supervision during break periods), the classroom level (through regular teacher-led meetings with students), and individually (with procedures for handling bullying and following up with perpetrators, targets, and their parents).

Olweus' evaluation of his program in Norway showed very encouraging results. After eight months, students reported 50 percent less bullying than they had before the program began. Teachers reported a similar drop. Students and teachers also reported less vandalism and theft, better order in their classrooms, and improved social relations. There was no data from schools that had not instituted the Olweus program, so it wasn't possible to know how much the general rise in awareness of bullying, as opposed to the specific interventions Olweus urged, had contributed to the drop. Still, in 2001, after another positive evaluation, the Ministry of Education offered the program to schools throughout the country. The king and prime minister highlighted the problem of bullying a year later in their traditional New Year's Eve addresses on television and radio, underscoring it as a priority. The government and the teachers' union signed an official manifesto against bullying, agreeing to do their best to address it. More follow-up studies of the Olweus program in the Norwegian schools have shown drops in bullying of 35 to 50 percent.

No wonder, then, that Olweus is hailed as the father of the bullying prevention movement. At eighty-one, he has racked up citations in professional journals and is in constant international demand as a speaker. The American Psychological Association recently gave him two major awards.

I met Olweus when he came to New York to give the keynote address at a conference on bullying and suicide prevention at Columbia University. He was in his element, vigorously presenting new data to fellow psychologists who packed the auditorium, cramming into the aisles and the standing-room section at the back. We met afterward, over lunch. Olweus walked in looking like an older blue-eyed Mr. Rogers, in a navy cardigan and jeans. But the iron behind his kindly, slightly rumpled demeanor was soon evident. Olweus started our conversation by lashing out at critics who, he said, were trying to undermine the implementation of his bullying prevention program in Sweden.

"Their attitude toward me is hostile," he said. "They are trying to reduce my influence in my own country. So they sketch the development of the program inaccurately. This is lousy, lousy research."

The spirited introduction made me ask Olweus a question I'd been asking myself: why did it take American research psychologists decades to take note of his work? Until the 1990s, the Americans in his field ignored bullying as a research topic. When I mentioned this to Olweus, he smiled. He reached into a leather satchel and took out a page from the talk he planned to deliver the following week. For a quarter century, Olweus would argue, researchers in the United States and Europe had gone off on a tangent, focusing narrowly on popularity and looking at status hierarchy among children for its own sake, instead of using it to gain insight into how some children try to hurt other children. The American social scientists had simply missed the boat. "They did not include my emphasis on the power differential. This created a lot of confusion. They did not capture the problems and behavior that causes children real harm."

In the last decade, however, Olweus had prevailed over his academic rivals. His theory of bullying was in ascendance, in academic circles and beyond. And Olweus had the statistics to prove it. "Now, you see, we have more than 1,500 academic articles about bullying in the 2000s, compared with only a few dozen in the 1990s," he said, pointing to the numbers on the paper he'd given me. "You can see that people followed my approach, because the other methods fell apart."

The pendulum swung Olweus' way when American researchers woke up to the merits of his research and the success he'd achieved in the Norwegian schools. But that wasn't the only reason. Olweus also owed the belated recognition to a single, shattering event—the kind of once-in-a-generation tragedy, like the Tromso suicides, that sends people scrambling for answers and gives rise to a national moment of reckoning.

"We just didn't get it in the U.S.," Susan Swearer, the University of Nebraska–Lincoln school psychologist, told me. "Until Columbine."

Eric Harris and Dylan Klebold didn't plan a school shooting. They planned a *bombing,* on the scale of Oklahoma City. In a chilling video made shortly before their attack, Klebold boasted about inflicting "the most deaths in U.S. history" and imagined a movie with Steven Spielberg or Quentin Tarantino directing. As Dave Cullen explains in his meticulously reported book *Columbine,* Klebold and Harris set propane bombs in the cafeteria that would have killed hundreds of people if they'd been wired right. After the bombs went off, the two seniors intended to wait at the exit and gun down the survivors as they fled. Then they hoped that nearly a hundred more bombs they'd made would explode, tearing through the crowd of rescuers, reporters, and parents that would gather at the school—and that it would all be caught on live television.

The bombs didn't go off. But the shootings that killed thirteen and wounded twenty-four at the Colorado high school in April 1999 sent shock waves through the country. It was a huge, deeply disturbing, crystallizing moment. Columbine was an ordinary school in an ordinary suburb; Harris and Klebold, shyly smiling in their yearbook photos, looked ordinary, too. And yet they'd somehow turned into mass murderers. Was it their parents' fault? The boys'? The school's?

The questions seemed especially pressing because the shooting at Columbine wasn't a lone incident. It was the most devastating example of an unhappy trend—one of more than fifty school shootings in the 1990s, compared to about thirty in the 1980s. Afterward, in an effort to understand why students in growing numbers were turning guns on their classmates, the Secret Service conducted an exhaustive investigation into the causes and circumstances of thirty-seven student attacks since 1974. The agency found that 71 percent of the attackers felt persecuted, bullied, threatened, attacked, or injured before they turned to violence. The report elaborated:

> In several cases, individual attackers had experienced bullying and harassment that was long-standing and severe. In some of these cases the experience of being bullied seemed to have a significant impact on the attacker and appeared to have been a factor in his decision to mount an attack at the school. In one case, most of the attacker's schoolmates described the attacker as "the kid everyone teased." In witness statements from that incident, schoolmates alleged that nearly every child in the school had at some point thrown the attacker against a locker, tripped him in the hall, held his head under water in the pool or thrown things at him.

The school shooters also had mental health troubles in common: about three-quarters of them had a history of suicide attempts or suicidal thinking, more than 60 percent had a history of depression, and a full 98 percent had experienced a profound sense of failure or loss. Yet in the wake of Columbine, it was bullying, not suicide or depression or other problems, that schools were asked to tackle.

The Kaiser Family Foundation made headlines with a 2001 survey that highlighted bullying as students' primary concern, more pressing than drugs or discrimination. Sensing the concern of parents, the media started to point the finger of blame, for example in a *Los Angeles Times* column that made this wish: "If we could only round them up and herd them into detention, then haul their parents in for counseling, maybe we could isolate the menace of bullies in our midst." In response to a shooting rampage at a California high school that left two people dead, a year after Columbine, Attorney General John Ashcroft spoke of an "onerous culture of bullying."

Americans were finally paying attention, and legislatures responded. Colorado, California, Mississippi, Connecticut, West Virginia, Louisiana, Oklahoma, Minnesota, New Jersey, Illinois, Delaware—a parade of states passed anti-bullying laws, mostly requiring schools to come up with procedures for handling the problem.

Along with the school shooter, who was almost always a boy, a female archetype emerged as well: the mean girl. Fueled by the findings of Scandinavian researcher Kaj Björkqvist—the psychologist who made waves by arguing that girls could be just as aggressive, in their own way, as boys—mean girls loomed large in a pair of 2002 best-sellers. Rachel Simmons' groundbreaking *Odd Girl Out* sounded the alarm about the harm girls can do with gossip, slights, and exclusion, tactics that were especially wounding because girls often deployed them against former friends. "Unlike boys, who tend to bully acquaintances or strangers, girls frequently attack within tightly knit networks of friends," she wrote. "In this world, friendship is a weapon, and the sting of a shout pales in comparison to a day of someone's silence. There is no gesture more devastating than the back turning away." In the same year, Rosalind Wiseman's *Queen Bees and Wannabes* charted mean girls' habits, from their preferred perch in the minivan carpool (second-row "captain seats") to their in-school hangout ("Bitches, Incorporated" hallway). This is the book that inspired Tina Fey to make the movie *Mean Girls,* which truly put them on the cultural map.

The newfound attention to girls' pecking orders was supposed to help us dismantle them. This, of course, proved easier said than done. The anti-bullying efforts of the early 2000s, however, did convey the message that teachers and counselors had to start taking the issue seriously. "In the 1980s and '90s, one very common adult reaction to a kid being mistreated by another kid was to say to the mistreated kid, 'Pretend it doesn't bother you,' or 'Just tell them to stop,' or 'Walk tall and make eye contact,'" Stan Davis, a researcher who spent four decades as a school counselor and therapist in Maine, told me. "The concept of bullying as power-based peer abuse was really important. It moved many adults away from doings these things that the mistreated kids say just don't work."

If the budding drive to stop bullying made inroads, it also hit some bumps. As schools clamored for help, a cottage industry of self-styled experts sprang up to meet the demand. Some were rigorous, but others were hucksters promising to solve a school's bullying problems with one assembly for students or an inspirational talk for teachers. Unless they were part of a longer-term effort, these quick fixes rarely showed results. "Some schools still think they can hire one speaker— a juggler, a person who wrote a book," the researcher and child development professor Dorothy Espelage told me. "Dr. So-and-So comes for ten or fifteen thousand dollars and you can check bullying off your list. Well, you can't. Maybe you see a change among the kids for a few days, and then everyone goes right back to what they were doing before."

Conservatives in particular were skeptical of the money being poured into unproven initiatives. They especially objected to the treacle ladled out by ex-hippies such as Peter Yarrow of the folk group Peter, Paul and Mary, whose nonprofit organization developed a curriculum called Don't Laugh at Me, which was given for free to more than fifteen thousand schools and summer camps. It featured a song that Yarrow compared to "We Shall Overcome" but which others mocked for verses like "I'm a little boy with glasses, the one they call a geek / A little girl who never smiles 'cause I got braces on my teeth / and I know how it feels / to cry myself to sleep."

The skeptics made mincemeat of Yarrow, but the questions they raised about the anti-bullying movement also went beyond the silliest extremes. Ann Hulbert, author of *Raising America,* a history of child rearing, wondered in Slate if the adult-led effort to prevent bullying was robbing children of the chance to solve their own problems. "The conventional wisdom used to be: Just walk away or slug the big lout while no grown-up is watching," she wrote. "That's now lore from the dark ages." Hulbert worried that bullying prevention efforts would encourage "a hypervigilant wariness, which hardly seems the best way to promote the community spirit of courageous solidarity the crusaders tout." In the *New Republic,* Ben Soskis argued that "by defining bullying so broadly, the anti-bullying movement risks pathologizing behaviors that, however unpleasant, are in some sense normal parts of growing up."

These were serious critiques in need of serious answers. Was the problem that hucksters and old hippies were giving bullying prevention a bad name? Or was the whole effort fundamentally flawed?

Dan Olweus actually got his first crack at bringing the bullying prevention program he'd developed in Norway to American schools in the mid-1990s, before Columbine. The initial results were disappointing. After seven months, students at eighteen elementary and middle schools in South Carolina reported no less bullying. A follow-up study in Washington State had mixed results. Skeptics questioned whether the Olweus approach could translate across the Atlantic. Maybe peaceful, homogenous Norway could eradicate bullying, but the more violent, melting-pot United States could not.

Olweus, however, thought the problem was in the execution, not the model. With collaborators at Clemson University, he stepped up trainings for teachers and did more to coach schools along the way. Olweus and his American colleagues increasingly emphasized "implementation fidelity"—the all-important question of whether a school that said it was adopting the program actually took the materials out of the box and carried out the steps it was supposed to.

Olweus is convinced that, carried out properly, his approach can succeed at reducing bullying in the United States. He has the backing of schools that have found his method helpful, as well as the federally funded Blueprints for Violence Prevention, a project at the University of Colorado established in 1996 to evaluate violence prevention programs. In assessing more than nine hundred programs for juveniles according to strict standards, Blueprints chose Olweus' as one of only a dozen proved to be effective, and the only one specifically directed at bullying.

The Olweus program has now been adopted by more than eight thousand schools in more than forty states. In Pennsylvania, where grants paid for nearly all the schools to adopt it, a long-term evaluation has begun. The first two years of results are promising. Anecdotally, teachers back them up. "It used to be a pretty rough place," one chemistry teacher said of his high school east of Pittsburgh, where the number of violent altercations decreased by one-third between 2009 and 2011. "A lot of teachers would leave because it was a rough environment. It's calmed down considerably since then. This is the best year yet."

Among American academics who have been skeptical about whether the Olweus program works well for schools here with large and diverse student populations, there are lingering questions about how independently it has been evaluated—Olweus and his American colleagues are involved in the Pennsylvania assessment—and how much the method demands of schools. "The bottom line is that his program is difficult to implement," Dorothy Espelage told me.

And in fact, this point isn't really in dispute. The Olweus Bullying Prevention Program, as it's officially called, uses a train-the-trainer model. Schools choose teachers and counselors to send for intensive training over three days; they also get follow-up and backup consulting from Olweus staff. These selected teachers and counselors then become the emissaries who are responsible for launching the program at their schools. They form a school-wide committee, hold a kickoff event, post rules throughout the school, and show teachers how to hold classroom discussion about bullying and how to intervene when they see it happening. It's a long-term, labor-intensive commitment. "This is *not* a one-year program," the Olweus trainer I watched, Marlene Snyder, told forty educators gathered for three days in Des Moines, Iowa. "To initiate and implement, you will need three years. You will meet twice a week with your committee. Teachers will meet regularly by grade level. They will hold classroom meetings with the children. This is a *systematic change process*. Schools have had Olweus in place for ten years, and they've seen bullying go down every year they do their meetings and trainings. But if they skip the steps we have in place for a year or two, bullying goes back up."

Espelage argues that the curriculum designed by the Committee for Children, a nonprofit group in Seattle, is easier for schools to put in place. Called Second Step, the program is also less expensive. It builds from year to year, starting with kindergarten, and addresses bullying through empathy building, problem solving, and anger management. Second Step is scripted for teachers with a sequence of slides, questions, and videos that make it relatively easy to handle as an add-on to their regular subject areas. "We're evaluating Second Step in a rigorous study of effectiveness, and I can tell you it takes only three to five minutes for teachers to prep a lesson," Espelage said.

Research has shown less acceptance of bullying and aggression among third through sixth graders who have gone through a related Committee for Children program (called Steps to Respect), compared with kids of the same age who have not. When students are taught these curricula year after year, you can hear them using the vocabulary and strategies. "In kindergarten they learn the words *frustrated* and *furious*," said Rachel Prince, a counselor at Annie Sullivan School in Minneapolis, where Second Step had been in place for three years. "By first or second grade, kids will come up and say, 'I saw someone getting mad and I reminded them to stop.'" Prince put up her hand, palm out, in the universal stop sign. "We teach them that if you have a problem, first you say 'Stop' to yourself, so you're not being impulsive. Then you think what *is* the problem—you try to state it. Next, what are the solutions? You ask yourself, 'Is the one I've chosen safe and fair? How will it make other people feel? Will it work?' Those are the steps we're giving them to follow."

After watching both the Olweus and Second Step programs in action, it seemed to me that either could come across as boring and rote or genuinely helpful—it depended on the teacher's skill and commitment and the kids' level of interest. As I traveled from school to school and talked to expert after expert, I concluded that the most important thing is for a school to pick *one* approach that administrators, teachers, and parents buy into and *stick with it*. This is hardly a new idea, but it bears repeating and then repeating some more, because American education is notorious for trying too many new things at once. To wit: on average, along with all the academic initiatives that are their central focus, schools use nine different strategies at once to prevent violence and promote a safe learning environment. It seems to me that this is eight more than they can successfully execute. No matter how good the program, it will disappoint when a school sends a teacher to a staff training, buys boxes of manuals and videos, announces with fanfare that bullying will stop, and then shelves the whole effort when a new principal or superintendent comes along.

So let's say you're a principal—or a PTA member—and you're looking for a program, for your school, designed specifically to prevent bullying. You do the research and consider the options, and you decide to go with Olweus, because of its long history and its track record, and because you're not afraid of hard work. You choose a couple of teachers or counselors to get the necessary training, come back to school loaded down with binders and DVDs, and get cracking. What will your school look like a few years later? Will the students be better served, and if so, how?

In August 2005, Freedom Middle School opened its doors to students from Cherokee County, a growing suburban area a few dozen miles north of Atlanta. A new principal, Karen Hawley, arrived two years later from the nearby elementary school she'd been running. "That's where I encountered Olweus for the first time," she told me. "When I came here, my kids said that middle school felt cold and sterile. I knew we had to do something."

Georgia has a law requiring "character education" in the public schools, including strategies for stemming bullying and violence, at all grade levels. To help principals get moving on this front, Hawley's school district offered the services of Michael Carpenter, author of a book about how schools can address bullying called *Setting the Tone* and one of the first Olweus trainers in the United States. He administered the program's student questionnaire (based on the initial prevention campaign in Norway) to gauge the baseline level of bullying at Freedom. About a quarter of the students said they'd been bullied once or twice in the past few months, and another 8 percent said they'd been bullied regularly. About 20 percent admitted to taking part in bullying once or twice, and 5 percent to doing it more frequently. Asked how often teachers put a stop to it, the students said teachers frequently did so only 58 percent of the time.

That last statistic, in particular, helped get the teachers' attention. One of the central tenets of Olweus is that the attitude of the staff is just as important as the attitudes of students and families, because if teachers and other adults at school see bullying and don't act to stop it, the message they send to kids is that they don't care. This was a lesson Hawley had taken to heart. "We poke further into it when a kid says something mean, instead of just saying, 'Boys will be boys, girls will be girls,'" she said as we walked her school's quiet hallways together.

Schools can get hung up on the Olweus stipulation that for meanness to qualify as bullying, it has to happen repeatedly. If you see one student knock the books out of another student's hands, how do you know whether that's part of a pattern or a onetime thing? The answer is that the distinction matters for deciding whether to discipline a student but not for reacting in the moment. "If it's mean, intervene," as Olweus trainers instruct. On the spot, a teacher should talk to the student about what he did and make sure he knows not to do it again. But the teacher shouldn't necessarily impose a formal punishment. For that, the teacher (or another school staff member) should know whether what she has seen is part of a pattern.

Hawley explained how the distinction between intervening and punishing worked at Freedom. "When we hear that one kid is calling another kid names, we call home," she said. "The first time, we call instead of referring to discipline. I really think that makes a tremendous difference in whether the student makes the same mistake again. Most parents see it as an opportunity to turn things around. Ninety percent of our parents are happy that we call. They say, 'Thank you so much for letting us know.'"

I asked Hawley how she draws in parents whose children aren't having problems with bullying themselves, and who might not have an incentive to pay attention to the issue. She had a trick I hadn't heard before for enticing parents to attend presentations: they earn "attendance points," which count toward their kids' final grades. As we talked, we passed by a poster that listed the "Bystander's Steps to Courage," and Hawley pointed it out to stress that the Olweus approach teaches students they should keep other kids from being bullied rather than only looking out for themselves. I thought of Woodrow Wilson in Middletown, and the problem of urging such action on kids when the overall culture doesn't support it. Freedom, however, was trying to tackle this throughout the student body, not in an after-school group with a dozen kids. The guidance counselors designed a log for reporting bullying, and students who made use of it were praised for standing up for themselves and others. "They're being sort of a hero," is how Hawley put it. In their answers to the Olweus questionnaire, almost 60 percent of students said they ought to help or actually did try to help when they saw someone their age being bullied—a statistic teachers could use to show students that if they stood up for a target of bullying, they'd actually be doing what most of their peers thought was right.

This is very much in line with the results of an exciting study conducted at five New Jersey middle schools. The researchers surveyed students about the prevalence of bullying. Then they designed posters with messages like "Most Lake Middle School students (9 out of 10) do NOT exclude someone from a group to make them feel bad" with the tagline "Results are from a December 2006 survey." After the poster campaign, students were surveyed again. At all the schools, the second time around students reported less acceptance of bullying and less personal experience of acting like a bully or of being a victim. The biggest drop took place at the school where students were most likely to remember the messages in the posters.

At Freedom, I started talking to students at an early morning meeting of the school's For HOPE Club. HOPE stands for Helping Other People Enthusiastically, and the club has collected clothes and gifts for anonymous poor families at the school. (While most Freedom students live in comfortable single-family homes, a smattering come from low-income trailer parks, with 15 percent qualifying for free or reduced-price lunch.) Earlier that year, the students had raised almost $3,000 in bake sale proceeds for an eighth grader who was hospitalized with a serious illness.

The For HOPE students, who were eighth graders, analyzed the Olweus program for me, from the parts they liked best to the parts they liked least. They gave Hawley and the guidance counselors high marks for helping individual students—people who, in the words of one student, "don't have a lot of friends and have trouble getting along well with other kids but maybe it's not really their fault." They were decidedly less enthusiastic about the curriculum for the teacher-led meetings on bullying that every Freedom student has in lieu of a regular class twice a month.

"We don't take those classes as seriously as the teachers think we do," one eighth grader with a ponytail told me. "We hear 'Don't bully,' and we're like, '*We know.*'" Another girl sighed. "I don't even remember what we did in that class the last couple of weeks," she said.

I could see what the girls meant when I sat in on a sixth-grade meeting later that morning. The teacher, whose regular subject was math, gave the kids an Olweus true/false quiz. She went over the answers by asking them to raise their hands and call out a quick "true" or "false." Some of the questions struck me as particularly ripe for discussion—"True or false: A bully is usually insecure under the surface"—but the teacher didn't ask the kids to explain their answers or give their thoughts. The class reminded me of driver's ed: serviceable but rote.

Far more popular among the For HOPE students was a one-day annual event called Rachel's Challenge, a day of intense discussion run by a nonprofit founded by the parents of Rachel Scott, one of the students who died in the Columbine shootings. The presenters push students hard to think about the importance of small acts of kindness and about how they treat each other, and students at Freedom and at other schools, too, told me they gave it good reviews. "No matter how much of a bully you are, it touches your heart," the eighth grader with the ponytail said.

"Rachel's Challenge tells us to second-guess ourselves," a boy with a Texas football T-shirt added. "Like if someone is sitting by themselves, should we go sit with them?"

Rachel's Challenge cost Freedom $4,000 each year. No study shows what it accomplishes, but teachers and counselors at Freedom agreed with the students that for a few weeks after the event, Freedom felt different. Kids who made friends easily did go up to kids who were alone in the cafeteria. Teachers noticed students greeting each other a little more kindly in the hallway. The For HOPE Club swelled to twice its size.

Inevitably, though, the sense of urgency ebbed. Some students would see the familiar social reward in meanness and try to cash in. When that happened, what tools did the Olweus program at Freedom provide?

Lauren Moss worked as a special education teacher for emotionally disturbed high school students before coming to Freedom as a guidance counselor in 2007. Once there, she'd gotten the Olweus training, which she valued for its step-by-step practicality. "No one talked about how to set up a procedure for dealing with bullying when I was in grad school," she said. "So I loved that Olweus showed us how: okay, here's how to design a bullying log so students have a good way to make reports, here's how we investigate, here's what we do if we find bullying is happening, here's what we do if we find it happening again."

I asked Moss to introduce me to a few of the bullied middle schoolers whom she'd tried to help, so I could get a sense of how the Olweus approach works one-on-one. We started with a sixth grader named Maddy, who was wearing a dress with a flower and butterfly design. Under black and gray striped stockings, a brace was strapped to one of her legs, and she wore special orthopedic shoes. "It was a little tricky to fit in here at first, because I was born with spina bifida," she said frankly. "I'm different. There's only one other kid here with spina bifida, and he's in special ed classes."

"Maddy was in a wheelchair for a month in kindergarten, and at other times up to third grade, because she had surgery on her foot and back," Moss explained.

"I've had five surgeries on my back and two on my foot," Maddy said. "I used to have pretty big seizures, but now they're small and I don't have them that much."

Maddy came to Freedom with a few friends from elementary school but soon found herself having run-ins with a girl she didn't know named Nicole, who'd come from a different feeder school. In the beginning of sixth grade, Nicole asked Maddy about her foot, but in a way that felt cold rather than sympathetic. Maddy tried not to let it bother her. Then one day, Nicole walked out of class surrounded by her friends and scanned the hallway as if she was looking for someone. Her eye fell on Maddy. "Who wants to hold my books?" Nicole asked.

"It was pretty subtle, but you knew what she meant, right?" Moss said gently.

"Yeah, and then she dropped her books and told me to pick them up," Maddy said. "Like I was supposed to do whatever she said."

Maddy didn't pick up the books, and after that Nicole started saying hi to her in the lunchroom in a fake, sarcastic tone, and made it clear that Maddy wasn't welcome to sit at her table. She often did it in front of her friends, as if to underscore her power. "One time, I dropped my pencil in class when Nicole was sitting behind me," Maddy said. "I bent down to pick it up and she smacked the back of my head with her pen."

"Maddy is very sweet to everyone," Moss said, "and she's always doing what she's supposed to do. So with kids like her, teachers think, 'Oh, maybe she'll be a big influence on another student who is having trouble with lots of kids.' In this case, the teacher paired her with Nicole." Moss couldn't resist rolling her eyes. "It wasn't a great situation. The teacher didn't know what was really going on. Maddy was coming in to tell me, but she wasn't ready to make a formal report. I said, 'You need to make a bullying log and write down what's happening.'"

"I wasn't sure," Maddy said. "I've never really been in a situation like this before. I wasn't used to it. I tried talking to my parents, but that was no help." Maddy was also disappointed in the reaction of one of her friends, who heard some of Nicole's comments but didn't speak up.

Maddy wasn't the only girl Nicole was making miserable. Moss also introduced me to Beth, a heavyset sixth grader who walked into the room wearing glasses, a stained orange polo shirt, and pink pants. Beth had gone to fourteen schools since kindergarten and spent most of the previous year in a group home while her mother struggled to kick a drug habit. She and her brother now lived with their mother in a trailer park near Freedom. "I have problems with the other kids here," Beth said. "I'm not good at making friends. I don't trust anyone, that's the problem. They talk about me and my brother. They make fun of our weight."

Unlike Maddy, Beth was a girl who could give as well as she got. When Nicole started a rumor about her—"She said I cut my legs, but I would never do that"—Beth retorted that Nicole thought only about herself rather than about how she made other people feel. Soon after, waiting for the bus at the end of the school day, Nicole asked Beth where she got her clothes—a barbed question, since Beth's clothes were never new. "My mom, she doesn't have enough money to buy good clothes and nice shoes," she told me. "I'm not trying to be mean to rich kids, but Nicole gets things handed to her. My brother and me have to do chores. We have to do the dishes. Nicole doesn't understand what it's like to live in our house."

When Beth left the room, Moss showed me the complaints in the bullying log about Nicole. On green sheets of paper, Beth, Maddy, and a few other students had recorded things such as:

"Makes fun of my hair, clothes and shoes."
"Asks, where do you get your clothes? And then she laughs."
"Throws pieces of paper at me."
"Whispers to a friend, looks at me, laughing."
"Threw a chocolate chip cookie at Alissa and laughed."
"Called Beth trailer trash."

Moss had collected the reports over a few months and, once she'd established that Nicole's meanness was a pattern, called her mother. "She didn't tell me a whole lot," Moss said. "I wasn't sure I was getting through to her. Then Nicole's father called me about something else, and I said, 'Well, listen: while I have you on the phone, I have to share with you that I have some real concerns about Nicole's behavior in school.' And he said, 'What are you *talking* about?' He had no idea. As an example, I told him that she'd asked another student where she got her clothes, and because that student doesn't have much, it was crushing to her. He was very upset, but I felt I had to show him the worst of what his daughter had said."

Nicole and her father came into school the next day, and he told Moss about how he'd lost everything in the recession. In front of his daughter, he said he couldn't believe that, after what her family had been through, Nicole would make another person feel bad about her clothes. As he spoke, Moss watched Nicole. "She didn't say anything. She just smiled and nodded. I told her I hoped she'd really think before she speaks. She said, 'But sometimes I'm just asking a question.' And I said, 'If you see that a question is hurtful, then you need to think about that.' She looked at her dad and said, 'I'm gonna work on that.' And for a while she did."

But a month or so later, Maddy and Beth were back in Moss' office, reporting that Nicole was saying hurtful things again. At the time of my visit, Moss was on the verge of recommending discipline, though she didn't have enough solid evidence yet. "The first time, following Olweus, we hope to deal with an issue like this in counseling. But if a student brings me another bullying log on Nicole, I'll send it to the administrators," she told me. "I don't know what will help her, and I don't know if I'll find out."

When I finally met Nicole, I could see why Moss felt frustrated. She took zero responsibility for her actions. She told me that when Moss confronted her about Maddy, she couldn't even remember who Maddy was, much less doing anything mean to her. About Beth, she said, "This boy said I called Beth trailer trash, and that really made me upset, because my dad got upset, and I didn't say that. I kind of think she made it up, because she doesn't like me." Nicole reminded me of a piece of accepted wisdom about addicts: you can't help people who don't want to be helped.

When I checked back in with Moss nearly a year later, though, she said that to her surprise, Nicole had turned herself around: no bullying reports for seventh grade. "She has really matured," Moss said. "She has some new friends now, and that's made a real difference. I do think the fact that we have the Olweus program sets the tone. Everybody knows there is a process, and we take it seriously. Maybe the most important part is that the adults don't say, 'Oh, there's nothing we can do.' And the kids all know that."

In the early days of bullying prevention, programs such as Olweus' could focus exclusively on how students treat each other in school. This, of course, has changed. School prevention programs now have to address the online aspect of bullying as well. It's straightforward enough to discuss cyberbullying in class: Moss has added lessons about social networking and texting to Freedom's anti-bullying curriculum. Figuring out when and how to intervene when students attack each other online, however, is much trickier. Recognizing this, Principal Hawley tried to draw a clear line for her guidance counselors. "If it's off campus, we don't get involved," she said. "Unless we're trying to protect the safety of a student."

I could see the virtue of such a rule. It kept counselors and teachers from routinely intruding into students' off-campus lives, yet asked them to step in when they saw a real risk. It meant making a lot of nuanced judgment calls, though, and raised a question that still nagged at me after all my reporting in the aftermath of Phoebe Prince's death: what *can* schools, and especially guidance counselors, do to help students who may be at risk of hurting themselves?

Moss answered that question with a story about a seventh grader named Megan and a social networking site called Formspring.me. Entrepreneur Ade Olonoh originally launched a website for a purpose far removed from middle school: business data collection. In 2009, he noticed that thousands of bloggers were using his service to answer the questions of readers, bringing with them the culture of anonymity online, where commenters often use handles instead of their real names. Olonoh wrote the code for Formspring.me, built around a simple feature later dubbed "hide my name." It allowed users to pose questions and answers with no identifying information. The posts would pop up unsigned, without even a handle. Formspring users could also then broadcast these questions, and their answers, to whomever they wanted. For example—if, say, you're a teenager stirring the pot—you could ask, "Who are you pissed at?" You could send the question to all seventy-five people in your network, and then their answers—also anonymous, if they chose—would appear, under the question, on your Formspring page and on all their pages, too.

A million people signed up for Formspring in the forty-five days after it went live.

"It was a free-for-all," the site's spokesperson, Sarahjane Sacchetti, told me. "There weren't controls. There was no easy way to block someone."

In the next couple of years, the site grew to twenty-five million users, one-third of them age seventeen and under. Size-wise, it was a pimple on Facebook's nose, but at Freedom and other schools I visited, it had outsized influence. It was the venue of choice for anonymous cruelty—the place where you could settle scores or shred someone else's self-confidence and not get caught. Facing criticism over how teenagers used the "hide my name" feature, Olonoh added privacy controls, so the recipient of a question could choose what other users would see, and could block and report people for posting abusive content. This was a nice idea, but Moss and the students I talked to at Freedom had never heard of anyone preventing other users from seeing mean posts. The whole point of Formspring for the middle schoolers seemed to be that it was risky and public—like walking on a tightrope, as one fourteen-year-old girl described it to me. "It's like an interview where you find out how other people really see you," she said. "It's just honest. Even if what you find out about yourself is bad, you think that you want to know."

Except that in the end, you don't.

Megan's daily routine was to come home from school in the afternoon and take a break before starting her homework. She would grab a granola bar in the kitchen, go up to her room, turn on some music, and log on to her computer. One day she found this question waiting for her on Formspring:

> *Megan sticks up for people so it looks like she isn't a bitch. we all know the truth. She is a fat ass whore who needs to die. Lets all work together to kill her off. Agree?*

And, a few days later:

> *Megan is a fatass who has no life. She cuts and needs to go hang herself already. She whores around with every guy but will NEVER get one. Who agrees?*

Not surprisingly, Megan started to feel self-conscious at school. "I'd walk down the hallway alone and think, 'Will people think my friends don't want to talk to me because of what this person is saying?' Or at lunch, 'If I eat this, will someone make a rude comment online later?' 'If I get a bad grade, will they judge me for it?'" Feeling increasingly wound up and distressed, Megan confided about the Formspring posts to a friend, who told her own mother, who insisted that Megan go to the counseling office at school to talk to Moss.

Megan came in crying, and Moss could tell right away something was really wrong. Megan described the slashing queries she'd gotten, but Moss wanted to see for herself. She couldn't get onto Formspring at school, where the site was blocked, so at home that night she set up an account for herself and went to Megan's page. She found the ugly posts on Megan's Formspring page and on the pages of other students in her network.

They got creepier as they got more intimate. In the late-night glow of her computer screen, Moss started to feel seriously alarmed. "I was starting to obsess, wondering whether Megan was okay— could this push her over the edge?"

The most disturbing messages said things like "Nobody in your family loves you," "Your mom gave you away," "Your dad didn't want you," and "Your uncle was murdered and he didn't love you either." Some of these statements were true—Megan's uncle had been killed; she wasn't raised by her mother; and she had grown up with her grandmother—but Moss knew that Megan didn't go around telling people about her family history. Now someone had apparently betrayed her. Clicking from post to post, Moss could see that Megan had egged on her tormentors by responding with posts like "One day, you guys are gonna be sorry because someone will slit their wrist."

Moss finally turned off the computer in the middle of the night. Weary and aching for her students, she wondered what to do. Should she tell the kids and their parents what she'd seen? "My family was in bed and there I was, obsessing," she told me. "I finally decided, 'I'm not going to be a voyeur. I'm going to let it be known that I've been here.' I wrote to Megan, on her page: 'This is your guidance counselor and I want you to pass it on that your counselor has been on Formspring for the last couple of hours, reading these posts and the history. I knew things were bad but I couldn't have imagined it had gotten to this point.'"

Moss also looked up Formspring's rules, which stated: "Don't bully, harass or target other members of the Formspring community with hate speech or threats." Having just read dozens of posts that violated the company's rules, she wrote to alert the site. "I said, 'I'm a guidance counselor, and I've just spent hours looking at my students' Formspring pages, and all I conclude is that this site is just a vehicle for cyberbullying. You're promoting that, by giving the kids a way to ask these terrible anonymous questions in front of each other.' I never heard back."

Moss consulted with Principal Hawley in school on Monday about how to deal with what she'd discovered online. They agreed that the posts posed a risk to the safety (in terms of emotional well-being) of Megan and a few other students, so Hawley asked her to call Megan's grandmother, as well as the parents of students who'd talked openly about cutting themselves, and tell them what she'd found. One mother told Moss she knew about Formspring and was secretly reading everything her daughter wrote, as a way of keeping tabs on her. "I said, 'Well, ideally, that's not the best strategy,'" Moss said. "'At this age, kids aren't always making good decisions for themselves, and it's your job to help them.'" The other parents, however, thanked Moss for alerting them, asked to come in to talk to her, and in some cases, followed up with counseling when Moss recommended it.

To Megan's grandmother, Moss explained the content of the harassing Formspring posts, and said she wanted to make sure Megan didn't hurt herself. "Not because she'd said anything to me about doing that, but because there were these people blasting her," Moss told me. "Her grandmother got Megan and they pulled up her Formspring page while I was on the phone. Her grandmother said she'd known nothing about it, she was shocked, and she wanted Megan off the site immediately."

When I asked Megan about this moment, she remembered her grandmother's exact words: "Don't waste your time with people who won't say what they have to say to your face." She took her grandmother's advice and tried to delete her account, but she couldn't figure out how: the site made it clear how to go on hiatus, but not how to quit permanently and erase your history.

This was disconcerting. For Megan, going on Formspring was a daily habit; now she'd have to stay away knowing that she could always go back. But at Moss' and her grandmother's urging, she resolved to quit the site. She also tried not to fixate on the identity of her anonymous enemies. "In some ways, I kind of want to know, so I know who to trust and who not to," she told me. "But I also don't want to know. Maybe they have their own issues going on. I just have to move on. I'll admit I did let the bullying stuff get to me, and I don't want to be like that. My friends say, 'Come on, you're the one who's always smiling.' And I think, 'Right! I *want* to be happy.' Like this." Megan gave a wide smile. She had orange-colored braces. She looked not just cheerful but strong. "When you're happy, people look up to you."

After Megan went back to class, I asked Moss about how her Olweus training factored into her Formspring intervention. Was there a straight line from instituting the program to helping Megan, or had she simply put her talents as a counselor to good use? Moss credited Hawley's engagement and their mutual instinct to protect their students. It depended too, though, on the culture of awareness that Dan Olweus had fostered. His program opened channels of dialogue between Moss and Hawley, Moss and Megan, and Moss and Megan's grandmother. It helped the school come up with a protocol to follow that the counselor and the administrator had faith in. "On some level, I crossed the line by going on that site," Moss said. "One of the kids told me that forty students stopped using their Formsprings when they found out I'd been there. I decided that was okay with me. It's not that I want to know all their business. I have my own life. I went on there because I was worried about Megan, and if I'm concerned about a student, that comes first. That's what I'm here for."

I called Megan and her grandmother several months later to check in. Megan, in ninth grade now, was chatty and self-assured. High school felt *big*, she said, but she liked her teachers and she'd made some new friends. I asked her if she'd stayed off Formspring, as she'd wanted to. "Yes, I'm never going back there!" she said. "Now we're in high school, none of my friends get on it anymore. We're all like, 'What were we *thinking* last year? Why did we use it?' The whole thing was stupid, asking anonymous questions to stir up a lot of pointless drama. If you have a problem with someone, you solve it face-to-face."

At that point, Megan's grandmother got on the phone. "It was ugly and hurtful and I was upset that she was picked on last year," she said. "But Megan is doing very well now. She's getting excellent grades, and she joined a club to donate her time in the community. She worked eight hours last Saturday for the elementary school carnival, and she does horse rescue and she volunteers at the historical society." Looking back, Megan said, she was grateful to Moss for stepping in and helping her. I asked her grandmother what she thought, and she paused for a moment. "You know, the school did all they could do," she said. "I don't know what else we could have asked."

Chapter 8

Old Mill

I‍T WASN'T LONG AGO THAT PARENTS BEGGED TO KEEP THEIR children out of Old Mill Middle North. The school was rife with gangs, weapons, and drugs. The Crips and the Bloods were recruiting, colors flying. One boy brought a four-inch razor blade to school, two others were caught with high-powered pellet guns, and ten more got lengthy suspensions for selling or buying pot. Fights were rampant; in fact, conflict seemed to be in the building's bones. "It was obvious," said principal Sean McElhaney, who remembers feeling a wave of surly disrespect hit him when he walked into the school for the first time. "If you walked down the hallway and kids were having a disagreement, they'd literally push you out of the way and keep at it. If you told them to stop, they'd give you the *F* word. Or, 'Who are *you*? You're not my dad!'"

When McElhaney arrived at Old Mill North a decade ago, he knew of no systematic strategy for turning a rough school into a serene one. Once in a while a principal or a group of teachers would be hailed for genius—and maybe become the heroes of an after-school special—but no one had tried to bottle the magic and convert it into a formula. Reform seemed to revolve around an elusive quality in short supply: superhuman inspiration. A calm and orderly environment (or school climate, as it's often called) is the necessary precondition for academic achievement and good social relations, both among students and between students and teachers. And yet no one had comprehensively mapped out how to fix a troubled school like Old Mill North with a manageable, even ordinary-seeming process, step by step.

This was about to change, and McElhaney would reap the benefits, with his staff and students. And along the way, he would help answer a crucial question: how do you begin to address bullying at a school with such a long list of other pressing problems?

Old Mill Middle North is in Anne Arundel County, a large, suburban slice of eastern Maryland that includes Annapolis, the Naval Academy, and several upscale shopping districts. Not many miles from the school, yachts, sailboats, and fishing trawlers crowd the ports along the Chesapeake Bay, but Old Mill North didn't pull the yacht owners' kids. More than a third of its 950 students, in grades six through eight, qualified for free or reduced-price meals. A couple of hundred came and went, with a handful ending up homeless, during the course of each year. The school was about 40 percent white, 40 percent black, and 20 percent Hispanic, Asian, and Native American.

McElhaney had grown up in a whiter and more stable place: the town of Butler, in western Pennsylvania, where high school football was king. McElhaney played tight end, and his father, a former professional player, coached at a local college. He also taught physical education, as did McElhaney's mother, but the house rule was academics first—homework always came before practice. Which made it all the more shocking for McElhaney's parents when they discovered that their son barely knew how to read in the eighth grade. "My teacher handed me a novel—*Bridge to Terabithia*—and I couldn't read the first paragraph out loud to her," McElhaney said. "It almost killed my parents. We kept it hush-hush while we worked on it."

McElhaney went to college on an athletic scholarship but decided to go into education, determined to find a way to reach the reluctant learners because, as he says, "I *was* that child." After graduation, he became a math teacher and, at twenty-three, took a job at Anne Arundel's top-performing middle school, where most of the students were white and affluent.

Ten years later, McElhaney became an assistant principal at a school in Baltimore. "That was really my first taste of a very diverse school and also a school that had kids with a lot of baggage," he told me. "The district brought me in to build rapport, and I took it pretty personally. I was supposed to make things better by being the guy who listens, who's easy to talk to."

McElhaney found that he enjoyed it and had the personality for it. He steered clear of suits and wore jeans on Fridays. He told parents and students to call him Mr. Mac. He had a piercing whistle from his football days that he deployed to break up fights. He stayed true to his Pennsylvania roots by remaining a Steelers fan, but when his team lost to the local favorite, the Baltimore Ravens, two years in a row, he made it a happening: he dyed his hair purple one year and shaved his moustache the next. "He knows how to have fun, which breaks down all the old barriers with the kids," said Susan Shelby, a French teacher with three decades of experience.

After Baltimore, McElhaney went to Old Mill North, taking a job as an assistant principal. He arrived at a time when the school's test scores were bottoming out along with its reputation and morale. "There was nothing academic going on here," Shelby told me. "It was

absolutely chaotic and there was no follow-through from the administration. The kids didn't respect the staff, and it doesn't matter if you
have the best lesson plan in the world if you don't have that."

McElhaney and the principal who'd arrived with him made a deal
with the gangs: they wouldn't meddle with the gangs outside school,
and the gangs wouldn't recruit in school. The administrators also established their authority by resorting to mass expulsions. In that first
year, fifty-two kids were drummed out—the highest rate in the county.
"It was all about the heavy hand of discipline at first," McElhaney
said. "We had these kids who said, 'I don't care, I've never cared,
you're not going to change me.' So we said, 'Okay, we're going to eliminate you.' That's how we set an example." Meanwhile, fully a third
of the teachers—twenty-two out of sixty-six—had also walked out
the door, an exodus driven by the abiding fear that Old Mill North
was no longer a safe place to work. In 2005, the principal left, too.
Sean McElhaney was put in charge.

At the end of a sweltering summer, in 1854, a cholera epidemic
snaked through the Soho section of London. As scores of people grew
sick and died, three-quarters of the residents of Soho fled the city. The
reigning theory at the time was that cholera was contracted through
the lungs, by breathing in foul air, or miasma. A British doctor named
John Snow had his doubts, however. Though no one understood yet
how germs transmit disease, Snow conjectured that contaminated
food or water caused cholera, by poisoning the human body. He tested
this idea by knocking on doors, asking questions about cholera, and
tracking the answers on a Soho map. Snow's study of the neighborhood led him to the discovery that almost five hundred people had
died near the intersection of Cambridge and Broad streets—and that
they had drawn their water from Broad Street's public pump. The well
for the pump was close to underground sewer pipes, and Snow guessed
that raw sewage might have seeped into the water. As it turned out,

the well was just three feet from an old cesspit where the diapers of a choleric baby had been washed. In a presentation to city officials, Snow connected the dots from the cesspit to the pump to the cholera outbreak. Based on his testimony, the handle of the pump was removed the following day.

With the well shut down, the spread of the disease immediately subsided, and a public health legend was born. The story of Dr. Snow and the Broad Street pump has come to stand for the idea that the right mass intervention can break the hold of an epidemic. Stop people from drawing their water from a contaminated well, and you can control the spread of a deadly disease. A few unlucky people will still get sick, but removing the pump handle helps them, too, because once the number of patients becomes manageable, they're more likely to get the care they need.

In 1996, an education professor named George Sugai, along with several colleagues at the University of Oregon, translated this set of insights from public health to education. Before he joined academia, Sugai spent five years teaching emotionally disturbed teenagers. He worked intensively with them on social skills as well as academics, but no matter how much time and effort he put in, Sugai gradually realized, his students' progress depended in large part on a factor outside the classroom and beyond his control: the larger school environment. "It was really hard to educate my students in a place that was chaotic and unsupportive," he told me. "The key insight was that the best practices will fail in a bad environment. We had to shift from thinking about individuals to thinking about systems."

The system, for Sugai, was the school as a whole, and the lesson of the Broad Street pump was that he had to find the intervention that would convert school-wide chaos into order. If classrooms and hallways were calm, Sugai reasoned, most students would respond accordingly. Many would try to keep the peace; others wouldn't want to get caught breaking it. The kids who continued to act out would often be the ones with more serious problems, and the school, no longer burdened by an epidemic of misbehavior, could concentrate on getting them the attention they were essentially begging for. Schools could pinpoint the hardest cases, and this would bring the school further under control—which, in turn, would help the other students, too.

Sugai offered a handy way for schools to visualize this approach with a pyramid that follows the public health prevention model:

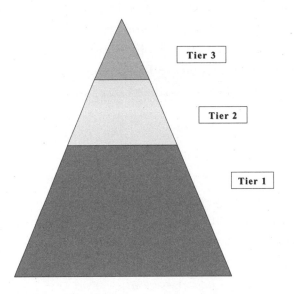

The bottom tier represented the broadly effective intervention that everyone gets. Sugai's favorite illustration, after the Broad Street pump, comes from diabetes prevention. "If everyone exercised, ate a good diet, and slept more, you'd prevent a lot of diabetes," he told me. "That is the first tier of preventive care." The second tier represented the more targeted approach to the minority of people—say, 20 percent—who still remained susceptible to diabetes. "They will need to be reminded to take care of themselves, or even, for example, have their food prepared for them." This secondary intervention further whittles down the pool of potential diabetics. "Then you're left with a third group of people— the remaining 10 percent—who still don't respond," Sugai said. "They're the ones who need more intensive support and treatment."

Sugai and his colleagues decided that the surest first-tier intervention for schools—the best way to get most kids to behave better—was
to transmit what was expected of them, explicitly, from grade to
grade. Schools had to get into the business of teaching social skills—
how to manage conflict, how and when to say please and thank you,
make eye contact, and acknowledge the feelings of others. To reinforce the skills, kids would be rewarded for demonstrating them the
right way, at the right time, and in the right places. A second-tier intervention for the 20 percent of students who didn't respond could
involve more intensive work in small groups, with a teacher who
would reinforce expectations and track progress. And a third-tier intervention for the students who didn't respond to *that* would be a one-
on-one intervention, such as counseling or even therapy.

There was one more wrinkle to Sugai's approach: he stressed
strengthening the relationships between teachers and students, and
offered a particular method that involved substituting rewards for
punishment—carrots for sticks—throughout the school. The idea
was that instead of noticing students for the things they did wrong,
teachers would focus on what they did right. They would make praise
for small accomplishments, rather than admonishment for infrac-
tions, the currency of their classrooms.

Sugai and his fellow professors tested their approach at about
thirty schools in Oregon. They also started writing papers and giving
presentations about their work, in hopes of getting the attention of
policy makers. In 1997 and again in 2004, Congress took notice and
included in two special education bills instructions for schools to look
at "positive behavioral interventions and supports" in hopes of reducing the nationally high rate of suspension and expulsion and improving behavior. Congress also funded a research center at the University
of Oregon, where Sugai and his colleagues looked for the best existing
practices for school-wide discipline and classroom management, adding them to their stockpile of knowledge, and preparing to take their

approach nationwide. The unwieldy catchphrase in the law, "positive behavioral interventions and supports," became an acronym, PBIS.

Sugai organized the PBIS strategy for teaching social skills and managing discipline into four parts. "First," he explained, "schools use their own data. They look at what's actually happening inside the school to figure out what needs to change. Second, they agree to use evidence-based practices that relate to the needs the data reveal. Third, they determine socially important, well-defined outcomes for kids—what do they want kids to do? And fourth, they establish the systems for achieving those standards by asking, what do adults need to do for students to reach these goals?" Sugai is the kind of person who speaks in fully formed paragraphs, with the enthusiasm of a teacher who feels sure he has plenty to teach that's of value. "Those four features define how we do business. They are what we push with schools. I walk in and say, 'Show me your data. What are the outcomes you want? What evidence-based practices will get you there? And what do you need to build for the adults?' Everything we do is based on that framework."

PBIS schools start by crunching data. Specifically, they look at referrals to the principal's office—the sign that students are breaking rules and the precursor to suspending or expelling them. These numbers, according to Sugai, are key indicators of the health of a school. When a teacher sends a parade of kids to the office, she's not in control. Not to mention the fact that the kids who leave class miss out on the instruction they're supposed to be getting, which only makes them less likely to succeed.

Sugai helps schools figure out why exactly kids are getting referred for discipline and also where the bad behavior occurs. Do kids act out in the lunchroom because the lunch period is too long, teacher supervision is lacking, or because the attention is socially rewarding? Do they mouth off in class? Do they push and shove and jeer in the hallway? Finally, what would it take to calm the trouble spots? Sometimes, the solution is surprisingly simple. After one PBIS school I visited saw a spike in misbehavior in the hallways, a teacher reminded the principal that he'd recently added one minute to the "passing time" students had to get from class to class. The data showed that the extra minute was a liability, so the principal took it away. The hallways calmed down.

Schools kick PBIS into gear with a team of dedicated teachers, administrators, and support staff, including counselors, bus drivers, and cafeteria workers. (The cost of the program varies, depending on how schools implement it.) The PBIS team crunches the referral numbers to determine what needs to change where and who's going to do it. They use this information to come up with interventions that are easy to market to teachers and students. At Old Mill, McElhaney and his staff had distilled the school's goals into three short phrases, called the Patriot Pledge, which is spoken aloud every morning: "Be respectful. Be responsible. Be on task." Classroom posters and lessons added a layer of specifics: Being respectful meant saying please, thank you, and excuse me. Being responsible meant turning in homework. Being on task meant participating in class and completing assignments on time.

Sean McElhaney stressed that "Be respectful" was a message that his teachers, too, had to absorb. In his early years at Old Mill, many of the kids sent to his office were there because they'd mouthed off. But when McElhaney asked them why, many said a teacher had disrespected them first. "When you yell at a child, you're not on their side, and they'll yell back," he said. "I had courageous conversations with teachers about how they have to take a step back."

One of McElhaney's memorable conversations with his staff was prompted by the cues they missed when a girl showed up late at school one morning. Her skin was red and blotchy, and her eyes were wet with tears. She sat down, put her head on her desk, and refused to hand in her homework. When her teacher prodded, she got surly, and this landed her in McElhaney's office. He asked her what was going on, with concern rather than frustration, and she crumbled. "She said,

'Mr. Mac, I can't do it anymore. I'm getting questioned and yelled at and *I just want to be here.*'" McElhaney asked what her morning had been like. She told him that the police had kicked in her door at dawn, shot tear gas into the apartment, and arrested her father. The cops gave him one minute to say goodbye. Then he was gone.

McElhaney called the police to verify the girl's story, and it checked out. He brought the teachers together that afternoon. "We just expected her to come to school and do what she was supposed to do," he told them. "But no one asked her what was wrong in a way that allowed her to tell her story." The staff, he told me, was devastated, and teachers who McElhaney had worried were too harsh began to soften their tone over the coming days and weeks. The tenor of the school didn't change all at once—that would be the after-school special version—but these days, teachers at Old Mill say they look out for kids more than they did before, even kids they don't teach themselves. The culture is less atomized, more cohesive. "Recently, the father of one of our students was murdered," Susan Shelby, the French teacher, told me. "It used to be that, as a teacher, you might find out about something like that or you might not—it was haphazard. But now we take it upon ourselves to make sure everyone knows. We bring it up in a meeting, or we send an email, so that even if it's a kid you've never met, if you pass her in the hallway, you can make sure to be kind, instead of seeing a girl who looks upset and asking, 'What's wrong with you?'"

For McElhaney, the staff's reaction to his story about the girl whose father had been arrested—their willingness to recognize that they hadn't been sensitive enough to ask the right questions—was a turning point. It showed he was assembling a team of teachers who believed in the system he was putting in place. "We'd weeded out the people who weren't in it for the kids," Shelby said. "The teachers who stayed or who came in, we had each other's backs. We were together. Turnover became very low." One of the challenges of turning around a school with a lot of poor kids is that a fraction of teachers are convinced that some of the students are just thuggish and *should* be sent to the principal's office. McElhaney had gotten rid of those teachers, much as he'd gotten rid of the fifty-two students he'd expelled early on. Old Mill Middle North had to have a purge of sorts before it could remake itself.

The staff was now ready to concentrate on the reward system that PBIS promises will strengthen teachers' relationships with their students. To chart their academic progress, kids get feedback such as points and check marks or grades, and to chart their social progress, McElhaney's staff started giving out blue slips of paper called Patriot Passports. Students received them for good acts, however small and ordinary: turning in an assignment on time, answering a teacher's question in class, listening attentively, and keeping their hands and feet to themselves when walking down the hallway.

To be effective, the Patriot Passports have to function as an internal currency that students *want* to earn. So McElhaney and his staff have tried to be creative. Students can use Patriot Passports to jump to the front of the cafeteria line, or eat lunch with their favorite teacher, or buy school supplies from a cart that the PTA stocks. A few times a year, Patriot Passports can be used as tickets to movie screenings or ice cream socials. McElhaney even set up Café Old Mill: a separate section of the cafeteria outfitted with comfy chairs, laptops, game consoles, and earbuds. Students can use their passports to gain entrance for themselves and their friends. The only thing missing is the coffee.

Some schools get rewards fatigue. The ice cream socials can start to seem gimmicky, and restless students and distracted teachers can revert to their old ways. Sugai's answer is that rewards are really about prompting a moment of recognition between teacher and student, not about free dessert. "When you give the kid that piece of paper, what matters most is the handshake and the praise—'I like the way you did that,'" Sugai said. "People think kids work for the reward. In part, that's true. But the reason this works for older students too is the handshake. To be honest, the piece of paper is most important as a reminder to the teachers to catch kids doing something well."

At Old Mill, McElhaney put a star on a teacher's door when he or she requested another pack of the Patriot Pledges. He also instituted an advisory program that pairs one teacher—as well as an assistant principal and a guidance counselor—with one set of students for all three years of middle school, thereby providing continuity and the capacity for building a strong relationship over time.

In the end, *all* of the PBIS strategies are about strengthening the relationships between the staff and the students. "That's my foundation: you have to make the connection with the child," McElhaney said. "If you do, they'll go to the end of the world for you." While in the pre-PBIS days, according to Shelby, students would act as if it was no big deal when other kids brought weapons or drugs to school, now they report it. "We had a student bring in a knife in October, and we found out because other kids told us," she said. "They were like, 'He did *what*?' It's nice to hear that because it's like there's more innocence."

Six years after Old Mill North launched PBIS, office referrals had decreased dramatically. In 2004–5, the year McElhaney became principal, students were sent to the office almost 2,200 times. In 2010–11, they went about 1,000 times. The number of suspensions also took a dive, from 739 to 358; expulsions dropped as well, from 16 to 0. In the middle of the following year, Old Mill North was on track for the lowest office referral rate in the district, and again, there were no expulsions. When he'd arrived at Old Mill, part of McElhaney's job had been to "eliminate kids," as he put it. Guided by PBIS, he and his staff had learned how to keep them.

PBIS wasn't designed to address bullying directly, but a 2012 study found that teachers in PBIS schools reported less bullying and peer rejection than teachers in schools without PBIS. At Old Mill, the PBIS framework seems to have had much the same effect as a bullying-specific program such as Second Step or Olweus can have when it is faithfully implemented. In 2006, 31 percent of Old Mill North students said they'd been bullied and 24 percent reported bullying other students. Almost 60 percent of the student body saw bullying as a moderate to serious problem. More than half of students said they'd seen adults "watching bullying and doing nothing." Almost three-quarters said they responded to bullying by getting into a physical fight or an argument. All of these numbers dropped significantly over the following five years.

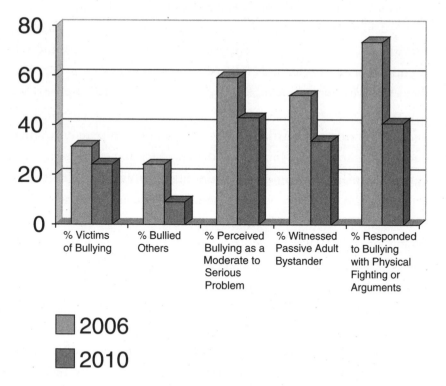

Changes in Student Reports of Bullying at
Old Mill Middle North School
2006 to 2010

By 2007, Old Mill North's bullying statistics were well below the district's average. Meanwhile, two other numbers rose: almost 70 percent of the students now said they felt safe at school, and four in five said they felt like they belonged. "PBIS works as our framework, and everything else we do falls underneath it," McElhaney told me. "The district brings people from other schools here to watch us now, because we're creating a blueprint for how schools can function. You take the name away, and we're just as good, if not better, than the much more affluent school my son goes to. He gets picked on there, and the principal will sit down and talk to the kid who did it and then it will happen again. Here I can say with the utmost confidence, the students can say whatever they want in this room. They can cuss and scream. But when they walk out it will be with the understanding that we all have to coexist here, and they *will* help make that happen."

Walking around Old Mill North with McElhaney was like following a young entrepreneur around the small, thriving business he built from the ground up. The school was his baby, his source of pride. When we passed students in the hall, they smiled or nodded hello and kept going, while McElhaney filled me in on their backstories. One eighth grader had suddenly started getting into fights in the beginning of the year; it turned out his father had been deployed to Afghanistan. "One day he wouldn't back down from arguing with someone and it got nasty," McElhaney said. "I turned into the Mr. Mac you don't want to see. He settled down and apologized." Another student who passed by had a new haircut, which McElhaney told me one of his staff members had arranged with a parent who owns a salon, when it became clear that the boy's father, a single parent who often worked nights, was overwhelmed and letting it go. McElhaney asked another boy if he'd slept well: he'd recently moved into a shelter in Washington, D.C., and took a 5:00 a.m. bus to school every day. Since Old Mill North was the last school he'd attended before he became homeless, he had a legal right to continue to go there. We ran into a teacher in the hall and McElhaney asked her how a girl in her advisory group, who'd recently been in a fight outside school, was faring. When the report was good, McElhaney grinned. "Maybe because we picked up on her early, we've got her on a flight path now."

In the library, a wide-open space with paintings that students had made with a resident artist who'd visited from Texas, McElhaney said he'd taken out the high shelves so you could see across the large room. In one corner, a sofa sat between two armchairs with a coffee table in front of it. On the table was a vase with flowers and the *Oxford English Dictionary*. In a corner, a polite distance from the other art, was a mural with graffiti bubble letters and Jackson Pollock–like splatter. The letters, in bright green and pink, spelled words such as *thinker, caring,* and *balanced.*

The words in the mural came from Old Mill North's International Baccalaureate curriculum, which connects content across courses and asks students to view what they're learning through an international lens. "It sounds elitist, but in fact it works well for average to below-average learners," McElhaney said. "It's like putting on a pair of global sunglasses. For example, when the sixth graders learn about Africa, they're asked, 'If you were African, how would you react?' I hear them in the hallway talking about genocide, and I get a call from a parent, and I say, 'Our job is to broaden their minds.'" McElhaney brought in IB, as it's called, after the successes of PBIS gave him and his staff the breathing space to concentrate on the school's course offerings. The ultimate data prize for every public school these days, of course, is higher test scores, and PBIS, which has been adopted by more than forty-five hundred schools across the country, looks promising in this regard, too. In a Johns Hopkins study in 2010 of thirty-seven Maryland elementary schools, fifth graders at schools randomly assigned to adopt PBIS made significant academic gains compared with fifth graders at other schools. McElhaney's school had made strides in closing the achievement gap for minority and special education students, and test scores in reading and math were on the rise for the student body as a whole, bringing Old Mill's results up to the district average even though its student body is among the poorest in Anne Arundel. With the advent of the International Baccalaureate program, McElhaney hoped to improve the school's academic standing further, and its adoption also turned Old Mill North into a magnet school. About sixty students now applied to get in each year. The school had gone from shunned to sought after, step by careful data-crunching step.

On the way back to his office, McElhaney dropped me in front of two small, side-by-side offices on a windowless hallway. Renekki Wilson, assistant principal and McElhaney's right-hand man, worked here next to a guidance counselor named Karen Jones. Together, Wilson and Jones were responsible for three hundred kids, a mix of sixth, seventh, and eighth graders whom they shepherded through all three years of middle school. Jones called Wilson her "office husband" and explained their good-cop/bad-cop roles. "He's the disciplinarian," she told me. "And I'm the one who says, 'Come talk to me, how can I help?'"

Wilson and Jones kept track of what they called the Red Zone, a list of students with three or more disciplinary referrals, students who needed special attention. The successes of PBIS had helped shrink the number of kids in the Red Zone over the last few years. The ones who remained were the school's third tier—the hard-to-fix cases at the top of the pyramid. How did the school deal with them? To answer that question, I talked to a trio of Red Zone students, named Melissa, Cathy, and Amy, whose conflicts had taken a lot of time to untangle. "Lots of drama with these girls," Jones said. "We were putting out fires for about a month."

Melissa, who'd just turned fourteen, had been an A and B student, one of the fifty kids (in a class of about three hundred) who took advanced math. She'd been friends with other good students who kept their heads down and stayed out of trouble, but in the summer before eighth grade, something changed: she seized on a chance to hang out with Cathy, who was the same age but seemed a lot older. She messaged high school boys on Facebook and met up with them at night. She got decent grades, but her teachers thought she was bright enough to do better.

"Cathy and I got really close," Melissa said. "We hung out all summer. She's the kind of person who influences a lot of other people. To be honest, I followed her. All her friends kind of do." Cathy's parents were immigrants who ran a small business and didn't speak English; what she didn't want them to know about her life, in or out of school, they usually didn't find out. "Cathy got a tattoo and a nose pierce and a belly pierce," Melissa said. "Her mom doesn't know, except about the nose pierce. She didn't know about the guys, either."

Jones watched with some trepidation as Melissa and Cathy bonded. "One day in October, they were giddy in the lunch line over these T-shirts they had on," Jones said. "It was before a big football game at the high school. The T-shirts said something like, 'I'm here if you're looking for a good time.' I just knew that was so out of character for Melissa. There was no way she'd been wearing that when she left her house."

Cathy, on the other hand, looked perfectly comfortable playing the part of the bad girl. When I met her, she was wearing ripped jeans, a red streak in her long dark hair, a tiny diamond stud in her nose, and flip-flops, which no one else had on. "We were really good friends," she said of herself and Melissa. "But then I stopped trusting her because she started doing bad stuff, like messing around with my other friend's boyfriend."

Whether or not this was true—Melissa said she'd just talked to the boy, whom she'd known since elementary school—there was a fight over him on Halloween night. His girlfriend jumped Melissa, pulling her hair and hitting her. The police came, and on Monday Melissa told Wilson, the assistant principal, that she'd been attacked, and that Cathy and the girl who did it were now harassing her on campus.

I was surprised that Melissa had gone to the assistant principal for help. In Middletown, where I'd spent time following Monique, students generally considered it an act of betrayal to report a fight unless it was major. Melissa wasn't hurt badly. Yet she had come into Wilson's office on her own, and she'd gone to him instead of talking to her parents. Cathy shrugged when I asked her what she thought about this. "We don't go crazy about snitching here," she said. "People talk to guidance and it's okay." This is how social norms work—once they're in place, students take them in stride.

After the Halloween fight, Jones suggested that Melissa distance herself from Cathy. In the next few weeks, Melissa tried to do that. But Cathy and her friends weren't ready to let her just walk away. Rumors started about Melissa on Facebook, saying she was a slut who stayed out all night with high school boys. "Somebody hacked my Facebook," Melissa said. "I think it was Cathy because she knew my password. She was messaging people saying she was me, saying I did stuff with a guy. She put my cell phone number up with this note that said, 'Hey, if you want a girl who's DTDE, call this number.' "

I asked what DTDE stood for.

Melissa started to cry. "It means 'down to do everything.' I didn't know my number was there because my mom didn't let me on Facebook after the fight on Halloween. But then I found out because a lot of guys called me on my cell phone. Most of them were in high school. I didn't know what to do."

Melissa stopped speaking to Cathy, but she didn't go back to being a follow-the-rules girl who took advanced math. Instead, her grades dropped to C's—and she worried that she was pregnant. She didn't tell her parents, Jones, or any other adult, but she did confide in a few girls at school, one of whom was an eighth grader named Amy. Like Cathy, Amy got a lot of attention from boys, but she also had a nurturing streak. She'd watched dubiously as Melissa became tight with Cathy, and now she was glad Melissa was appealing to her for help—she saw it as a chance to look out for a girl who'd gotten in over her head. "That whole fall Melissa wasn't acting like herself, but she wasn't a bad kid, and I knew trying to act like one with Cathy would end badly," Amy said. "When she said she was pregnant, I went with a friend of mine and we got her a pregnancy test."

Melissa took the test in the school bathroom, while Amy waited outside the stall. "She came out and said it was positive," Amy said. "But afterward these other girls found the test in the trash, and the piece that says whether you're pregnant or not was gone." Amy concluded that Melissa was faking it, claiming to be pregnant to get attention, and she took this personally. "That's not something you should joke around about. My mother got pregnant when she was fifteen. It's a serious thing."

Speculation about Melissa—was she or wasn't she? Why would she lie?—traveled through the eighth grade and even into the high school. Wilson and Jones got wind of a fight looming between two groups of boys in Melissa's class. One group was calling her a liar and the other was defending her, and they were talking about thrashing it out in the woods after school. This made Melissa's pregnancy rumor a school-wide discipline problem, which meant that Jones and Wilson had to bring in Melissa's mother. She took Melissa to the doctor, who determined that Melissa was not, in fact, pregnant.

What should have ended the drama actually ramped it up. Amy, now sure that Melissa had made up the whole pregnancy thing, heard that Melissa was talking dismissively about her and stormed into the cafeteria. She sat down with Cathy and a couple of other girls, and they all started talking about Melissa, stoking their collective rage. When Melissa walked in and sat down at a different table, the group rose and moved toward her, and Amy and Cathy shouted for a fight. One girl heeded their call and climbed over a table to get to Melissa, determined to let her have it for lying.

Jones, who was on lunch duty, heard the shouts, saw the group closing in, and pulled Melissa away. She spent hours over the next few days talking to all the girls involved, piecing together who'd done what, who was angry at whom, and why. She decided that Amy wasn't acting like a bully; she had more power than Melissa, but she'd encouraged the fight in the cafeteria because she felt used and betrayed, not to take revenge or add to her social capital. Jones decided it was safe to sit down with Amy and Melissa at the same time, so that, with her help, each could hear how the other was feeling. The meeting succeeded, the girls told me.

"I didn't go up to Amy myself and she didn't come up to me, so we hadn't heard each other's stories," Melissa said.

"After we went into Ms. Jones' office, we were okay with each other," Amy agreed. "I asked Melissa all the questions I wanted to know and she answered. We had a real conversation and we restarted our relationship from there."

Jones didn't think the same one-on-one strategy would work with Cathy, though, because she was still trying to intimidate Melissa. Jones consulted with Wilson, and they decided to play their strongest card: Mr. Mac.

As a rule, McElhaney stays out of day-to-day discipline. It's rare for a student to be called into his office. "I never talked to Mr. Mac before that," Cathy told me. "But I really liked talking to him—he understood. My friend and me were still planning to fight Melissa, but he told us that we were the people with the most power to stop this whole thing. He said, 'You're so much better than this.' We left and I felt like I wanted to do what he asked. So we called off the fight. I felt good about it."

A generation or even a decade ago, schools like Old Mill weren't expected to help solve the conflicts of kids like Cathy and Melissa and Amy. Bullying, drama, and their effect on emotional well-being were seen as beyond a school's purview, not part of the mission. But today schools are wading into all of this and more, alongside parents. It's a role that McElhaney and his staff embrace. "I've worked hard to get the staff to understand that we are the family," he said. "We are raising these children. We have to smile and say good morning to every child, every day. We don't raise our voices unless we have a very good reason. This has to be a place kids come to be safe, to be happy, and to learn. Being happy is what I focus on the most, because if they have that, the rest will fall into place and their achievement will increase. This is what we've seen—we know that it's true."

At Old Mill North, the benefits for kids and their families were clear. But I wondered if a PBIS school, given the resources, could do even more. To hark back to John Snow and the Broad Street pump, could a school with broadly effective first-tier and second-tier strategies— a school that had used PBIS to bring down the rate of disciplinary problems—mount a serious and sustained effort to change the lives of the 10 percent at the top of the pyramid? This was beyond the call of duty for a school, perhaps, and yet that was where the kids went every day, where their issues played out. And these kids were signaling clearly, by their behavior, that they needed more one-on-one attention. I wondered if what was missing for these students was longer-term services, such as therapy, that guidance counselors—however skilled, however dedicated—don't provide. If schools were the social institution responsible for improving their lives, what other resources could help them do that job as well as possible?

When I got home, I asked that question of Susan Swearer, the school psychology professor at the University of Nebraska whom I'd come to rely on as a guide through the mountains of social science research on bullying. It turned out that in addition to conducting studies herself, Swearer was in the process of testing some of her ideas about how to help the small number of students at the top of the pyramid, at a middle school called Irving in her hometown of Lincoln, Nebraska. Irving is mostly white, but its Hispanic population had grown in recent years, and the number of low-income kids was also rising, to more than 40 percent. Swearer had designed a targeted intervention program for a small number of Irving students funneled to her, by the principal or the guidance counselors, because of their problems with bullying.

Swearer got involved at Irving when the principal, Hugh McDermott, came to her with a nagging problem. Irving is a PBIS school and has been following the framework since the 2007–8 school year. For the most part, students had responded well. McDermott had a lower-key style than McElhaney, but he'd made PBIS work for his school, too. This was reassuring: charisma always helps, but for a reform to work from school to school, it can't hinge on rock-star principals. The Irving hallways were quiet. Disciplinary referrals were down. To return to the pyramid analogy, Lincoln's first-tier strategy was going strong. The school had a second tier in place, too: a time-out room, with a specially chosen teacher at the helm, where students could go for ten minutes to cool off if they acted out in class.

At Irving, as at Old Mill, the third tier started with the guidance counselor's office. The counselors, however, found themselves spending an inordinate amount of time on a small number of kids—maybe a dozen per grade—who constantly sucked their peers into conflicts, some of which qualified as bullying and some as drama. Like most principals, McDermott initially punished these third-tier offenders with suspensions, but that felt useless. "When you suspend kids and two weeks later they're doing the same thing, you can suspend them again, but if you keep at it and nothing changes, it's frustrating for everyone," he told me. "What do you really accomplish by sending the student home? So I asked Sue if there was something else we could do—something more reflective for the students and their families. And for us, too."

Swearer came up with an idea: what if McDermott tried a one-day intervention session in lieu of suspensions? She sketched out a program and, with McDermott's help, started piloting it at Irving. The third-tier students McDermott and his staff referred to Swearer began in the morning by taking an hour-long psychological assessment, conducted by trained graduate students. "We look at depression, anxiety, and self-conception—how kids see themselves scholastically, athletically, and in every other way," Swearer explained. The idea was to fill in a mental health profile that could be shared later with parents and, if they gave permission, with the school. Next, students watched short videos about bullying and talked through the conflicts with the graduate student. This would force kids with a pattern of bullying, or being bullied, to recognize themselves on-screen and come up with concrete steps they might take to change their behavior. After the day ended, the graduate student wrote up a report for parents, based on the psych assessment and the graduate student's observations, containing specific recommendations about how to help the kids fare better in school from here on out. "The write-up gives amazing feedback, and the parents usually share it with us," a guidance counselor named Valerie Moser-Bergo told me. "It's an opportunity for us to say, 'Okay, how do we help your child function in a more prosocial way? What does she really need?'"

McDermott offers spots to kids with a range of bullying problems: chronic aggressors, frequent targets, and bully-victims. So far, every parent asked has said yes. At Irving and two other middle schools in Lincoln, about eighty kids have participated over five years. It's a small number, but then only about a dozen kids per grade persistently caused or suffered from serious bullying over the course of a year. Swearer is now doing a follow-up study, and her preliminary results show the kids who participate in the sessions get into trouble about half as often as they used to. A couple of caveats: Since Swearer is picking students at their low points, some of them would be expected to improve on their own. (Researchers call this "regression to the mean.") And because no one has said no to her program, Swearer can't do a randomized study comparing students who get the targeted intervention to students who don't.

I wanted to meet some of the students who had gone through Swearer's intervention program, so Moser-Bergo introduced me to a boy named Joshua. He'd had a rough start when he got to Irving at the beginning of sixth grade. His mother spent that year serving in Iraq while he lived with his father and stepmother. Still angry about his parents' divorce, Joshua spoke bitterly of his father to teachers. He seemed fragile and inclined to play the victim. Someone threw a pencil in the hallway, for example, and Joshua reported that the pencil had been thrown at *him*, even though no one else who'd been there saw it that way. Or another student would say something like, "That's stupid," and Joshua would report this as bullying, without mentioning that he'd done something to provoke the comment, or called the other student a name back.

By seventh grade, Joshua's mother had returned from Iraq and started following up Joshua's complaints with angry emails. The accusations of bullying seemed to snowball. Moser-Bergo began to wonder if Joshua was blowing up small incidents into big ones to get his mother's attention. "He liked her to rally around him, and she always portrayed it as the other kids being against her son, when that wasn't the only thing going on," she said. "It's really difficult as a parent to step back and say, 'Okay, there are things that could be causing my kid to be picked on—what could they be? What could he do differently that might help?'"

Moser-Bergo offered Joshua a spot in Swearer's program, hoping that he'd respond to the session with the graduate student, and also that the write-up of Joshua's psychological profile would help her get through to his family. Joshua told me he wasn't sure why he'd been recommended. "I don't know why I was in that class, but some people here were pushing me around, and my mom was worrying about me," he said. "In the class we talked about provoking and retaliating. I don't have as many problems with that now."

Joshua's mother said that after his assessment, she talked with his counselor, and together they came up with ideas to help Joshua become more socially involved. "He's more active this year—he does Boy Scouts and tennis and plays an instrument," she told me. "I wanted to make sure he wasn't a child who's at home, isolated, playing video games." Moser-Bergo said she'd coached Joshua and his mother on strategies for keeping small conflicts in perspective. "I suggested that since the details of some of the reports he made were sketchy, he could try keeping a log to show his parents," she said. "Anytime you ask kids to write things down, they'll only do it if it's a really big deal. It helped him stop magnifying everything and let some of it just roll off his back, which kids have to learn to do. With his mother, I asked her to think about the times she herself had grown and changed the most, and that helped remind her that some of those times are painful. Sometimes we have to let kids experience some pain and some consequences of the things they say and do, to help shape them. Because as adults, it won't be as useful a life skill to respond by playing the victim or retaliating. I always tell families, 'Bullies don't go away. Adults bully, too. So we all have to figure out how to deal with them.' "

In the beginning of eighth grade, a student whom Joshua had tangled with years earlier, in elementary school, launched an attack on him after school, on the sidewalk, by getting down on his knees behind Joshua while another boy pushed him over. "The kids call it table topping, and it just happened out of the blue, without Joshua doing anything to provoke it," Moser-Bergo said. "I saw so much growth in how Joshua handled it. He came in and told us, without involving his mother. He's really matured and become smarter about how to handle himself."

One afternoon I went with McDermott to the cafeteria to watch the seventh grade eat lunch. On the surface, it all looked pretty copacetic, with kids slinging their trays onto long tables and talking, elbow to elbow, while they chomped away. McDermott, however, filled me in on the dynamics, pointing out students who'd given the staff cause for concern, at one time or another, because of bullying or drama. Seeing the kids through his eyes reminded me of Robert Faris' social network maps—the ones he'd used to show how students enhance their status by acting aggressively toward other kids who are a step removed from them in the status hierarchy. Faris concluded that kids often bully for the social reward.

Even at a school such as Irving, where the staff was working hard to disrupt this dynamic, that negative idea still had a toehold—as I noticed when I talked to a seventh grader named Brittany.

Susan Swearer had mentioned her before I arrived at Irving. Intensely social and self-aware, Brittany had gotten into trouble in sixth grade with her best friend for mocking a meeker girl, day after day, for wearing the same clothes. After going through Swearer's program, and much urging from her guidance counselor and her mother, Brittany had been persuaded to break off the toxic friendship, and the other kids soon stopped complaining about her antics. When Brittany was asked in a follow-up interview if there was anything she missed about being a bully, she answered, as if she'd walked off the pages of Faris' study, "Feeling like you're powerful and you control your group or whatever. That's the thing I miss."

Brittany's psychological assessment had shown that she was struggling with depression and anxiety, and that she was prone to oppositional defiance. (She answered yes, for example, to "I can't help losing my temper a lot" and "People are always trying to hassle me.") On the positive side, she didn't choose many answers blaming other people for her misbehavior, faring better on that part of the assessment than her guidance counselor's reports suggested. And she also said she saw bullying as a problem at Irving, acknowledged that she'd been a bully herself, and said that the bullying made her feel bad.

Brittany told me that during her day in Swearer's program, she'd seen herself in one of the characters in the bullying videos. "There was a girl who would say a mean thing first and then afterward everyone else would say exactly the same thing," she said. "And that was like me, like how people would follow me. I knew why I was doing that but I also knew I really shouldn't be."

Connecting those dots had helped her stay away from bullying in the year since. So had breaking off the friendship with the girl she'd gotten into trouble with. "I switched friends, and yeah, that's hard. But I've stuck with it, because of how much trouble we got into," Brittany said. "My mom won't let me and I can understand why."

Brittany's mother, Lisa, dropped in to talk to me; she had a new baby in tow, who slept in her stroller while we pulled up chairs around a small conference table. Lisa said she worried about coming down too hard on her daughter, who'd had a tough childhood. She was frightened of her father, Lisa said, and when Brittany was six, he left home and cut all ties with his daughter. "She has a right to her anger with all the things she's been through," Lisa told me, but she also knew this didn't excuse the way Brittany was acting toward weaker kids. Lisa had dark memories of her brother being bullied in high school. He'd struggled ever since, and she hated to think of her daughter causing the kind of pain and self-doubt he'd endured. "I couldn't believe what I was hearing, that she would do this to someone, when this is the thing I've been telling her *not* to do since she was born."

Along with Brittany's guidance counselor, Lisa had insisted that Brittany end the friendship that seemed to give her license to be mean. When Lisa went over Brittany's psychological assessment with the counselor, they talked about the risks depression poses, and Lisa decided to take a step she'd been resisting and get her daughter into therapy. This is one of the key outcomes of Swearer's program, which she has helped bring about by making her graduate students available to offer weekly therapy to a few Irving students. If there's no slot open, the school refers families to a university counseling center, where they pay as little as $10 for a weekly session. These opportunities for therapy are a huge windfall for Irving and its students. Since the school doesn't pay Swearer or her graduate students, Irving is offering a sophisticated third-tier intervention, with potentially long-term follow-through, at practically no extra cost.

Thinking back while her baby obligingly kept napping, Lisa told me about how she'd kept Brittany close over the summer before seventh grade. "I work with the elderly, and I took her with me a lot," she said. "I wanted to show her how you care for people to make their lives better." Brittany also doted on the new baby. "She really has a lot of nurturing in her."

Lisa's baby started to wake up, and she reached into the stroller as Brittany knocked on the door, coming in to ask if she could walk home with a girl her mother liked. Lisa nodded her approval. Before Brittany left, I asked if she still missed feeling powerful. She shook her head. "That kind of power was a version of making someone else get hurt," she said. "Two days ago, a boy who doesn't have too many friends came in the front door from recess, and a kid book-checked him. That means he slammed the boy's books on the ground. In front of everyone. Lots of people laughed. I went to pick up his books for him and asked if he was okay. I didn't know one of the teachers was watching, but the next day she came up to me and said I did a really good thing."

Lisa smiled, but Brittany wasn't looking at her. She'd seen the friend she was going home with waiting in the hallway, and raced out the door to meet her.

Chapter 9

Delete Day

WHEN I PULLED MY BORROWED CAR INTO THE PARKING LOT OF Facebook, I felt a little like I was arriving at college all over again. I was on a small campus with buildings that could have been dorms and manicured lawns kept green by sprinklers. The sneaker-wearing young people walking along the neat paths could have been the slightly scruffier cousins of the law students I teach, or the older brothers and sisters of undergrads at Stanford University, which I'd just driven through. I breathed. I loved college. And I could smell jasmine. Then I spotted Facebook's familiar logo, on a red sign low to the ground, and remembered that this was no hall of learning. It was the Silicon

Valley center of the online universe for as many as twenty million American teenagers, the universe where a lot of the bullying they experienced took place.

It had taken me six months to get here, to convince the gatekeepers to grant me access to the inner sanctum. I started with a PR representative, asking to spend some time with the Facebook team that handles complaints about bullying and harassment. After a series of follow-up emails and phone calls—I'd launch a message, wait, launch another one—he quizzed me about my intentions, and, once satisfied, told me to contact Nicky Jackson Colaco, a member of Facebook's Privacy and Security team. Many moons and emails later, I reached Colaco on the phone. She told me Facebook wasn't interested in participating in a book with a "techno-panic" slant—in other words, a book that blamed technology for social problems like bullying. I said that wasn't my take. She gave me a list of experts—psychologists, journalists, youth advocates—who she said could elaborate on her concern about techno-panic. I was to call them, and then try her again.

It felt like jumping through hoops, but I went along. I dutifully made the phone calls and, a week or so later, circled back to Colaco. More weeks of polite nudging ensued. And then one day the Facebook PR rep called back: I could come for a visit, he said. I'd apparently passed the entrance exam.

So here I was, at the appointed address on the appointed day. Facebook's receptionist took my ID and pointed me to four thick white binders arrayed before her, each of which contained a different nondisclosure agreement. The lawyer in me started worrying about what I'd be asked to sign. But before I'd finished reading, Colaco and the PR rep appeared, saving me from the binders and their fine print.

Colaco, who had green eyes and a blond ponytail, came to Facebook in 2009 with Sheryl Sandberg, whom Mark Zuckerberg hired away from Google to be his chief operating officer. Colaco told me she loved her job. She'd had a baby a year earlier and could leave work at

5:30 p.m., though she also worked at home from 8:00 p.m. to midnight. "People here understood when I had to miss the White House bullying summit for my child's first birthday," she said. "We'd already bought the tickets to Hawaii, and there are some things you just don't cancel."

Colaco led me through glass doors, down a short hallway, and then into a large, open space. On one side was a white wall, covered in handwritten graffiti—a relic from the company's original office, back when Facebook got its first round of venture capital funding. I felt as if I'd walked onto the set of *The Social Network*.

That feeling deepened as we walked around a corner into a vast, brightly lit room in which row upon row of engineers sat at long tables in expensive ergonomic chairs, tapping away on their keyboards. Most wore headphones, not to mention sneakers and baseball caps. The engineers sat out in the open, Colaco said, because that's the way it worked at Facebook. The idea was to facilitate collaboration, though I didn't see any of the engineers speaking to each other. It may have looked like a newsroom, but it sounded like a library. We turned another corner and happened on a mini-kitchen, stocked with cereal, milk, and bananas, just one of countless perks that no newsroom or library would ever pay for. My personal favorites were the café that served sushi, the refrigerated cases of free drinks, and especially the individually wrapped toothbrushes in the bathroom. Alongside various walls, or in open spaces between tables, there were couches for sleeping and beanbag chairs for sprawling. It all reflected my notion of the Silicon Valley dream: go west, young engineer, and pull all-nighters.

Colaco led me into a small room with squishy green love seats to meet Arturo Bejar, Facebook's director of engineering. It was his job to come up with a custom-made tool for addressing bullying and harassment. In 2011, *Consumer Reports* estimated that of the twenty million teenagers and preteens who used Facebook in the previous year, one million of them were bullied, harassed, or threatened on the site. A Pew Center survey from the same year found that 15 percent of teens between twelve and seventeen said they'd been harassed on a social networking site in the last twelve months, and since "Facebook dominates teen social media usage," as Pew put it, it's safe to say that a lot of the harassment happened there (93 percent of kids who use social networking sites have a Facebook account).

Facebook's own numbers show the extent of harassment and other misconduct on the site, too. At the time of my visit, Facebook was getting two *million* "abuse reports" a week—complaints from users about content posted on the site. (To put this number in context, that's 2 million out of 7.5 billion pieces of content—Web links, photos, notes, posts—that users shared weekly.) The abuse reports came from adults as well as teenagers, and they included everything from hate speech to nudity to drug sales to solicitations for sex. Accusations of bullying and harassment by teenagers, however, made up a significant portion of the total, though Bejar wouldn't say how much.

Facebook takes the reports seriously. After all, the site has built its brand by holding its users to a higher standard of decency: cruel and intimidating posts are a violation of Facebook's explicit rules. "You will not bully, intimidate, or harass any user," the site requires you to pledge when you sign up. You also agree not to fake your identity, or to post content that is hateful or pornographic, or that contains nudity or graphic violence. In other words, Facebook is decidedly *not* the public square, where people can say anything they want, short of libel or slander. It's much more like a mall, where private security guards can throw you out for calling someone a whore.

A mall, that is, with an enormous enforcement challenge, given that with 800 million users and counting, Facebook has more people than most countries. For years Facebook has given users an automated button to click on to report abuse, and for years parents, teachers, and teenagers have complained that Facebook's responses are slow, or impersonal, or nonexistent. There's no hotline to call if you're unhappy, and while a settlement the company reached with the New

York attorney general in 2007 requires a twenty-four-hour turn-around for complaints about nudity, pornography, harassment, or un-welcome solicitation, other kinds of abuse reports can wait much longer. When I surveyed fifteen hundred Slate readers about Facebook in 2011, about 150 said they'd reported bullying or harassment by clicking on the designated button, and two-thirds of that group said they were dissatisfied with the site's response. "It took a full 6 mos to take down an account of a 10 year old that was horribly bullying an-other 10 year old," one parent wrote. Another said Facebook had taken down a post she'd complained about, but faulted the site for the generic response it sent to her. "They don't report on what action was taken," she wrote. "If inappropriate pictures or comments are made, they should say what kind of discipline was issued." "No response from FB for anything," a teacher said. "No threats, harassment, or profane comments I've reported have ever been removed. Ever."

This is where Bejar comes in, but not quite in the way you might think. Settling in on the love seat, he explained that his goal was to wean users from appealing for help to what he called the "Great Facebook in the Sky." Bejar wanted unhappy users to turn for help not to an automated reporting system but to the people they trust. "Everyone I talk to has a big divider in their head, as if the way to resolve conflict is different if a kid is online versus sitting in a park," he said. "But our biggest insight, in the work we're doing now, is that there isn't a big separation between online life and real life in terms of social structures. Facebook shouldn't be in the business of dictat-ing and enforcing community norms. People should enforce their own norms."

Bejar wanted users to do this by bringing solutions from their off-site lives onto Facebook, just as they'd brought their conflicts. "Our goal should be to help people solve the underlying problem in the of-fline world," he said. "Sure, we can take content down and warn the bully, but probably the most important thing is for the target to get the support they need. We want to get the right people talking to each other about what's really going on—the people who know the million things about context that we can't know."

To this end, Bejar designed a new flow, or set of responses, that users see when they make an abuse report. The flow was called Facebook's social reporting tool. For offending comments on photos, it began with this screen:

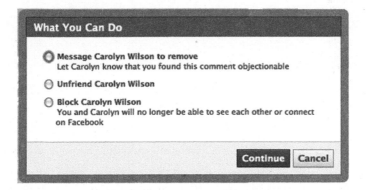

If you clicked on the first choice, "I don't like this comment," another window opened:

Tracking how people used the tool, Bejar found that when one user asked another to remove a photo (an additional option), the picture in question often came down. "We're finding that people often just need to talk to each other," he said.

This was an appealing idea: if users were taking down offending photos upon another user's request, then just as Bejar had said, Facebook was helping people solve their own online social problems. The people using the social reporting tool could also write their own "please remove" messages and send them via Facebook's inbox feature, which operates like internal email. But in tests, Bejar's team found that people were more likely to send a scripted message than one they had to compose themselves.

Bejar's tool offered more options, too. If you thought the content you wanted to report *was* bullying or harassment, a different window opened:

> **What You Can Do**
>
> If you are in physical danger, please contact a local authority right away.
>
> ☐ **Block Carolyn Wilson**
> You and Carolyn will no longer be able to see each other or connect on Facebook
>
> ☐ **Get help from an authority figure or trusted friend**
> Forward this comment to someone who can help you in person
>
> ☐ Report to Facebook   **Continue** Cancel

In presenting these options, Bejar was thinking about bullying from the point of view of the target. "The best thing to do is to make it really easy for the target to reach out to a parent, or a friend, or someone else you trust, and get them to respond quickly," he said. "To me, the ideal interaction would be sending the post to a person you trust, and then that person prints it out and confronts the person who sent it and asks, 'Do you understand how this makes the target feel?'"

The lesson here was the online equivalent of the adage that it takes a village to raise a child. In this case, the village wasn't Great Facebook in the Sky; it was the communities of people who populated the site and were connected with each other outside it.

Bejar's thinking lined up with a central tenet of bullying prevention: kids, parents, and school staff must band together and treat harmful aggression as unacceptable. Parents can play a crucial role as monitors of technology. In a 2009 study, researchers asked middle school and high school students what would deter them from bullying other kids online, and the answer the teenagers ranked first was parental discipline in the form of taking away access to social networking sites. Second was taking away their computers or phones. "My perspective is that children interpret parental monitoring as a form of caring, even if they protest," Elizabeth Englander told me. "I don't buy the argument that you can't intervene this way because nobody else's parents are doing it."

Some parents are flummoxed by the technology. They friend their kids on Facebook without realizing they can't see everything the teenagers post. (For that, you need your child's password.) They set up filters for the Internet or controls on cell phone use without realizing their kids have figured out how to sidestep them. Or they hear stories of children outwitting their parents and decide that monitoring is a lost cause. (It's not.)

Facebook's social reporting tool counted on adults to know how to handle cyberbullying. When a teenager clicked the bubble "Get help from an authority figure or a trusted friend," Bejar imagined parents, teachers, and counselors coming through on the other end. "My ideal world is one in which parents and teachers understand the tools we give them and how they map onto conflict resolution in the real world," Bejar said. Discounting for parental cluelessness, this still seemed reasonable: it demanded maybe one part tech savvy and three parts relationship savvy.

Bejar told me that since the tool had been launched five months earlier, "self-resolution"—users voluntarily taking down content—had accounted for more than half the deletions on the site. That sounded promising, but since he also said that deletions were relatively rare, it didn't tell me how often the tool was being used. When I did my survey on Slate a few weeks later, 70 percent of my fifteen hundred respondents had never heard of the tool and only 3 percent had used it. I've asked a lot of teenagers and their parents about it since then, and gotten blank looks.

Since I talked to Bejar, Facebook has added a bit to social reporting for thirteen- and fourteen-year-olds. If a kid that age doesn't like a post that's about him, he can click "This post is a problem." The prompt pulls up a series of questions about the post, designed to gauge how abusive the content is and how bad he feels about it. When he finishes the questions, the following screen appears:

Thank You

We have received your report.

It's never ok for someone to say mean or hurtful things about you. You deserve to be treated with respect and kindness. You did the right thing by reporting this post. It might also help to:

- Make sure you don't write mean things back to the person – it could make the situation worse.
- Talk to a trusted adult, like a parent or teacher, in person.

Would you like to answer a few questions about this experience?

Okay

In other words, Facebook is expressing sympathy and giving good advice, but leaving it to kids to help themselves. I still wonder whether the company can hand off a large part of enforcing the site's rules to individual users. Libertarian engineers may shrink from the image of Great Facebook in the Sky, but like it or not, the site has real authority, especially over people who devote considerable effort to building their profiles over time. That investment is a lot to lose. Bejar himself made the case for the site's power to shape and alter behavior, explaining to me why Facebook had moved from wholesale banishment of rule breakers toward a calibrated combination of warnings and "temporary crippling of the user experience." After all, if you were banished, you could sign up again under an assumed name. You'd have to start over, but you might not absorb the message that it's in your interest to abide by the site's anti-harassment policy. Whereas if you were allowed to keep your account, knowing that Great Facebook in the Sky had its eye on you, the message would be *You're still part of this community—but you'd better shape up.* For example, if you were caught setting up a page that mocked someone (someone who wasn't a celebrity, that is) Facebook could warn you that your account would be disabled if you did it again, and block you from setting up any more group pages for a month. The site had data to suggest that teenagers were acutely sensitive to this kind of policing. According to an in-house study, after getting *one* message from Facebook that content they posted prompted an abuse report the site had investigated and confirmed, 94 percent of users under eighteen generated no more complaints. As one staffer put it to me, "The rate of recidivism is very low."

This didn't surprise me. In the course of my reporting, I'd been asking middle school and high school students whether they'd rather be suspended from school or from Facebook, and most of them picked school.

The people at Facebook who decide how to wield the site's power every day are called reps, and they worked on the opposite side of the building from Bejar, handling the never-ending stream of abuse reports. They'd done the recidivism study, and they appreciated its lesson. "What we have over you is that your Facebook profile is of value to you," Dave Willner, the twenty-six-year-old head of the Hate and Harassment team, told me. "It's a hostage situation."

Colaco and I found Willner among the rows of tables where his reps scrolled through the reports of bullying, harassment, and hate speech. They sat across from the Safety team (for suicidal content, child exploitation, and underage users) and near the Authenticity team (for complaints of fake accounts). The Authenticity reps, I noticed, had clear bright lines to follow: accounts that aren't attached to real names and email addresses must come down, period. The Safety reps, meanwhile, were backed by a Microsoft software called PhotoDNA, which Facebook has piloted for tracking child pornography because it can identify images based on their digital signature, even if they've been cropped or changed. For the twenty to thirty warnings about suicidal posts that Facebook averaged per week, the site had a partnership with a suicide prevention center, which could pop up via IM chat on the page of a potentially suicidal user.

The Hate and Harassment reps, however, could not rely on clear calls or technological whizbangery as they slogged through their reports. "Bullying is hard," Willner said. "It's slippery to define, and it's even harder when it's writing instead of speech. Tone of voice disappears." Willner's team tried to come up with algorithms the site could run to determine whether a post was meant to harass and disturb, but hadn't found anything that worked. Context was everything. He gave me an example from a recent abuse report he'd seen, complaining about a status update that said "He got her pregnant." Who was it about? What had the poster intended? Looking at the words on the screen, there was no way for Willner's team to tell.

"Is it knowable whether that's harassment or not?" he asked.

In an attempt to impose order on their frustratingly subjective universe, Willner's team developed one rule of thumb: if you complained to Facebook that you were being harassed or bullied, the site took your word for it. "If the content is about you and you're not famous, we don't try to decide whether it's actually mean," Willner said. "We just take it down."

All other complaints, however, were treated as "third-party reports" that reps had to do their best to referee. This included abuse reports from parents saying their children were being bullied. That surprised me, because I'd heard from parents who'd made reports so their kids wouldn't have to, but that was news to Willner, who didn't bring in focus groups of teenagers, parents, or teachers to ask about how they used the site. No one at Facebook did, as far as I could tell.

To demonstrate how the harassment reps do their job, Willner introduced me to an affable young guy named Nick Sullivan, who had a grim reaper with a pirate sword on his desk. Sullivan opened the program that he used for sorting and resolving abuse reports, which used to have a great name—the Wall of Shame—until someone thought better of this and rechristened it the more prosaic Common Review Tool. And yet a glimmer of personality lingered: on the screen under the bubble labeled "Permanently Delete," which a rep could click to wipe out a whole Facebook account, an engineer had added "No Take Backsies."

We scrolled through a few of the reports in Sullivan's queue. He stopped on a page called "I Hate Mariah." Three people had friended it. This was an easy call: next to the name of the person who'd created the page, Sullivan checked the CRT's box for "confirmed cyberbully." He checked another box to send an automated message: "We have removed the following content you posted because it violates Facebook's Statement of Rights and Responsibilities. To keep your account from being blocked or deleted, please remove any content that includes attacks or threats to an individual or group. Please reread the Facebook Community Standards." The message included a link to these standards, which the user would have to click on before he or she could write a status or post any other new content.

I asked Sullivan whether he would ever spend, say, ten minutes on a particularly nuanced or vexing report, and Willner raised his eyebrows. "We optimize for half a second," he said. "Your average decision time is a second or two, so thirty seconds would be a really long time. We don't ask anyone to do the same thing all day anymore, but we used to, and the reps could do ten thousand to twelve thousand photos in a day." When I asked for the total number of reps on the Authenticity, Safety, and Hate and Harassment teams, I didn't get an answer. Looking around, I counted about two dozen; Facebook also has "user support" teams in Austin, Dublin, and Hyderabad, India. Still, with two million abuse reports a week, no wonder complaints fell through the cracks, as my Slate survey respondents had told me. Staffing up, to allow the reps to slow down, would cost money, but that's not the only reason Facebook doesn't do it. The company's philosophy doesn't accord with hiring warehouses of people to process individual complaints one by one. That would be reactive. The Silicon Valley ethos prizes efficient, systemic solutions.

Next Sullivan showed me a photo of three girls, posted by a boy with the caption: "That's right bitch I see u." "He's clearly targeting one of them," Sullivan said, clicking on the button on his screen that would delete the post and send a warning to its author. He deleted a group page called "The People Who Are Scared of Robert and Are Gonna Get Fucked Up This Summer." I asked if this constituted bullying, and Sullivan said it didn't matter, because the person who'd set up the page hadn't used his real name.

That reminded me of "Let's Start Drama," the Facebook page with the anonymous author that was riling up the students I'd met in Middletown. Justin Carbonella, director of the city's Youth Services Bureau, told me he'd filed two abuse reports about "Let's Start Drama" the previous winter, and nothing had happened. He'd gotten no answer, and six months later the page was still up. I asked Willner and Sullivan why. Since "Let's Start Drama" wasn't a real-name profile, didn't it clearly violate Facebook's rules?

Sullivan did a quick search. The blurry photos I'd seen many times at the top of "Let's Start Drama" appeared on the screen. The page was still active: Sullivan scrolled through some recent "who's hotter" comparisons. Colaco expressed surprise: she hadn't heard of this use of Facebook before. "Really, they call them voting pages?" she asked, jotting down a note.

Sullivan clicked on the history of the page, which the Common Reporting Tool allowed him to call up. A window opened on the screen's right, showing three abuse reports. Two were from Carbonella, sent in February. A third, sent in March, was from someone else.

Colaco asked if Carbonella and the other person had failed to fill in the bubble saying that "Let's Start Drama" was fake. But that wasn't the problem: the abuse reports had been filled out correctly. Yet next to this history was a note made by the rep who'd previously reviewed "Let's Start Drama": "Auto ignore."

We sat and stared at the screen.

Willner broke the silence. "Someone made a mistake," he said. "This profile should have been disabled." He leaned in and peered at the screen. "Actually, two different reps made the same mistake, two different times."

Colaco asked what the "auto ignore" message meant. "If our decision hasn't changed after two reviews, we automatically ignore any other complaints that come in," Willner said. There was another long pause. Sullivan clicked on "Let's Start Drama" to delete it.

The drive to referee cyberspace began, oddly, with a mother—not a teenager—gone berserk.

Before she had the incredible lapse of judgment that made her a national pariah, Lori Drew was seen as "slightly annoying" and "kind of pushy" by her neighbors in Dardenne Prairie, a St. Louis suburb. But when she got drawn into the tensions between her thirteen-year-old daughter and an eighth grader on the block named Megan Meier, Drew turned to the Internet to exact a breathtakingly immature kind of revenge.

Megan, who had a volatile, on-again, off-again friendship with Drew's daughter, opened a MySpace account for her fourteenth birthday. On the site, she called herself Megan Babi and chose the instant-messaging handle prettynbling16. Megan exulted when she started getting messages on MySpace from a sixteen-year-old boy named Josh Evans. In his profile picture, he was "adorable," Megan's mother, Tina, later said. "He had big blue eyes, very cut features, brown wavy hair." He said his goal for the next year was to "meet a great girl." Josh said he'd just moved to a town about an hour away and was being home-schooled. When Megan posted a picture of herself wearing a tiara, Josh wrote, "You're my beautiful princess."

Megan asked to talk to Josh on the phone; he said he didn't have one yet. Tina began to wonder if Josh was real. Concerned, she called the police to ask if they could verify a MySpace account. They said they couldn't. Meier was right to worry: Josh Evans was the creation of Lori Drew and an eighteen-year-old named Ashley Grills who worked for Drew's direct mail business. Lori Drew's daughter had been fighting with Megan, and Drew later told the police that she created the Josh account to win Megan's trust so she could find out what Megan was feeling about her daughter.

But before all this came to light more than a year later, someone used the Josh Evans account to write this fateful message to Megan, "I don't know if I want to be friends with you anymore because I've heard that you are not very nice to your friends." Megan sent back a series of confused and distressed messages. "What???" she wrote, and "Umm how bout no were the hell u gewt this?" The next day, Megan, fake Josh, and other kids began volleying insults back and forth. Megan called one girl a slut, and the insult was returned. The last message from the Josh account read, "You're a shitty person, and the world would be a better place without you in it."

Megan hanged herself in her bedroom about twenty minutes later, with a belt her mother had gotten her from Old Navy.

A month of grieving passed—and then the Meiers learned from a neighbor about Lori Drew's role in conjuring Josh, who had disappeared from MySpace the morning after Megan's death. The Meiers went to the police, and for nearly a year—following their advice—

kept quiet while the case was investigated. But after law enforcement decided Drew hadn't committed a crime, the Meiers told their story to the *St. Charles Suburban Journals,* which published an article about the case in November 2007. To protect her daughter's privacy, the paper didn't name Drew, but enraged readers soon matched details in the article with property records, and posted her name online. When the police dismissed Drew's MySpace shenanigans as merely "rude" and "immature," the story became national news. Her neighbors shunned her, a brick was thrown at her kitchen window, and her home address was posted on the Web with the heading "Child Killer."

After the state of Missouri declined to charge Drew, a team of prosccutors in California came up with the idea of indicting her under a law written to punish computer hackers. The theory was that Drew had committed a hacking offense by violating the MySpace terms of service (and could be indicted in California because that was where MySpace's servers were). A jury convicted Drew of three misdemeanor charges, but the trial judge overturned that verdict, saying that the prosecution's theory stretched the law too far.

The enduring outrage over Drew—over how she had lured Megan in and gone unpunished—helped prompt a wave of tougher cyberbullying laws. Missouri and eight other states made cyberbullying a crime. Thirty-six other states, however, directed their cyberbullying enforcement at schools. Some required local school boards to come up with policies to address bullying and cyberbullying, while others instructed schools to punish students for online misconduct. The new laws in California and Nebraska, for example, explicitly stated that cyberbullying may be the basis for suspension or expulsion.

In other words, even though the alarm about online harassment initially sounded over the actions of an adult, lawmakers have mostly turned to schools to solve the problem. It's understandable: school is where students meet and interact, and often where a bullied student feels most threatened.

However natural this may seem to distressed kids and parents, though, it's a huge task for schools to take on. To punish a student, school officials are supposed to be sure about who has done what, but what can seem straightforward based on a screen shot or printout often leads administrators down a rabbit hole. Tony Orsini, a middle school principal in Ridgewood, New Jersey, told Jan Hoffman of the *New York Times* about a girl at his school who was scared and upset by sexually explicit text messages she received. Her parents demanded that Orsini investigate. He wanted to help, and at first the task seemed easy enough, since the messages came from a single cell phone. But the boy to whom the phone belonged said he'd lost it and hadn't sent the texts, and many hours of staff time later, Orsini concluded that as far as he could tell, the boy was telling the truth: someone else *had* sent the texts, and there was no way to know who. When he broke this news to the parents who had begged him for help, the principal said of the family, "They were still in so much pain. They wanted us to keep investigating."

After many other such forays, Orsini finally sent a school-wide email to parents reflecting his frustration over all the work administrators and counselors were putting into refereeing kids' cyberbattles. "There is absolutely NO reason for any middle school student to be part of a social networking site," he wrote, and instructed parents that if they thought their children were being harassed online, they should "IMMEDIATELY GO TO THE POLICE!"

The police, however, often have more important things to do than deal with Facebook thugs. When they do intervene, they generally have a lot of discretion. They can choose to play a limited role, by warning kids to straighten out, as the cop did who told Gianna to stay away from Monique after the threatening MySpace message she sent. But there's also a risk that in the hands of an overzealous prosecutor, a police investigation will blow up into a community-wide meltdown and heavy criminal charges, as it did in South Hadley.

Schools may be better situated than cops to discipline students for what they write online, but for principals and their staffs, cyberbullying investigations raise free speech concerns. Students, after all, have some First Amendment rights both on campus and off. The question is how far these rights extend in cases of online bullying.

The Supreme Court first took a crack at setting the parameters for students' free speech in the famous 1969 case of *Tinker v. Des Moines Independent Community School District,* which began when a sister and brother named Mary Beth and John Tinker, along with a third student, wore black armbands to school in Des Moines, Iowa, to protest the Vietnam War. The school responded by passing a rule banning the armbands, but the students came back wearing them anyway. They were suspended. With the help of the ACLU, their parents went to court to challenge the suspension as a violation of their children's free speech rights. A federal court said the suspension was within the school's authority.

The Supreme Court reversed, ruling on behalf of the students and against the school. "It can hardly be argued that either students or teachers shed their constitutional rights to freedom of speech or expression at the schoolhouse gate," Justice Abe Fortas wrote for the majority. The armband was a form of free speech, the justices found, and students could be punished for their speech in school only if they substantially or materially disrupted the school's operation, or if school authorities reasonably forecast such a disruption.

In the years since, the Supreme Court has taken a few less stirring cases, and though the court has never said that students have a right only to political speech like an antiwar protest, the justices have added exceptions to *Tinker*'s broad rule. Schools can discipline a student for making "lewd" remarks at a school assembly, even if the vulgarity doesn't cause a substantial disruption. They can delete articles from a school-sponsored newspaper, and they can restrict speech that is "reasonably viewed as promoting illegal drug use," the court said in 2007, in a 5–4 decision allowing administrators to suspend a senior named Joseph Frederick who unfurled a fourteen-foot banner reading "Bong Hits 4 Jesus" in front of his high school.

The "Bong Hits 4 Jesus" ruling, in particular, incensed free speech advocates. There was nothing lewd or offensive about the words on Joseph Frederick's banner; they weren't school-sponsored, and he was standing across the street from the school, not on its grounds. Shouldn't he have had a right to free speech, by the logic of *Tinker*? Even one of the Supreme Court justices who ruled against Joseph Frederick complained that the rules were blurring. "We continue to distance ourselves from *Tinker,* but we neither overrule it nor offer an explanation of when it operates and when it does not," Justice Clarence Thomas wrote. "I am afraid that our jurisprudence now says that students have a right to speak in schools except when they do not."

As if the law wasn't confusing enough for schools to follow, cyberbullying cases have created a whole new dilemma. Students generally write harassing messages from their home computers or send them from phones they're using off campus. And so schools now need answers to questions that rarely surfaced in the past: under what circumstances can they punish students for cruel off-campus speech?

Judges have recently come up with conflicting answers to that question. Compare the two cases of J. Cohen, an eighth grader in Beverly Hills, and Kara Kowalski, a senior in West Virginia. J.'s misadventures began one day after school at a restaurant, where she made a four-and-a-half-minute video with a few of her friends. The video showed the girls talking about a fellow student named Carina. On camera, J.'s friends called Carina a slut and "the ugliest piece of shit I've ever seen in my whole life." Off camera, J. encouraged the other girls to keep going. "Am I the only one who doesn't hate Carina?" one of them asked in response.

J. posted her video about Carina on YouTube and told other students, including Carina, about it. The video got about ninety hits overnight, and kids were talking about it the next morning at school. Carina came in with her mother and, crying, showed it to a counselor. The school suspended J. for two days for making and posting the video. Her father, a Los Angeles lawyer, sued. "What incensed me was that these people were going to suspend my daughter for something that happened outside of school," he told the *New York Times*.

Kara Kowalski brought the same kind of lawsuit in West Virginia. As a senior, Kara created a page on MySpace called "S.A.S.H.," with the subheading "No No Herpes, We Don't Want No Herpes." She invited a hundred of her MySpace friends to join the page, and about two dozen did. "S.A.S.H." apparently stood for "Students Against Shay's Herpes," and Shay was the name of a girl at Kara's school. A classmate, Ray, posted a photo of himself and a friend holding their noses, with a sign that read "Shay Has Herpes." Kowalski wrote back to him, "You are soo funny!=)" Ray added two more pictures of Shay. In one, he drew red dots on her face and added a sign in front of her pelvis that read "Warning: Enter at your own risk." The second photo showed Shay's face with the caption "Portrait of a whore."

A few hours later, Shay's father called Ray to express his fury over the MySpace page, and Ray called Kara. She tried to take down the page and the photos but couldn't figure out how. In the morning, Shay and her parents went to the school and showed the principal "S.A.S.H." on her computer. Humiliated, Shay skipped her classes that day.

The principal questioned Kara and, when she admitted what she'd done, decided that she'd violated the school's policy against harassment, bullying, and intimidation. Kara was suspended for ten days; when her parents protested, the suspension was cut in half. Kara also was kicked off the cheerleading squad and stripped of the privilege of crowning the school's next Queen of Charm, which she otherwise would have had because, implausible as it sounds, *she* was the outgoing queen. Her parents filed suit in her name.

In Kara's lawsuit, just as in J.'s, the girls' lawyers argued that their suspensions violated their First Amendment free speech rights. Legally speaking, the two cases are virtually identical: they are about whether schools may discipline students for cruel speech expressed online, outside school. Yet the judges who decided these cases reached opposing conclusions.

The U.S. Court of Appeals for the Fourth Circuit treated Kara's MySpace page in the same way it would have treated a note passed at school. "Kowalski indeed pushed her computer's keys in her home, but she knew that the electronic response would be, as it in fact was, published beyond her home and could reasonably be expected to reach the school or impact the school environment," Judge Paul V. Niemeyer wrote for the majority. A MySpace page mocking a fellow student's herpes, the judge continued, "is not the conduct and speech that our educational system is required to tolerate."

That sentence jumped out at me when I read it. Why did Niemeyer think the *school* had to "tolerate" Kara's MySpace page at all? Kara had been at home when she'd written it, so how exactly did the school have to countenance her misconduct? Couldn't the principal have told Shay's parents that while she was sorry about what had happened, and would bring in Kara and her parents to discuss it, she didn't have the authority to punish students for what they did online any more than she had the authority to punish them for what they did at the movies or on the beach? And yet to Judge Niemeyer, it didn't matter where Kara was when she set up the vile MySpace page. The fact that she used it to insult another student established a connection to school—a connection strong enough to justify the principal's decision to suspend her. But would Niemeyer have said the same thing if Kara had yelled that Shay had herpes while walking by her on the street?

Probably not. Once the Fourth Circuit decided to treat Kara's speech as if it had happened in school, however, the judges applied the rule in *Tinker*—schools can discipline when speech causes a substantial disruption, or when officials can reasonably forecast that it will. The disruption, Niemeyer said, was the "targeted, defamatory" MySpace page, and the "potential for continuing and more serious harassment of Shay N. as well as other students." This hadn't actually happened, but it could have. And that was enough. Perhaps Niemeyer let his underlying feelings about the case show when he chided Kara for suing in the first place: "Rather than respond constructively to the school's efforts to bring order and provide a lesson following the incident, Kowalski has rejected those efforts and sued school authorities for damages and other relief. Regretfully, she yet fails to see that such harassment and bullying is inappropriate and hurtful and that it must be taken seriously by school administrators."

Judge Stephen V. Wilson, who heard J.'s case, agreed with the Fourth Circuit that schools can discipline students for rude online posts. But he didn't think J.'s YouTube video created a substantial disturbance. To him, it wasn't enough that Carina had missed part of a class while crying in the counselor's office, and it also wasn't enough for school officials to say that at the time, they thought a larger disruption was reasonably possible. The school, in Wilson's view, had to show "something more than the ordinary personality conflicts among middle school students that may leave one student feeling hurt or insecure."

This is quite different from Judge Niemeyer's approach. Wilson took the expansive pronouncement of *Tinker* at its word—students have a right to free speech unless that speech substantially disrupts the workings of their school. First Amendment advocates celebrated his ruling because it served to limit the scope of schools' authority over what students say off campus. The idea that there should be such a limit seems right: otherwise school officials could become Big Brother, peering over students' shoulders wherever they go. But when you stop to think about the reasoning that Wilson used to arrive at the limit he set for schools' authority, it starts to seem strange. Schools punish students all the time for making other students feel insecure or hurt. Was the problem really that Carina wasn't upset and disruptive enough to justify J.'s suspension? Or was it that J. made and uploaded her video outside school? And yet the off-campus nature of the video wasn't the basis of Judge Wilson's decision to erase J.'s suspension from her record. Instead of treating cyberspace as a zone that schools may not police, he lifted her punishment by minimizing her meanness.

It's not clear which judge's interpretation will ultimately win out—or whether another approach will trump both of them. Kara Kowalski appealed to the Supreme Court, but the justices declined to hear her case, so for a while at least, the free speech questions she raised will remain unsettled. In comparing Niemeyer's and Wilson's rulings, I kept thinking about how I'd feel if one of my sons was a classmate of J.'s or Kara's, or one of their victims. Would I want to leave their punishment up to their parents? Or would I want them to face some kind of official sanction at school? It seemed to me that once other kids, and parents, found out about an online attack on a student, I would want the school to do *something*—to help the rest of us reckon with what happened.

But allowing schools to suspend kids for cyberbullying is a step down the slippery slope of allowing them to punish any online speech they deem undesirable. The First Amendment doesn't distinguish between insults and other kinds of free expression. As Judge D. Brooks Smith of the U.S. Court of Appeals for the Third Circuit wrote in another case about the free speech rights of students off-campus:

> *Suppose a high school student, while at home after school hours, were to write a blog entry defending gay marriage. Suppose further that several of the student's classmates got wind of the entry, took issue with it, and caused a significant disturbance at school. While the school could clearly punish the students who acted disruptively, if* Tinker *were held to apply to off-campus speech, the school could also punish the student whose blog entry brought about the disruption. That cannot be, nor is it, the law.*

So where does this leave us—what about that reckoning? I'd argue for punishment other than the tired old penalty of suspension. Sending kids home is a knee-jerk response, and that's about all it has going for it. (As Donna Lieberman, executive director of the New York Civil Liberties Union, put it to me, "Instead of solving problems, it just temporarily gets rid of kids.") Taking away a privilege, as Kara's school did when it barred her from cheerleading, seems far more meaningful.

This is where Facebook comes in, or could. In light of how many teenagers dread being blocked from the site, what if Facebook figured out a way to work with schools to suspend a student account, based on a joint investigation by the site and the school administration? If this was possible, it could solve the free speech problem the courts are grappling with. Facebook, after all, has clear authority to enforce its anti-bullying policy, and it's the place where as many as a million teens, each year, are being harassed.

The idea that social networking sites should work more closely with schools may sound impossible, but it's already being done. MySpace (though it has too little market share to matter much anymore) has a hotline and an email drop box for school administrators— a special address they can use to alert the site to problems. When I mentioned the email drop box idea to Nicky Colaco at Facebook, she dismissed it, saying this was simply out of the question. "Remember," she told me, "we're all over the world, in every time zone. The scale is huge."

The scale was indeed huge, but that didn't explain why Facebook had never so much as tested an email drop box with a small group of American schools. For many people I'd talked to who work with kids, this was a no-brainer. "We know things about what's going on with the kids that they don't know," the Middletown Youth Services director, Justin Carbonella, said. "If they wanted to, they could really help us help the kids."

Surely Arturo Bejar would have agreed that there are adults in kids' lives who are well positioned to help them with their online problems—that was the rationale he'd given for Facebook's social reporting tool. Yet in the course of my day at the company's headquarters, I encountered resistance to the notion that such adults could reliably be found at schools. "In our experience, principals have said untrue things," Willner told me. When I asked how often this happened, he said it wasn't the norm, but he didn't want to take down posts based on a principal's say-so. I'd gotten used to hearing parents and school staff vent about Facebook. Now I could see that to a degree, the suspicion was mutual. No one from the world of schools had a seat at the Facebook table. The company did have a Safety Advisory Board, consisting of five nonprofit organizations, but none of the groups was led by educators or even worked directly with schools. Colaco insisted that the lack of educators in Facebook's inner circles didn't matter. "We know what schools want," she told me.

Coincidentally or not, a few weeks after my visit, Colaco did ask thirty schools to sign up to test an email drop box for reporting cyberbullying and other time-sensitive problems. It was a start. A year later, however, Facebook hadn't expanded the pilot project, and it wasn't clear how much good it was doing. Carbonella, in fact, told me he'd sent an email one Thursday to the drop box with a long list of new disturbing voting pages, set up anonymously, with names like "Vote Heart," "Vote More," and "True Talk," and one page tied to an account with a real name, called "Chris Hollins Needs to Stop Making Stupid Groups." By the following Tuesday, Carbonella had heard nothing back, got fed up with waiting, and forwarded his note to the live email address of a Facebook staffer he'd managed to contact. In the end, it turned out that Facebook had taken down the anonymous pages without letting Carbonella know, but left up the "Stupid Groups" page. It was finally deleted after Carbonella emailed the Facebook staffer directly—after days in which Chris refused to go to class.

The more ambitious partnership I'm imagining would ask that Facebook truly share with schools—and parents—the burden that cyberbullying imposes. The site would own its power over kids and use it to make them reckon with their wrongdoing. Facebook profits from its teen users, so how crazy is it to ask the site to spend some of its social capital on helping the adults who work with teenagers? It seems to me a demand worth making.

Back at Facebook headquarters, I watched Nick Sullivan officially delete Middletown's old troublemaker, "Let's Start Drama," and then I moved to my next stop, a few feet across the aisle, and sat down with Charlotte Carnevale Willner, the twenty-seven-year-old head of Facebook's Safety team. (She is married to Dave Willner; they met in college.) I looked over Charlotte's shoulder as she scrolled through the profiles of kids who said they were thirteen or older when they signed up for Facebook but had since been reported for being underage.

Out of concern for children's privacy, Congress decreed in 1998 that without their parents' explicit permission, kids under the age of thirteen may not join an online service that collects, uses, or discloses personal data. The idea was that young children were particularly vulnerable to marketers, who were beginning to use the Web to pitch them products directly. Called the Children's Online Privacy Protection Act, or COPPA, the law aimed to "place parents in control over what information is collected from their young children online," as the Federal Trade Commission, which enforces COPPA, puts it. Some sites that attract lots of young children charge nominal fees by credit card; when parents agree to pay, they also give the site permission to collect personal information from their kids. Facebook doesn't offer a credit card option or any other way for parents to give permission to open accounts on the site. Instead, children under thirteen are simply barred from signing up.

Or rather, they're *supposed* to be. The reality is that despite the law and the site's rules, seven and a half million kids age twelve and under have Facebook accounts, according to *Consumer Reports.* COPPA doesn't force websites to patrol for underage users, however— the argument is that this level of enforcement isn't feasible. So when kids fib about their age and sign up, they can stay, unless someone reports them. Only when that happens is Facebook obligated to investigate.

Charlotte pulled up the profile of a girl named Hallie. Because I was sitting there, she wasn't in a rush, but normally she'd try to decide in a few seconds, based on her best guess about Hallie's age, whether her profile would stay up or come down. "To delete an account, we have to find *positive confirmation* that a child is too young," she explained. "It used to be that we'd take a parent's word for it, so if you reported your own child, we'd automatically take the account down. But then we found that sometimes parents would say their kid was underage, but really the girl would be fifteen. So we don't do that anymore." Charlotte turned her attention to Hallie's photo. "Hmm," she said. "She looks young, but it seems like she's gone through puberty. I mean, she's got boobs."

The boob check as age validation surprised me, but as Charlotte and I discussed, there wasn't much more to go on, and Hallie's profile stayed up. Another girl named Jenna was less lucky. "She liked *Diary of a Wimpy Kid*. She's a fan of Justin Bieber and *High School Musical 3*. Plus *Toy Story*. Plus she has baby cheeks. Okay, I'm deleting her." A third girl named Zoe had been reported for being underage by a man who shared her last name. Charlotte clicked on his page. "He doesn't look old enough to be her father. Maybe he's her older brother?" She clicked back to Zoe. "She doesn't look underage. She has boobs." Charlotte clicked on a photo album on Zoe's page and scrolled through it. "And here she's shopping for a prom dress. She's been on the site for 913 days. She says she's in high school and here's a photo with five other people who look like high schoolers. She stays."

I told Charlotte that this all seemed so tricky and semi-arbitrary, not to mention time-consuming. "True," she said, "but this is the process. We do this all day. We do what COPPA tells us."

That doesn't mean they're happy about it. Mark Zuckerberg, in a speech at the NewSchools Summit in California, had inveighed against COPPA's demands a couple of months before my visit. "That will be a fight we take on at some point," he said. "My philosophy is that for education you need to start at a really, really young age."

What kind of education? Zuckerberg didn't say, and I couldn't find any research to support the argument that Facebook has educational benefits for young kids. There's a lively debate over the benefits of social media for teenagers—proponents point to the chance to connect with people of shared interests whom you wouldn't otherwise meet, which can especially help kids outside the mainstream, while critics worry about the harassment and the endless hours of screen time. But it doesn't much reach down to elementary school.

I asked about Zuckerberg's statement over lunch with Colaco and Joe Sullivan, Facebook's chief security officer. Sullivan, a genial father of three, is a former federal prosecutor who helped launch the Justice Department's first effort to crack down on computer hacking. He and Colaco couldn't cite any evidence of Facebook's educational benefits, either. Instead, they reframed the issue. Facebook wanted to challenge COPPA because it was bad for kids to lie about their age.

"We think the vast majority of our users under thirteen have lied, and if their parents don't know, there's a problem at home," Sullivan said. "My view is that we should find a way for those kids to tell the truth about their age and get their parents involved."

In fact, a national survey by the researcher danah boyd found that two-thirds of the time, underage kids with Facebook accounts had their parents' help in signing up. boyd argued that this means COPPA is failing: maybe most kids with accounts aren't lying to their parents, but they are still lying. I wasn't so sure this was a fatal flaw for the law. Kids have lied about their age for generations—to get into R-rated movies, to buy beer—without toppling the social order or obviating the need for age barriers. It seemed to me that COPPA didn't have to stop all parents and kids from ducking the rules to serve some purpose when parents want to enforce them. If your kid is begging for something you don't want him or her to have, "It's illegal" is a pretty good retort. And while plenty of kids under thirteen are on Facebook and the other sites like it, the majority of them are not: a 2011 Pew survey found that 45 percent of twelve-year-olds said they'd joined a social networking site, compared with 82 percent of thirteen-year-olds. The age barrier erected by COPPA still means something.

Nor do you have to be a Luddite to have reservations about social media for kids at a young age. As I mentioned in Chapter 1, research suggests that lots of texting and social networking is associated with social and emotional pitfalls for preteen girls, like having fewer good feelings about their friends and being nervous about going to school. The mean stuff that happens on Facebook and other sites is more often damaging for girls at a young age. I talked to a lot of high school and middle school students who saw things this way. "The more you do it, the smarter you get about it," a fourteen-year-old girl at Freedom Middle School outside Atlanta told me. "So there's less bullying on Facebook the older you get."

"In sixth and seventh grade, people would be like, 'What do you think of this person?' " a fifteen-year-old graduate of Freedom said. "In high school, we don't do that as much anymore. People don't let their true feelings out because they know it just stirs everything up."

But I didn't hear the same nuanced appreciation of how age relates to social networking during my day at Facebook. When I asked Sullivan and Colaco why preteens belonged on the site, they looked at me as if I was daft. "Because that's the way people communicate now," Colaco said. "It's like asking, ten years ago, 'Why do twelve-year-olds need cell phones?' Communication norms evolve."

"My daughter is nine," Sullivan added. "With her maturity level last year, she wasn't allowed to have any online accounts. But now I see a different level of maturity and comfort level."

"A nine-year-old creating a Facebook profile might not *need* to do it," Colaco said. "But they want to."

Lost in the conversation, somehow, was a basic premise of parenting: eight-year-olds and twelve-year-olds don't always get what they want when they want it, because sometimes parents decide they're better off without. COPPA isn't perfect, but it's a lot better than the alternative promoted too often by Silicon Valley, which is no protection at all for kids on the Web.

I made this argument in an article about Facebook and young teenagers in the *New York Times Magazine* a few months after my visit to the company. I wrote that while we don't really have a full picture of how joining Facebook affects young kids socially and emotionally, it *was* clear that Facebook wanted access to kids' lives in order to remain the giant of the social networking world—the place so many people, of so many ages, feel obliged to be. The younger the child, the greater the opportunity to build brand loyalty. And most crucially, signing up kids early got them in the habit of "sharing" with the big audiences that are at their small fingertips.

Here's how this works: the more people you're connected to on the site, and the more "likes" you post, the more Facebook hopes to profit in advertising revenue. If you like the page of a business, for example, "the story about you liking the page (including your name or profile photo) may be paired with the ad your friends see," Facebook has explained. The more friends, the more potential ad imprints. As Zuckerberg once put it in a rare moment of candor, "We help you share information, and when you do that, you're more engaged on the site, and then there are ads on the side of the page. The more you're sharing, the more—the model all just works out."

Facebook, of course, has taken serious heat for what it does with all the content its users share. In 2008, there was a big ruckus over a program called Beacon, which informed everyone on Facebook about what users did on other websites—the vacation plans they made on Travelocity, say, or the shoes they bought on Zappos—without their permission. Faced with a lawsuit for violating users' privacy, Facebook shut down Beacon and settled for $9.5 million. Then, in 2009, there was a fight over who owned users' information, and an overhaul that made all the posts of millions of adult users entirely public, unless they changed their privacy settings (by clicking through more than fifty privacy buttons presenting more than 170 options). Facebook responded by trying to make the privacy settings less onerous. When the company went public in 2012 and its stock price fell, Zuckerberg stressed the money coming in from the advertising that turns a "like" into a product endorsement. Facebook had just agreed, however, to pay $20 million to settle a lawsuit over the ads—and conceded that users should control how their "likes" are used. And yet over time, as my Slate colleague Farhad Manjoo has pointed out, "the very idea of making Facebook a more private place borders on the oxymoronic, a bit like expecting modesty at a strip club. . . . The only sure way to keep something private on Facebook is not to post it to Facebook. Mark Zuckerberg would never acknowledge this, but I think it will ultimately benefit both his site and its users if we adjusted our expectations about 'privacy' there. You should approach Facebook as cautiously as you would approach your open bedroom window."

Teenagers, of course, often don't heed this warning, since impulse control doesn't tend to be their great strength. Many of them have hundreds of Facebook friends: they tend to think it's rude to turn down a request, or they collect names as a marker of status. And on Facebook, the default setting for teenagers shares basic personal information (name, networks, photo) with the public, and posts with kids' Facebook friends *and also* the friends of those friends. Include friends of friends, and for many teenagers the circle widens to thousands of people. Given what we know about how teenagers are neurologically more prone than adults to take risks in front of an audience of peers, the degree of exposure many of them have on Facebook seems like a bad idea.

This is pretty obvious, and it's become standard for guidance counselors and other adults who work with kids to urge them to restrict access to their Facebook pages to their real-life friends, as the social workers in Middletown did. To change the default settings for teenagers would be easy, yet Facebook hasn't done it.

In fall 2011, the Federal Trade Commission, as part of its job of enforcing COPPA, proposed tightening its regulations. "Kids are often tech savvy but judgment poor," the FTC chairman pointed out. The suggested change would prevent sites from collecting the personal information, such as IP addresses, that data aggregators gather over time, via tracking tools such as cookies, and then sell it so companies can target their advertising based on a person's history of Web surfing and purchases. Cookies are even more prevalent on the most popular websites aimed at young kids than they are on the top sites for adults.

Facebook, not surprisingly, opposed the FTC's proposal. The company chose this moment to triple its spending on lobbying, form a political action committee, and hire former White House officials (Republicans and Democrats) to push its agenda in Washington. Before my *Times* article ran, I called Facebook for comment about COPPA and teen privacy, and I was directed to a new spokesperson who'd worked for years on Capitol Hill. She opened our first conversation this way: "I've been told we gave you more access than we've ever given a journalist, so I really hope this story is nice."

When she realized I wasn't writing a puff piece, the spokesperson berated me over a series of calls for daring to write critically about the company's approach to teenagers. She pushed two lines: Facebook was great for kids, and if it wasn't, Google was worse. She kept asking why I was singling Facebook out, never mind that her company had the social networking site with twenty million kids. I wondered how this could seem like a smart PR strategy. I told friends I felt like I was being bullied. I was only half joking.

A month or so later, the Federal Trade Commission announced a settlement with Facebook over a variety of charges that the company deceived consumers "by telling them they could keep their information on Facebook private, and then repeatedly allowing it to be shared and made public." The company promised to set up new internal controls and submit to a privacy audit by independent experts every two years. In a post on Facebook's corporate blog, Mark Zuckerberg admitted to making "a bunch of mistakes" on privacy. He notably omitted any mention of teenagers.

Yet Facebook remains their principal online hangout, and so it's Zuckerberg's attitude toward kids that especially matters. My own sons will surely want to sign up soon enough.

As a parent, I wish I could conclude that Facebook gets it, that the company is ready to forgo some short-term profits for the sake of safeguarding the privacy and well-being of its young users. But I can't. Instead, I see it like this: When it comes to serious dangers that affect a small number of kids, like sexual predation and child pornography, Facebook *does* try to serve as an online guardian for kids. The site has put muscle into helping the police find runaways and into tracking child pornography. This is where doing good and doing well coincide—the company bids for parents' loyalty by trying to keep kids safe from dreaded (but rare) harms like predation. But the compact doesn't hold for lower-level, common risks. When it comes to the stuff that affects millions of kids, such as privacy and COPPA—where a hands-off approach drives profits—Facebook has been slow to shield kids or hasn't shielded them at all. Facebook's track record on bullying is a little better, but hardly perfect, as Middletown's experience with "Let's Start Drama" showed me. The company could still do much more to help schools prevent outbreaks of online meanness. And if Facebook stopped habituating kids to giving up their privacy, it would lower the chances that a misbegotten, humiliating post will go viral.

If the company made these changes—minor tweaks, really, considering its vast reach and resources—it could leave its own state of adolescence behind. But maybe it's naïve to imagine that Facebook will grow up on its own. The responsibility for making sure our kids use Facebook wisely is on us, the parents, too. When users have revolted over privacy breaches, or the government has demanded that Facebook do more to protect users' data, the company has snapped to it. Parents as well as teenagers have to ask for more from the site to get more. We have to be smart and careful about the Web. The Internet won't do it for us. The best thing we can do is help kids learn to look out for themselves.

The seniors at the Mary Louis Academy, a Catholic girls' school in Queens, New York, understand stealth marketing. In early spring, they hung a series of posters in the stairwells and hallways that featured only a mysterious "D." This started a buzz—*D* for what? What did it mean? A few days later, when the girls heard their younger schoolmates murmuring, they hung a second set of posters with the word "Deleted." Next they held an assembly where the students on the podium explained that for their end-of-year service project, they'd come up with the idea of holding a school-wide Delete Day. The seniors would take over the school's computer lab and help other students clean up their online personas. Everyone was welcome to stop by during lunch or a free period. No teachers would be looking over anyone's shoulder to spot an embarrassing post.

Leaving the stage, the girls wondered if anyone would come.

The idea for Delete Day originated with the students themselves. They brainstormed it during a workshop with a former Girl Scouts project manager named Alison Trachtman Hill, who works with schools through a group she founded called Critical Issues for Youth. When senior advisor and English teacher Ally Gutierrez picked up on the idea and sounded out school administrators about turning over the computer lab for a day, the powers that be were skeptical. "They said, 'Why would the kids want to do this?'" Gutierrez told me.

On the appointed Friday in May, the students in charge were still nervous about turnout. In the computer lab they put out cookies they'd baked (sugar and chocolate chip) and a basket of "Deleted!" pins. In big white bubble letters, one student decorated a long blackboard: "Pause B4 You Post: Delete!"

When I walked in, halfway through the morning, business was going strong. Two dozen tenth graders were tapping on keyboards while a smaller group of seniors roamed around with clipboards of deleting instructions, offering advice. Hill stood on the sidelines, beaming. "For me this is the Super Bowl," she said. "The girls had this idea and now they're leading it."

I leaned down to look at the screen of a fifteen-year-old who had her Facebook page open. "I have seven hundred and seventy friends," she said to the girl sitting next to her. "But I don't talk to seven hundred and seventy people!" She took several boys she didn't know off her friends list. Opening up a photo album, she scrolled through rows of shots until she got to a picture of herself leaning on a guy. "He's my friend," she said. "My *real* friend. But we're too close together." She deleted the photo.

Other girls took down vampy photos of themselves on their own pages and untagged themselves in photos posted elsewhere. They erased their phone numbers. They un-joined Facebook groups with names like "I'm a Woman of Dignity . . . LOL jk [laugh out loud, just kidding]," "Our Girls Are Hotter," and "Some Kids Want Drugs Some Kids Want Alcohol."

"Don't you feel so clean now?" one student asked another.

A couple of girls told me about an episode of major Facebook drama earlier in the year, involving some Mary Louis softball players and a rival team. One girl called the other team losers, the other side retorted, and the fight escalated until one player called out another by name as a slut. At which point, the Mary Louis athletic director found out and ordered the whole team to take the girls from the rival school off their friend lists. "Yeah, they were on it," another tenth grader said of the administration. The intervention worked: the fight died down and the two teams played a game against each other without incident.

At the end of the period, the tenth graders gathered their belongings, stopped off for cookies, and filed out. Another wave of students filled the lab. I sat down next to Camilla, a fifteen-year-old with blue mascara, and asked if I could watch her delete. She opened Form-spring, the social networking site I'd heard so much about at Freedom Middle School, and scrolled through the questions and comments on her page:

do you hate me??? i hate u
go kill yourself. u shld we all hope u do
your so ugly i hate you you dumb fatassbitch
ur like 15 stop being a little slut nd maybe guys would want u

"At first when I signed up, I had people telling me I was nice and smart, and that felt good," Camilla said. "But after I got my first boy-friend, it got bad. Girls were jealous. It got really hard to take." Ca-milla didn't know who was writing the cruel posts about her or who else could see them, and that made her feel worse. "If I could have blocked them, I didn't know how."

Camilla asked a girl named Jocelyn, one of the seniors walking around the room, to show her how to disable her Formspring account. While I looked over their shoulders, they tried to figure out how to shut it down permanently, but couldn't. Instead, they changed the password and hid the page from other users. "The consensus is that Facebook is sometimes good and sometimes mean, but that Form-spring is all mean," Hill said.

"Also cowardly," Jocelyn added.

The students' exit poll for Delete Day showed that about 250 girls participated, out of a school of 700 or so. Forty-four took themselves off Formspring and nine shut down their Facebook accounts.

The girls had spoken. Yet when Hill reported on Delete Day to a Listserv of experts, some seemed unwilling to believe that teenagers would conclude on their own that Formspring was a bad place to be.

"Are they reflecting a perception of the adults around them (or of news coverage in their area)?" asked Anne Collier of a nonprofit called ConnectSafely, which receives funding from Facebook, Yahoo!, and Google, and has a seat on Facebook's Safety Advisory Board.

Hill explained that the idea to delete Formspring pages came from the students themselves, who'd said the pages "transmit and disseminate hate, drama, and mean-spiritedness and that they felt there was nothing good that came from them."

Still, Collier remained puzzled: "It's just another site, granted w/ a special format, but lots of sites have their own unique features, none of which I'm sure u agree are in themselves bad for teenagers. Seems to me it's always what we make of them, and the 'we' includes teens."

To me, this sounded like the Internet equivalent of "Guns don't kill people, people do." Sometimes a weapon is just that, and the best thing to do is to help kids stay away from it. Sure, if Formspring disappeared—and given how fast the Web moves, it may well be on its way out the door—another site offering anonymity could take its place. But you deal with the situation in front of you. As Delete Day shows, in the right circumstances kids can see for themselves that they're better off opting out of a bad choice. The leaders among them can even use the influence they have over other teenagers—an influence that often goes down easier than the kind adults have—to do good.

The girls at Mary Louis Academy understood this. "If everybody does it, peer pressure really works the other way—for the better," one senior said. She and her classmates wrote this pledge for Delete Day:

D

*I, _____, am a woman of dignity at The Mary
Louis Academy, and I
pledge to become a responsible cyber-citizen.
As Gandhi once said,
"My life is my message."
I pledge to:*

1. Delete personal information that is dangerous in public.
2. Delete unknown "friends."
3. Delete inappropriate comments and pictures.
4. Delete formspring pages.
5. Delete hurtful or offensive groups.
6. Create an email address that is suitable for a college-bound young woman.
7. Encourage my friends to Delete!

These girls weren't about to renounce their Internet citizenship. They were regular teenagers and they would keep living in both the real world and the virtual one. They'd figured out, though, that they could make their own rules, to the benefit of both.

Part IV

What Next?

Conclusion

As I was finishing writing this book, I came upon a study that a federal agency commissioned on media coverage of bullying. The research showed that news outlets frequently give no useful information about how to prevent bullying, even as they call it "epidemic"—false—and portray it as the biggest problem kids face today—also false.

The misperceptions aren't surprising, because in the two and a half years I spent writing about the topic, bullying has become an ever more powerful cultural preoccupation. We've recently debated the fairness of a thirty-day jail sentence for Dharun Ravi, who invaded the privacy of his Rutgers roommate Tyler Clementi by spying on him with a webcam, and the significance of an episode in Mitt Romney's prep school past, when he pinned down a younger boy (who later came out as gay) and cut off his bleached-blond hair, even as the student's eyes filled with tears.

Bullying is pressing in on us partly because the rise of the Internet forced us to see it up close, in printouts or screen shots or video clips, and partly because of the stubborn nature of the problem, across cultures and centuries. And it merits serious and sustained attention, because awareness is the first step to preventing bullying and to helping kids through it.

But—and this is a big caveat—we need to be smart in our choice of strategies. That starts with taking care not to over-diagnose the problem. We have to separate bullying from teenage conflict that is not actually bullying—from drama.

The old problem was that adults were too prone to look the other way when powerful kids turned on weaker ones. This, of course, still happens, but we also have a new trap to watch out for: being *too* quick to slap the label of bully onto some kids and the label of victim onto others. It's a kind of crying wolf, and it does damage. For one thing, calling every mean comment or hallway clash bullying breeds cynicism and sucks precious resources from the kids who need our help. For another, it turns a manageable problem into an overwhelming one.

The Swedish psychologist Dan Olweus gave us a useful definition for bullying forty years ago: verbal or physical harassment that occurs repeatedly over time and involves an imbalance of power. It's a definition with clear boundaries. Olweus found that 15 percent of elementary and middle school students were persistently caught up in bullying, as bullies, henchmen, or whipping boys, as he put it. The numbers may be slightly higher in the United States today, but not by much. Research consistently shows that 75 to 90 percent of kids don't bully at all or with any regularity—and we should keep that statistic front and center, because good research tells us that when kids understand that cruelty isn't the norm, they're less likely to be cruel themselves. On the other hand, mutual aggression, with no clear victim or perpetrator, *is* common. Kids recognize this when they use the word *drama* to describe their conflicts, and we should pay attention to what they're telling us. We also should rethink some of the many legal definitions of bullying, which run from vague language about causing harm, to creating a hostile environment, to interfering with learning, to no definition at all.

Applying the bullying label carefully and sparingly is crucial because of the stigma it carries for kids, and also because accusations can often be harder to sort out than they first appear. It sounds crazy, but if I've learned anything in my reporting, it's that trying to get to the bottom of a bullying report can be as difficult as investigating a crime. There are conflicting accounts, full of he saids and she saids. There are teenagers with competing interests, which means there are problems of reliability. Is the target denying what's happening because she doesn't want to alienate the few friends she has? Or is she exaggerating in a bid for sympathy? Are witnesses denying an account of bullying because they don't want to be seen as snitches, or because it really didn't happen? If you're lucky, you find physical evidence that helps you get to the bottom of these questions, such as a text message or a threatening Facebook thread. But often that's lacking, and sometimes it proves misleading—only a tiny piece of a larger, complex puzzle.

These stories, in other words, are enormously hard to untangle. That can be infuriating for targets and their families; it can also leave a cloud of suspicion around accused bullies that, in some cases, leads to unjust punishment—the out-of-court version of a wrongful conviction.

I can't stress enough that it's imperative to gather information before reaching conclusions, and then gather some more. I didn't really know what had happened to Monique, Jacob, or Phoebe until I'd immersed myself in their lives and communities, until I'd talked to people on all sides of each controversy and sifted through the documentary evidence. And even still, I can't resolve every factual dispute in these accounts. Now imagine being the principal of a school with hundreds or thousands of students, and trying to investigate accusations of bullying day in and day out.

It's especially important that we resist the rush to judgment when a story about bullying goes viral. Often, widely circulated facts end up melting away upon closer examination. In the initial reports about the shootings at Columbine, for example, the teenage killers were portrayed as bullied outcasts who'd opened fire to exact revenge on the jocks and popular kids who'd tormented them. This proved false. In 2007, when a senior at Virginia Tech named Seung-Hui Cho shot and killed thirty-two people on campus as well as himself, early reports claimed that he, too, was responding to a culture of bullying. False again. In the days after the 2010 suicide of Rutgers freshman Tyler Clementi, it seemed indisputable that he'd jumped from the George Washington Bridge because his roommate Dharun Ravi had humiliated him by filming his first sexual encounter with a man via webcam, outing him as gay. It turned out that Clementi had already come out before the spying took place. And while he was bothered enough by the incident to ask for a new roommate, we just don't know how much Ravi's "colossal insensitivity," as the judge who sentenced him put it, factored into his roommate's decision to jump. In the documentary *Bully,* released by the Weinstein Company in 2012, the suicide of a seventeen-year-old from Georgia named Tyler Long was portrayed as if bullying were its only cause. You'd never know from the film that Tyler had been diagnosed with Asperger's, which is linked to suicide. Or that his suicide note mentioned neither bullying nor school. Or that his family brought a $1.7 million lawsuit against his school, blaming the principal and other officials for his death, which was later thrown out of court. The examples of error and omission and distortion are seemingly endless.

At the heart of each of these disturbing stories were teenagers with troubles that included, in the cases of Dylan Klebold at Columbine, Seung-Hui Cho, and Tyler Long, serious mental illness. Yet in every instance, that essential underlying fact—despite all its explanatory power—was shunted offstage, and bullying was pushed front and center. Once the press and many online commenters looked at these cases through the lens of bullying, they could no longer see the larger truths it obscured.

It's wrong to fault parents, especially the parents of a child who has died, for any of this. They are reeling from grief and desperately searching for answers. The accuracy of the media is not, and should not be, their job. And sometimes, of course, the cruelty of schoolmates and the indifference of school officials *does* contribute to a distraught teenager's decision that life is no longer worth living. As a causal explanation of first resort, however, the seductive narrative of the "bullycide" is dangerous. It romanticizes victims in a way that can beckon other teens to follow them and it treats suicide as a normal response to bullying, rather than a reaction that's extremely rare. By all means, let's be gentle with the parents of these kids, as Michele Dauber of Stanford cautions, but at the same time, let's be tough on anyone with a megaphone who is prone to sensationalize and oversimplify their lives.

I also want to point out that while bullying prevention programs have their place, they aren't the only—or even in some cases the primary—intervention kids need. Before we started using the term *bullying* indiscriminately, we framed some of the taunting and violence kids experience in other more specific ways. Think about how the concept of sexual harassment moved from the workplace to schools. In 1999, when a girl who was subject to crude taunting by a fellow student argued that this was sex discrimination, and the Supreme Court ruled in her favor, sexual harassment became a problem schools had to be alert to. *Bullying,* by contrast, is a term that "doesn't do anything to stop gender harassment and sexual violence," as education professor Lyn Mikel Brown has argued.

Most critically, bullying prevention, even done well, is no substitute for the more intensive services, or support groups, that a minority of kids need. That is the insight behind targeted programs such as Sue Swearer's in Nebraska, with its goal of helping families see the value of therapy for troubled kids. At Jacob's school, official support for a Gay-Straight Alliance—a proven buffer for LGBT students—could have gone a long way. (And yes, we need more GSAs in middle schools as well as high schools.) After Phoebe Prince took her own life, South Hadley High School probably would have been best served by a painfully honest discussion about how to make sure depressed or otherwise ill students get the help that most directly reduces the risk of suicide—mental health services. Because no one talked about Phoebe's psychological history, the story of her death turned into a morality tale about bullying, and suicide prevention didn't get enough attention. The town of South Hadley ended up with a set of flawed and vindictive criminal charges, a wave of fury directed at school administrators—and not much more.

By all means, we should respond when terrible things happen to teenagers. But let's choose the response that fits the facts, not our less rational fears.

We also have to reset our response to bullying by affirming that parents, alongside schools, are responsible for leading the sustained effort to solve this problem. I worry about our tendency not just to ask schools to stop bullying but to point the finger at them and demand it. Much of the time, these orders are issued without the money or resources needed to carry them out.

I'm not excusing schools for brushing off instances of bullying—the stories in this book bear witness to how devastating that lack of vigilance can be. But we need to reckon with the magnitude of what we're asking of schools: to succeed where some parents have failed, to remake our kids' characters along with their test scores. Schools are supposed to do all of this even as pop culture stokes conflict, real or trumped-up, on every kind of screen. Some of the teachers and kids I talked to connected the prevalence of in-person bullying and Facebook thuggery to the put-downs and posing that dominate shows such as *Jersey Shore* and *Real Housewives*. It's far too simple to say that *Jersey Shore* actually causes instances of teenage cruelty. And yet there's a kernel of uncomfortable truth here, and it holds for the fighting and power plays kids see among the adults they know, too. The point is that many factors influence self-development. The environment inside schools matters, but media culture, neighborhoods, and upbringing matter, too.

Parents, in particular, are central. It sounds so obvious, and yet one of the oddest parts of covering this subject has been seeing how often parents slip off the hook of responsibility. To frame it simplistically: when a story about bullying blows up, we demonize the kids who bully, we blame the schools where bullying takes place, and we give the parents a pass.

Generally I'm in favor of less parental guilt, not more, since I often feel we're collectively drowning in it: "My babysitter isn't Mary Poppins" guilt, "We eat too much sugar" guilt, "My kid quit the violin" guilt, "Frozen pizza again" guilt. But in the context of bullying, there is something strange going on. We are asking schools to referee conflicts that extend far beyond campus. We get wind of casual or deliberate cruelty, in the conversations we overhear our kids having with their friends, or the messages they send via the phones we've given them or the social media sites we've let them sign up for, and we're understandably freaked out. But our first move often isn't to take the phone away, or talk to each other, or ask the social media sites to police their users. Instead, we call the principal or the guidance counselor and ask *her* to please do something, right now.

Yes, good schools can do their part to reduce bullying by adopting one of the approaches to prevention that have been shown to work, some of which I've explored. (For more ideas, see the list of resources at the end of this book.) It's vital that we keep devoting resources to creating new curricula, to developing a field that's still young and searching for solutions. But we also have to remember that *schools can't solve the problem of bullying by themselves*. It's neither fair nor wise for us, as parents, to demand this of them.

We could, however, demand much more from the social media sites that are so eager to sign up our kids and encourage them to share, share, share. These companies are selling our kids' "likes" and habits to advertisers, and enticing all of us to give up more and more of our privacy. In exchange, the least they could do is to spend more than two seconds on abuse reports such as the ones about the nasty, fight-starting page "Let's Start Drama," which Facebook should have instantly deleted according to its own rules. These sites—Formspring, Twitter, Google+, too—should staff up so they can do more to help kids and parents deal with cyberbullying and harassment. They should invite in some of the administrators and counselors who are currently sweating over cyberinvestigations, and ask them how to make their jobs easier. These companies should stand with schools, instead of apart from them. Mark Zuckerberg likes to say Facebook is all about a "social mission," with the goal of strengthening "how people relate to each other." Here's a way to make good on that promise.

Most significant of all is our *own* role—our responsibility, as parents, for our children's well-being. And on that all-important front, we have to know how to engage with kids—and also how to leave them alone. In our understandable eagerness to fight bullying, we have to resist going too far and taking away kids' freedom. By all means, when a child is being tormented, she needs help. Psychic wounds can be as damaging, and as lasting, as physical ones. At the same time, kids have to learn to cope with emotional bruises in order to grow up. They have to learn to handle conflict, to stand up for themselves and their friends, to recover from rejection. They have to feel in their bones the deep power of resilience and the magnetic pull of empathy. They have to develop strong character. "We have a serious problem with parents' promoting the importance of happiness and achievement and demoting morality and character," Harvard psychologist Richard Weissbourd told me. "That wasn't true in other times in our history. We're organizing kids around their self-esteem. But maybe the primary goal should be that kids are good people, and maybe all the focus on their own happiness doesn't actually make them happier. If you're caring for others, you're forging good and durable relationships, and there is no better path to happiness than that."

And those are the ideas I'd like to leave you with: character and empathy. Most of the time, the old adage that adversity makes us stronger does hold true. We have to watch out for the kids whose internal makeup means they are the exceptions, but we also have to give the majority of teenagers the space to prove the rule. We have to be there for them, and we have to stand aside. We have to know when to swoop in and save them, and when they have to learn to save themselves. And we have to make tricky decisions about the gray area in between those two poles.

We also have to instill in kids the paramount value of kindness—to show them that it's more important to come together than to finish first, that other people's feelings can take precedence over one's own, that relationships can matter more than tasks.

These are tall mountains to climb—don't I know it. These days, we have to make decisions about how much freedom to give our kids on two planes: the physical and the virtual. I sometimes fear that parents go too far in confining kids' real-world exploration—and then do little or nothing to track their travels online. And so kids strike out on their own where they can, including on their phones and on the Internet. The researcher danah boyd told me that if you look at the patterns of social media use among teenagers around the globe, it's the kids who live in places where physical roaming is more restricted who tend to socialize the most online. Among the groups with more physical independence, more space, "there's a lot less idle chat," she said. "The more restrictions on kids' movements, on the other hand, the more they use the phone and the Web to hang out."

I'm sure you can tell by now that I am not in favor of trading in physical independence for social media obsession. It's not that Facebook or texting is bad for teenagers, full stop, or turns them into bullies. But the balance between how they spend their time and the way we oversee them is off. If you wouldn't let your kids out at night alone, why would you give them unfettered access to every corner of the Internet? If you understand that kids have to do some online exploration to get the hang of it, doesn't it also follow that they need to venture outside alone sometimes, too? Kids have to develop confidence and self-esteem. They have to build relationships, offline as well as on. We know all this, but sometimes we block them because we're trying to shield them.

My kids are thirteen and ten, and I'm never sure I'm getting any of this right. Lately I've taken to letting my older son walk or bike by himself to a friend's house—it's exactly six blocks away. I've also let him have limited email privacy while talking to him about what he's writing and to whom. (By limited, I mean that I promised not to read messages to a particular close friend if he asked me not to.) I'm feeling my way here like everyone else. But I am as concerned about doing too much as I am about doing too little because, as hard as it is to recognize this, my boys have to learn to fend for themselves. They have to figure out when it makes sense to push back against cruelty or to hold their own worst impulses in check. They have to figure out when to ask for help and when to intervene on behalf of someone who needs it. I can take every opportunity they give me to weigh in or coach from the sidelines, but I can't take them out of life's game.

That's why character and empathy are the qualities I care most about instilling in my children. To me, the effort to prevent bullying isn't primarily about punishment, and it's definitely not about some kumbaya dream of the perfect childhood. It's about learning how to make it through life's rough patches, and how to help other people through them, too. "Childhood is, or has been, or ought to be, the great original adventure, a tale of privation, courage, constant vigilance, danger, and sometimes calamity," Michael Chabon wrote in his book of essays *Manhood for Amateurs*. "For the most part the young adventurer sets forth equipped only with the fragmentary map—marked HERE THERE BE TYGERS and MEAN KID WITH AIR RIFLE—that he or she has been able to construct out of a patchwork of personal misfortune, bedtime reading, and the accumulated local lore of the neighborhood children."

I want my kids—all kids—to have the best map they can make and the fortitude to find their way.

Frequently Asked Questions About Bullying

ADVICE FOR KIDS

I'M NOT A THERAPIST, AND I DON'T RUN A PROGRAM OF ANY sort for kids. But I've had the chance to talk to a lot of smart people about the issues in this book, and I asked many of them what advice they'd give about bullying. In consultation with Dr. Susan Swearer, the University of Lincoln–Nebraska school psychologist whose work you know by now, I've distilled the wisdom I've gleaned from them, along with my own ideas, in the FAQ that follow.

Q: *What is the first step I should take if I'm being bullied?*
You have surely heard this before (at least eight times?) but if you are being bullied or harassed and you can't make it stop on your own or you're upset by it, talk to someone you trust.

If at all possible, choose an adult as well as someone your age. I know that can be hard, but I'm hoping that if you stop and think, there will be some adult you can safely turn to—a parent, a friend's parent, a teacher, a counselor. I'm with Arturo Bejar, the Facebook engineer, on this one: the people who are best equipped to help you are the ones who are close by and will understand the context for what is happening to you.

You might also look for a sympathetic youth group in your area—one for LGBT kids, maybe, or kids with disabilities, or a group that's based at a church or synagogue or mosque, or a suicide prevention effort. Or maybe you'll be lucky enough to find a mentor like Johnny Callas, Monique's boxing coach. The point is that many of us are one or two degrees removed from people who are prepared to help, if they understand what's happening and know how to find you. They may not be able to fix everything right away, or even in the near future, but having allies and someone to talk with is crucial. And for immediate hope and inspiration, you might also want to check out Dan Savage's It Gets Better Project, or Lady Gaga's Born This Way Foundation, or make a video for one of those yourself (Marina, one of the kids you met in Chapter 2, has a great one, which you can find in the list of resources at the back of this book).

Q: *What can I do if I'm being harassed online?*
First off, you can ask the website to take down any content that violates its rules, as many harassing posts do. If that site happens to be Facebook, report the abuse yourself and they will take your word for it that you're being bullied, they told me. You can also take Facebook up on its helpful invitation to forward the mean content to an adult you can trust. Print out mean content so you have a record of it, or take a screen shot. Even if you feel like you'd rather make it go away by deleting

it, if you want help dealing with it, you need to show other people what's happening. It's usually better not to get into a back-and-forth with someone who is bullying you—it's almost never a good idea to reply to a harassing post. What seems like the perfect retort can end up backfiring. If you find yourself obsessively checking back to look for follow-up posts, try taking a break. And if you are having continuing trouble on a social networking site, you might be better off dropping out for a bit. You can always go back when things have calmed down. Plus, your good friends will know how to reach you by phone or by getting together. You don't need to be online to know who they are.

Q: What should I do if I see someone else being bullied?

If you see other kids being cruel, think about the steps you could realistically, and safely, take to stop it. You don't have to jump into the middle of a fight (though if you're up for that, don't let me stop you!), and you don't have to commit to befriending the person you're helping, either. Sometimes just sending a sympathetic text or asking someone in the hallway if they're okay is enough. If you can show empathy to someone who is vulnerable, in the moment or afterward, that can mean a lot. Most people appreciate just knowing that someone cares—even if it's someone they don't know very well.

Q: When should I go to an adult—my parents, a teacher, a counselor, or the principal? What about the police?

If you can trust your parents, you should talk to them early and often about bullying that you see or experience. Let them help you. Older siblings, like Jacob's sister, can also be a source of wisdom and protection. Don't let shame or embarrassment stop you. It's your family's job to have your back. If you're worried they may overreact, that's a legitimate fear, but it's one you may be able to talk through with them. If you really think your parents will make things worse, then try to think of someone else you could go to.

Talking to an adult at school is a little different. Teachers, counselors, and administrators don't have as much discretion as parents. In some states, they have to report bullying once they know about it. That can be good if your school has a solid system in place for dealing with this issue, but unfortunately, that's not always the case. When you talk to an adult at school, you want to have some confidence that your situation will improve. Sometimes you can help ensure that, by going to an adult you know is sensitive and sympathetic and by puzzling through with her what she could do that will make things better. I'd like to tell you not to worry about being labeled a snitch, but that's not always realistic. I will say, though, that you should never have to suffer in silence. If that's happening and you don't think anyone at school can help, try to find a person who is another degree removed who could. It's a big step to go to the police on your own—and again, if you can trust your parents, talk it through with them. But if you are worried about your safety or someone else's, or you have evidence of digital harassment, the police may have tools for helping you that other people don't.

Q: What do I do if I find myself tempted to bully someone else?
If you're a person who is caught up in a lot of drama, and you might be making other people unhappy—people who are weaker than you, physically or socially—take a good look at yourself. Do you really want to be like Heather and Lucy, the girls my friend Allie remembers, almost thirty years later, as the queen bees who humiliated her in eighth grade? You know the saying about walking a mile in someone else's shoes— how about trying that, just in your own mind? This doesn't

mean you have to beat yourself up, just that you can do better. Almost everyone on this earth has the capacity for empathy and for caring. Dig deep and find yours, and don't let go of it.

Q: What should I do if I think someone is hurting him- or herself because he or she is being bullied?

You should talk to an adult you think can help right away. Any hint that someone you know may be suicidal, or otherwise causing herself harm, is worth acting on. Don't ignore it and don't wait—this is one time when it's truly better to err on the side of caution. Don't leave the person alone. You can also call the National Suicide Prevention Lifeline, at 800-273-TALK. The bottom line is to get help from a psychologist, counselor, teacher, administrator, or any trusted adult.

FOR PARENTS

Q: If I think my child is being bullied, what should I do?

Start by asking a lot of questions. The facts behind an accusation of bullying can seem simple at first, but they're often maddeningly complex. What can seem like a one-way street—my child is being tormented! My child is being unjustly accused!—may in fact look more multidimensional once you understand the full context. Your job, of course, is to support your child. And sometimes it will be very clear that he or she is in the role of victim and needs your protection. Sometimes, however, the facts will prove more complicated, and you will learn that she is caught up in drama and has played an active role, rather than being simply at the mercy of bullying. The first step toward offering the most useful help is to make sure that you have a thorough understanding of what's going on. Many kids worry that their parents will overreact and the bullying will get worse. Start out by listening nonjudgmentally and trying to get the entire story. It's important to protect your child, but it's also important not to cry wolf. And if what's happening really is bullying, the more specific examples you can cite, the better for making your case.

Once you feel confident you have the whole picture, you should think about whether it makes sense to reach out to the parents of other kids who are involved. If you have reason to think they're part of the problem, or you don't know them at all, this may not be a wise course of action. But don't decide against it just because broaching the subject would be awkward. If you have reason to think the other parents involved are reasonable and trustworthy people, you may be able to work together for everyone's benefit. It's great to be able to model to your children how to resolve conflict in a healthy way. Of course, it would also be great if everyone was a reasonable human being and was able to work out conflict well; however, this isn't always the case. So you'll have to trust your instincts. Being able to talk openly with other parents depends on the relationship you have with them. Sometimes, especially if you're dealing with a difficult family, it makes sense to urge your child to extricate herself from a bad friendship. If she is close to someone who is making her feel rotten, maybe she needs to walk away.

You may also want to go to your child's principal, teacher, school psychologist, or guidance counselor for help. Remember that even legitimate complaints can boomerang if they're not carefully framed. (Alexa and Alycia McClain had a perfect right to publicly denounce the Middletown school board, but doing so made their lives difficult for a time and didn't help Monique as they'd hoped.) If school officials aren't responding the way you think they should, you may have to keep pushing. But remember they are people, too, with a heaping plate of responsibilities and duties, and the more you respect the role they play, the more likely they may be to sympathize. At least give them the benefit of the doubt for starters and save the frontal attack until you really feel you have no other choice.

Q: *Should I monitor my child's online posts? What about texts?*
Here's my next suggestion that's easy to say and hard to do: keep the lines of communication open. Show your kids they will be wise to rely on you by listening and thinking hard about how to handle the problems they bring you. About their lives online, maybe you'll want to follow Susan Swearer's approach and monitor your children's texts and social networking posts routinely and regularly from the start. After you feel comfortable that their online behavior is healthy, you can ease up. There is truth to the teachers' adage "Start out strict, because if you start out easy, it's hard to get stricter." Or you may decide on the "trust but verify" or "probable cause" approaches in Chapter 1—assume everything is okay, and check if you have reason to think otherwise.

Personally, I want to know what sites my kids are on and have their online passwords—not because I don't trust them or because I'm planning to look over everything they write, but because I want to help them learn the rules of this new virtual world they're entering. When they are older teenagers, maybe I'll move to the "faith and credit" model I described earlier in the book, and trust them to live out on their own the values my husband and I have tried to instill. After all, I can't expect them to turn over their Facebook passwords when they've made it to college.

Whatever level of monitoring you decide on as your kids grow up, you should make sure you talk to them early and often about your expectations for their online behavior. Don't assume they'll figure it out on their own—the Internet is a fast-paced, ever-changing world they'll need your help figuring out. Talk to other parents, check out the resources at the back of this book, read the stuff administrators or counselors send home from school, and do whatever else it takes to treat the Internet as a subject you're on top of. You don't need to know the latest text-speak, but you do have to understand the basic lay of the land: which sites they're active on, how they work, what kind of content can be found there. Don't laugh off how you don't understand YouTube webcams if your kid is posting videos online—take the time to figure out the basics. It can be intimidating if you're a technophobe, but it's not rocket science.

Q: What should I do about a teacher or a coach who is acting like a bully?

Start by documenting what's happening—you can keep a log. It's a good idea to get several concerned parents together—the idea of power in numbers. With evidence and allies, you can go to the principal or the athletic director and lay out what's happening. I also think you can help kids assert their own authority by reminding them that no one can make them feel inferior without their consent. (I'm stealing from Mae West here.) Kids also need to know how to distinguish between a not-so-good teacher or coach and one who is bullying or abusive.

FOR EDUCATORS

Q: How should I start to prevent bullying at my school?

The first step to addressing bullying is to get a handle on it. Do a survey—there's an online tool in the resource list that follows. Talk to your staff. Figure out your overall priorities for improving behavior and how bullying prevention fits in. Maybe this isn't your school's biggest problem. Maybe if you have the money and the bandwidth for one good intervention, your school population would benefit most from something else. What I like about PBIS, the approach to school reform that's the subject of Chapter 8, is that it begins with data analysis, for the purpose of informed diagnosis. You have to know what's wrong in order to know what solution to adopt. Once you're clear about that, pick one approach, or one set of coordinated programs, and stick with that. Reducing bullying is an ongoing annual, monthly, weekly, even daily commitment. Creating a healthy, positive school climate takes time, but it's worth it.

Q: *What methods should I avoid when dealing with bullies?*

Peer mediation has become a popular problem-solving strategy for schools, and in situations where kids are equally situated, it can work. But putting a victim and her bullies in a room together and asking them to make up doesn't recognize the power differential between them. Kids who bully are good at manipulating this kind of setting, often saying what adults want to hear in the moment and then retaliating later. The bottom line is that you want to make sure your intervention is well tailored to the particular situation you're dealing with.

It's also crucial not to ignore bullying when you see it. Don't turn a blind eye—kids will notice, and they'll often conclude that you're condoning bad behavior, or at least that it's not beyond the pale at your school. I like the Olweus slogan here: "If it's mean, intervene." That is not, however, the same thing as automatic punishment. Before you mete out discipline, you should make sure you have all the facts. But in the moment, if you see a child being cruel to another, speak up. That will send an important message and give you an opening to find out the context for what you saw. In fact, if you intervene when you see mean behavior, you can often circumvent and derail more serious bullying and aggression down the road—and it's obviously better to prevent bullying from happening in the first place.

It's also important to understand the complexity of bullying and the behaviors it entails. We do a disservice to kids if our only "interventions" are the simplistic and even unproductive responses of suspension and expulsion. Those punishments should never be the only response to bullying, and in fact should be reserved for times when you're really concerned about student safety. Many kids who bully others have their own familial and psychological problems. If you can help them get treatment, maybe you can help redirect them from a path of perpetual aggression and the negative outcomes associated with it.

Q: What do I do if parents and students approach me about cyberbullying? After all, this takes place out of school—are there limits on what I can and should do about it?

If kids and parents are coming to you for help with bullying and drama that's happening online, you may be tempted to send them to the police instead. They have authority to address this behavior under the harassment laws of most states, whereas in some places it's not entirely clear that you do. While the courts are sorting out the parameters of schools' authority over students' online and off-campus speech, however, one thing holds true: you can always bring kids and parents in for a talk. Maybe it doesn't make sense to punish kids for their online speech unless you can clearly trace the effects into school. But you can help kids see why they're hurting someone and understand the consequences of leaving behind a compromising digital record. Those are both worthwhile lessons. As for the cops, if you think the situation warrants the involvement of law enforcement and that they'll be helpful, you can involve them. But this should be a thought-through decision rather than a knee-jerk reaction because it can also trigger a response that's more heavy-handed than the misconduct calls for.

You can also work to prevent negative online behavior by having a solid digital citizenship program in place. Most schools have technology classes and a technology instructor. Work with that person to teach appropriate online and cell phone behavior. Start in elementary school so that students are prepared before they jump full throttle into their online worlds. I like the analogy of seat belts: the auto industry, prodded to action by safety advocates, has done an amazing job of convincing us to wear them, with national campaigns such as "Seat belts save lives." My kids never get into a car without buckling up. The reduction in drunk driving, which I've talked about, is another example. We can do the same thing to change this generation's thinking about bullying and harassment, online and off.

Resources for Readers

RESOURCES FOR STUDENTS

BOOKS

Blubber, by Judy Blume. When Linda, an overweight girl, gives a presentation about whales, the class begins to ostracize her. The instigator is Wendy, the class president. And when Jill disobeys her, she becomes the object of torment herself. This classic is perfect for eight- to twelve-year-olds.

Hate List, by Jennifer Brown. After Valerie's boyfriend Nick opens fire on their school cafeteria, she is implicated because she helped him create a "hate list," which he used to identify his targets. Valerie has to deal with her guilt about the shooting. A good book for teenagers.

Bully, by Judith Caseley. In this picture book, Mickey struggles to overcome a bully named Jack. Though his parents try to help, it is Mickey's own problem-solving strategy that enables him to befriend his oppressor. For young kids.

The Chocolate War, by Robert Cormier. At a private high school, a secret society, the Vigils, controls the students. When Jerry, the main character, defies the Vigils, he is seen as a hero—but also mercilessly bullied. Often taught in middle school.

Before I Die, by Jenny Downham. This book isn't about bullying—it's about a girl who is dying from cancer. But it's so heart-stoppingly good—beautifully written, brimming with empathy, and full of insight into the main characters' relationships with her parents and her friendships—that I have to recommend it. For teenagers.

Stinky Stern Forever, by Michelle Edwards. No one in the second grade likes Stinky because he is mean to all of the other kids. So when he dies in a car accident, his classmates have to figure out how to mourn someone who bullied them. Great for ages six to eight.

Hooway for Wodney Wat, by Helen Lester, illustrated by Lynn Munsinger. Rodney Rat is teased because he can't say his *r*'s properly. But when a bully joins the class, it's Rodney who becomes a hero, by standing up to her. For young kids.

Wonder, by R. J. Palacio. August Pullman has a serious birth defect that left his face misshapen. When he goes to school for the first time in fifth grade, he has to negotiate his classmates' hesitation and even disgust—and his own fears, too. An incredibly moving and closely observed portrait, filled with empathy and also wit. For nine to ninety (and a great audiobook).

Vintage Veronica, by Erica S. Perl. At fifteen, Veronica is "fashion-minded, fat, and friendless," as the author puts it. When two older girls she works with at a vintage clothing store convince her to spy on a socially awkward stock boy, Veronica finds herself in the middle of much more than a prank—and has to navigate the surprising dynamics that result. For teenagers.

Blue Boy, by Rakesh Satyal. The story of Kiran Sharma, a twelve-year-old Indian boy growing up in 1990s Cincinnati who is mocked for playing with dolls and choosing ballet over basketball—and then has a divine revelation. Frequently taught in high school; much food for thought for teenagers.

Loser, by Jerry Spinelli. The kid hero of this short novel, Donald Zinkoff, is not a cool kid. At field day, his slow running makes his team lose a big race. And then Donald overcomes his limitations and comes through for a friend—even if it doesn't turn out as he planned. A funny, empathetic, and accessible read for seven- to thirteen-year-olds.

Story of a Girl, by Sara Zarr. When sixteen-year-old Deanna Lambert is found in the backseat of a car with her brother's best friend, she becomes known as the "school slut." She struggles to overcome the damage to her reputation. For teenagers.

MOVIES AND VIDEOS

Bullied: Teen Stories from Generation PRX. Produced by two Hartford, Connecticut, teenagers for other teenagers, this audio show explores the stories of bullied students from Alaska to Connecticut. http://generation.prx .org/bullied.

Bully Dance. A ten-minute animated film with ideas for kids about dealing with bullies creatively. www.bullfrogfilms.com/catalog/bully.html.

DISconnected. An MTV original movie for teenagers, in which four young people get to know each other through a live-streaming website. One of them uses the anonymity of the Internet to criticize others and avoid harassment himself. www.mtv.com/shows/disconnected/series.jhtml.

It Gets Better is Dan Savage's YouTube project of encouragement for LGBT youth, with clips posted by more than forty thousand people, including many celebrities. An hour-long *It Gets Better* documentary, narrated by Savage, tells the stories of three LGBT kids as they struggle to find acceptance. http://www.itgetsbetter.org/ and http://www.thegavoice.com/blog /television/4210-mtv-highlights-it-gets-better-project-with-documentary.

The Karate Kid. The 1984 movie in which a master of martial arts teaches a bullied boy to stand up for himself, and not just by fighting. www .imdb.com/title/tt0087538.

Lady Gaga: Inside the Outside. An MTV documentary in which Lady Gaga speaks of her experience as a bullied high school student. www .mtv.com/shows/lady_gaga_inside_the_outside/series.jhtml.

Marina's Video: My Life Is No Place for Hate. In Chapter 2, you met Marina. Here is her moving video about being harassed, coming out, and the support she got from an Anti-Defamation League club at school. http:// www.youtube.com/watch?v=J7IvRuWXOfk.

Mean Girls. Tina Fey's classic and hilarious 2004 satire on the terrors of high school. www.imdb.com/title/tt0377092.

My Bodyguard. A sweet and earnest 1980 movie about being harassed as the new kid, and recruiting the scariest-seeming kid in school to help. www.imdb.com/title/tt0081207.

"Stand Up: Don't Stand for Homophobic Bullying." An excellent four-minute Irish public service announcement about two young men who are harassed after a group of boys discovers them holding hands. In the end, straight couples stand up and join hands with the bullied pair in solidarity. www.youtube.com/watch?v=lrJxqvalFxM.

ORGANIZATIONS AND PROGRAMS

The Anti-Defamation League, founded in 1913, works to combat anti-Semitism and other forms of bigotry, and helps form clubs in schools to prevent bullying and harassment. www.adl.org.·

Cometfire offers LGBT students in New York a space to talk about issues of sexuality, youth sexual confusion, and self-esteem. The group is a collaboration of PFLAG NYC and Manhattan's Jewish Community Center and LGBT Community Center. It's an example of the kind of youth group that can help if you're struggling with these issues. www.pflagnyc.org/support/cometfire.

Sources of Strength, founded in North Dakota, is a school- and community-based program that seeks to prevent suicide, violence, and substance abuse. Adult advisors work with peer leaders. www.sourcesofstrength.org.

Stop Bullying: Speak Up is Facebook's campaign against bullying. www.facebook.com/stopbullyingspeakup.

A Thin Line is MTV's campaign to stop the spread of digital abuse. www.athinline.org.

The Trevor Project provides crisis intervention and suicide prevention services to lesbian, gay, bisexual, transgender, and questioning youth. Services include 24/7 phone counseling and online support as well as work in schools. www.thetrevorproject.org.

RESOURCES FOR PARENTS

BOOKS

Girlfighting: Betrayal and Rejection Among Girls, by Lyn Mikel Brown. An informed, academic view of how girls hurt each other—and how our culture exaggerates this harm—by an education professor and activist. For parents and educators with the patience for academic prose.

Columbine, by Dave Cullen. The product of years of investigation into the 1999 suburban Colorado high school shooting, this groundbreaking work of reporting and thoughtful analysis deserves all the praise it has received. Cullen is especially sharp in writing about the psyches of the two shooters, Eric Harris and Dylan Klebold. An excellent read for everyone, teenagers included.

Hanging Out, Messing Around, and Geeking Out: Kids Living and Learning with New Media, by Mizoku Ito. A set of essays about growing up in the digital era, and how their access to the online world is changing kids. An ethnographic investigation, with twenty-three case studies, written accessibly.

The Blessing of a Skinned Knee, by Wendy Mogel. My favorite parenting guide: indispensable, practical advice for parents about how to raise kids to be resilient. This book is written largely for parents of young children; for parents of teenagers, Mogel followed up with more excellent advice in *The Blessing of a B Minus.*

Schoolgirls, by Peggy Orenstein. The author vividly describes the lives of a variety of girls from two different schools in California, weaving in research to explore why adolescents think the way they do.

You Can't Say You Can't Play, by Vivian Paley. In this short classic, a kindergarten teacher at the University of Chicago Laboratory School dissects social rejection among elementary school children. To combat it, she encourages students to say "You can't say you can't play"—and, best of all, tells us their reactions. A great read.

The Geeks Shall Inherit the Earth, by Alexandra Robbins. Mapping the social hierarchy of high school, from popular to outcast, this book follows seven kids with an eye to the qualities that make them stand apart and their journeys to self-awareness. Perceptive and well told.

Oddly Normal, by John Schwartz. A *New York Times* reporter's acutely felt memoir about raising his gay son, who tried to kill himself after coming out to his classmates at the age of thirteen. Especially insightful about the challenges of advocating for a child with unresponsive school officials.

Odd Girl Out, by Rachel Simmons. An award-winning, pioneering book about the social intricacies of girlhood. Simmons is especially good on the subtlety with which girls can undermine each other—and the strength they can offer through friendship. In an updated 2011 edition she offers ideas for coping with bullying in person and on the Internet.

Free-Range Kids: Giving Our Children the Freedom We Had Without Going Nuts with Worry, by Lenore Skenazy. A screed against helicopter parenting: With zest and vigor, the author argues that giving children more freedom at a relatively young age will teach them to be independent, and that's all to the good. A polemic that will especially appeal to like-minded parents.

Talking Back to Facebook: The Common Sense Guide to Raising Kids in the Digital Age, by James P. Steyer. The head of Common Sense Media argues for setting limits on kids' Internet use and other screen time. With helpful age-based guidelines.

How Children Succeed, by Paul Tough. The latest thinking on what it takes for children, rich and poor, to achieve in school and grow up to be productive adults. Excellent reporting and analysis.

The Parents We Mean to Be, by Richard Weissbourd. Strategies for raising moral and happy children, avoiding the extremes of too much or too little parental involvement. Persuasive emphasis on character development.

Queen Bees and Wannabes, by Rosalind Wiseman. The inspiration for the movie *Mean Girls,* this book cannily analyzes the social structure of "Girl World." Wiseman offers smart advice to both teenagers and adults. A classic of the genre. In *Queen Bee Moms & Kingpin Dads,* Wiseman extends her sharp analysis to the world of adults, offering advice about how to deal with conflicts with teachers, coaches, and difficult fellow parents.

MOVIES AND VIDEOS

Growing Up Online. A PBS Frontline production about digital risks and opportunities for kids. www.pbs.org/wgbh/pages/frontline/kidsonline.

I also recommend watching the movies and videos I listed above for teenagers and kids *with* them, or listening to books like *Wonder* on a long car ride. (My kids were mesmerized by that book.) It's a great way to start a conversation.

ORGANIZATIONS AND PROGRAMS

The American Foundation for Suicide Prevention is dedicated to decreasing the number of suicides across the country. AFSP funds scientific research related to suicide prevention, hosts programs for those who have been affected by suicide or are at risk, and educates the public about suicide prevention. www.afsp.org.

The Berkman Center for Internet and Society, at Harvard University, explores cyberspace, studying its development, dynamics, norms, and standards, and assessing when and whether laws and sanctions are needed. http://cyber.law.harvard.edu.

The Born This Way Foundation, created by pop star Lady Gaga, focuses on youth empowerment and equality by supporting programs that address bullying and crises of identity. http://bornthiswayfoundation.org.

The Center for Safe and Responsible Internet Use helps youth, families, and schools manage Internet use and online risk. http://csriu.org.

Common Sense Media advocates for kids in the world of media and technology. It offers reviews and advice for parents about movies, TV programming, and games and has a campaign called Stand Up to Cyberbullying. www.commonsensemedia.org/cyberbullying.

The Crimes Against Children Research Center at the University of New Hampshire conducts research on the problems of child victimization and maltreatment and family violence. www.unh.edu/ccrc.

The Cyberbullying Research Center provides information about the nature and consequences of online harassment and cruelty. The center's website functions as a clearinghouse for information about the use and misuse of technology, providing data, narratives, and resources to fight online aggression. www.cyberbullying.us.

The Family Acceptance Project at San Francisco State University does research, education, intervention, and policy work on behalf of LGBT youth. The project tries to alleviate the risks of suicide, substance abuse, HIV, and homelessness by working with teenagers and their families. With the goal of helping families from varied cultural backgrounds mitigate suicide risk, FAP has developed a series of multicultural, research-based materials offering "best practices" guidance for families of LGBT youth.

The Gracie Academy Bullyproof program uses martial arts as a form of self-defense. Instructors advise students to deal with conflict through dialogue and, if attacked, to use martial arts to gain control until help arrives. www.gracieacademy.com/bully_proof.asp.

SAVE (Suicide Awareness Voices of Education), which works to reduce suicide through public awareness and education, reduce stigma, and serve as a resource for those touched by suicide. www.save.org.

The Sikh Coalition is a community-based civil and human rights group that focuses particularly on ensuring that Sikhs can practice their faith freely while being part of their local communities. The group works to mitigate backlash violence, including bullying, against Sikhs, Arabs, Muslims, and South Asians. www.sikhcoalition.org.

The **Southern Poverty Law Center** has brought successful lawsuits on behalf of bullied students, including a recent case for LGBT students in the Anoka-Hennepin school district in Minnesota. It provides materials on teaching tolerance, including the documentary *Bullied* about Jamie Nabozny's lawsuit. www.splcenter.org.

Stopbullying.gov, a federal government website, has information and resources about bullying—who is at risk, and how to prevent and combat it—from government agencies including the Department of Education and the Department of Health and Human Services.

RESOURCES FOR EDUCATORS

BOOKS

Bullying Prevention and Intervention: Realistic Strategies for Schools, by Susan Swearer, Dorothy Espelage, and Scott Napolitano. Strategies for educators on how to deal with bullying from the ground up. A helpful guide for schools.

Schools Where Everyone Belongs, by Stan Davis. Guidelines for school-wide bullying prevention, drawing on the writer's decades of experience as a school counselor and consultant. Davis is one of the most thoughtful voices in the bullying prevention world, and this is full of ideas for educators.

Bullying in North American Schools, edited by Dorothy Espelage and Susan Swearer. Documenting bullying cultures in schools across the country, the authors synthesize research data and present adaptable programs for combating bullying.

Bullying Beyond the Schoolyard: Preventing and Responding to Cyberbullying, by Sameer Hinduja and Justin Patchin. Focusing on the Internet, the authors explain why it can invite and magnify bullying. Aimed at equipping teachers and parents to deal with online harassment of students.

Homophobic Bullying, by Ian Rivers. A theory of harassment based on sexual identity, drawing on psychology, sociology, anthropology, and ethology.

Classrooms and Courtrooms: Facing Sexual Harassment in K-12 Schools, by Nan Stein. Summaries of the key legal cases about sexual harassment, data from major surveys, and testimony from boys and girls about their experiences, good and bad, of turning to school authorities for help.

Cyberbullying and Cyberthreats: Responding to the Challenge of Online Social Aggression, Threats and Distress, written by Nancy Willard and edited by Karen Steiner. A detailed guide for dealing with varying forms of cyberbullying, with sample incident report forms, Internet use policies, and fact sheets.

MOVIES AND VIDEOS

Bullied: A Student, a School and a Case That Made History. A thoughtful documentary about Jamie Nabozny, the first student to successfully sue his school district over anti-gay harassment. Excellent for classroom discussions with middle school and high school students. www.tolerance.org/bullied.

It's Elementary. The film organization Groundspark offers practical ideas for how to talk with kids about gay people. http://groundspark.org.

Respect for All. Another Groundspark film, challenging stereotypes and helping students think about prejudice, bullying, and violence. http://groundspark.org.

Richardson High School Video. A short clip by an assistant principal in Dallas who talks about his experience with bullying as a teenager and his brush with suicide. www.dallasnews.com/video/bc/?bcid=1569859431001.

Stories of Us. An Australian project that has expanded to the United States, featuring unscripted films about bullying, made by students, for students.

ORGANIZATIONS AND PROGRAMS

Bully Busters is a step-by-step program for reducing bullying through the joint efforts of students, teachers, and parents. The organization has also developed a teen mentoring program. www.bully-busters.com.

Bullyproofing Your School, a program run in conjunction with the National Center for School Engagement, is designed to battle bullying through the creation of the "caring majority"—a group of students who ensure that their school is a safe place. www.schoolengagement.org/index.cfm/Bully%20Proof%20Your%20School.

The Committee for Children works to create safe environments for children. The organization has designed two curricula, Second Step and Steps to Respect, which aim to prevent bullying by strengthening the bonds between adults and children in schools. Research has shown that Steps to Respect can reduce the acceptance of bullying and aggression among participating students. (More in Chapter 7.) www.cfchildren.org.

Espelage Against Bullying, the website for Dorothy Espelage's research team, describes her projects and provides resources about prevention programs and related scholarship. www.espelageagainstbullying.com.

GLSEN, the Gay, Lesbian and Straight Education Network, works with schools and the public to educate about the dangers of homophobia, and to develop school climates in which diversity is celebrated. www.glsen.org.

H&H Publishing provides an online bully survey to help school personnel create data-based decision-making models for bullying prevention and intervention. www.hhpublishing.com/_assessments/BULLY-SURVEY/index.html.

KiVa is a research-based anti-bullying program developed in Finland. The program has a universal component that reaches all students at a school, as well as targeted interventions for students who bully or are victimized. www.kivakoulu.fi/there-is-no-bullying-in-kiva-school.

The Massachusetts Aggression Reduction Center at Bridgewater State University, run by Elizabeth Englander, conducts violence and bullying prevention programs and research for the state of Massachusetts. http://webhost.bridgew.edu/marc.

The Olweus Bullying Prevention Program, founded in Norway, works with schools on three levels—the campus, the classroom, and the individual. In the United States, the federally funded Blueprints for Violence Prevention assessed more than nine hundred programs for juveniles and chose Olweus as one of only a dozen proved to be effective, and the only program specifically directed at bullying. (More in Chapter 7.) www.violencepreventionworks.org/public/index.page.

Peaceful Schools aims to stop school violence by training students and adults in mediation and conflict resolution. www.backoffbully.com.

Positive Behavioral Interventions and Supports (PBIS) is a framework for improving school discipline. Research has shown that PBIS can reduce the rate of office referrals, suspensions and expulsions, and bullying. (More in Chapter 8.) www.pbis.org.

Roots of Empathy is a Canadian program that brings babies into classrooms, with their parents, to teach kids about infant development and caring for others. Students who have participated have shown less aggressive behavior, more acts of kindness, and better understanding of babies and their emotions. www.rootsofempathy.org.

The Suicide Prevention Resource Center offers training, materials, and other assistance to suicide prevention practitioners and others in the field. The center helps college and university staffs, health care providers, and professionals in social services with technical assistance, toolkits, and research summaries. www.sprc.org.

Target Bullying: Best Practices in Bullying Prevention and Intervention, the website for Susan Swearer's research team, provides resources and suggestions to help school personnel think about best practices in bullying prevention and intervention. http://targetbully.com.

The Youth Voice Project asks students about their perceptions of the best strategies for reducing bullying and harassment in school. More than thirteen thousand teenagers in thirty-one schools have taken the Youth Voice Project survey; the goal is to use students' responses to determine the most helpful interventions. www.youthvoiceproject.com.

Cast of Characters

Middletown, Connecticut

Monique McClain: target of bullying at Woodrow Wilson Middle School

Alycia McClain: Monique's mother

Alexa McClain: Monique's grandmother

Destiny and Cheyenne: accused eighth-grade bullies

Gianna, Aminah, Jasmine, and Davina: accused seventh-grade bullies

Mohawk, New York

Jacob Lasher: target of bullying at Mohawk junior and senior high school

Robbie Lasher: Jacob's father

Penny Lasher: Jacob's mother

Tiffany Lasher: Jacob's sister

Alyssa: Jacob's friend

Aric Barnett: graduate of Mohawk who started a Gay-Straight Alliance

Aaron: accused bully

Kimberly and Tom: Aaron's parents

South Hadley, Massachusetts

Phoebe Prince: target of bullying who committed suicide

Jeremy Prince and Anne O'Brien: Phoebe's parents

Sean Mulveyhill, Ashley Longe, Kayla Narey, Sharon Chanon Velazquez, Flannery Mullins, Austin Renaud: students accused of harming Phoebe

Chris and James: friends of Phoebe

Destiny, Cheyenne, Gianna, Aminah, Jasmine, Davina, Alyssa, Aaron, Kimberly, Tom, Chris, and James are pseudonyms.

Acknowledgments

I'll never be able to say thank you enough to all the people who have helped me with this project. At Random House, I'm grateful to Susan Kamil for understanding this project from the start, and to Tom Perry, Karen Fink, Sonya Safro, Avideh Bashirrad, Erika Greber, Kelle Ruden, Benjamin Dreyer, Nancy Delia, Sue Warga, Amelia Zalcman, and Kaela Myers for all the ideas, excellent counsel, and support along the way. Andy Ward is the book editor who isn't supposed to exist anymore—incisive, patient, responsive, and exacting in the best way. Working with him has been a privilege and pleasure. Elyse Cheney is the perfect agent: She whipped this project into shape and guided me at every step.

I owe my excellent bosses at Slate, David Plotz and Jacob Weisberg, for their wisdom and friendship and for letting me spend countless hours in South Hadley. Thank you to everyone on the Slate staff—you are wonderful colleagues. John Dickerson and Hanna

Rosin are my collaborators and my rocks. At the *New York Times Magazine* and Slate, I've had the great good fortune to work with two incredibly talented and generous editors, Ilena Silverman and John Swansburg. I owe the high standards I may not meet, but still aim for, to Lincoln Caplan, who is the Best Mentor Ever.

I am indebted to Harold Koh and Robert Post for bringing me to Yale Law School, and to Alan and Louise Schwartz, and the Truman Capote Literary Trust, for supporting my work there. Judith Resnik, Denny Curtis, Linda Greenhouse, Reva Siegel, and Jack Balkin have made the law school feel like home.

Ariel Doctoroff, Marcelle Friedman, Katie Henderson, and Zara Kessler contributed skilled research assistance and excellent companionship to this project. Sarah Yager was the fact checker of my dreams, nerdy as that sounds. I'm grateful to Anne Fadiman for suggesting I report about the aftermath of Phoebe Prince's death in South Hadley, to Natalie Engdahl for translating from Swedish, and to Bill Brazell for digging around in his garage for old trial transcripts.

I've benefited from the help and advice of many experts along the way, and I am especially grateful to danah boyd, Elizabeth Englander, Dorothy Espelage, Robert Faris, Alison Trachtman Hill, Sameer Hinduja, Justin Patchin, Dan Olweus, Laurence Steinberg, George Sugai, and Nancy Willard. Thank you to Ta-Nehisi Coates, Dave Cullen, Charlie Duhigg, Jake Halpern, Jack Hitt, Ann Hulbert, Matt Labash, Steve Mufson, Mark Oppenheimer, Annie Paul, Rachel Simmons, and Emily Yoffe for collegial and critical chats. For essential help with reporting, I thank Johnny Callas, Justin Carbonella, Ally Gutierrez, Kajsa and David Heinemann, Chris Kraeuter, Hugh McDermott, Sean McElhaney, Lauren Moss, and Melissa Robinson. I salute Stefan Pryor, Emily Byrne, and John Flanders for getting Monique back to school. It was a group effort.

Thank you to my early readers, who made this book better with their sharp comments: James Forman, David Goldblum, Rachel Gross, Dan Ho, Alison MacKeen, Susan Swearer—who also offered invaluable expertise—and Richard Weissbourd. I feel like I owe all of New Haven for listening to me yammer on about this book, and I'm full of gratitude and wonder for the generosity of my friends: Darcy Chase, Julie Friedberg, Nathaniel Frank, Cori Schreiber, Kishwar Rizvi, Beverly Gage, Jenn Marlon, Myra Jones-Taylor, Leslie Stone, Paige MacLean, Sheila Hayre, Pericles Lewis, Alethea Desrosiers, Eliza Leighton, Erica Perl, Elizabeth Shreve, Julie Farkas, and Seth Goldman. I am grateful to Judge Richard Posner, Judge Frank Easterbrook, and Lee Epstein for inviting me to the University of Chicago law school to talk about student free speech. I want to thank all my thoughtful Slate readers for their comments and feedback, and I'm awestruck by the fans of the Slate Political Gabfest.

I am honored by the trust of the kids and families who are central to this book. Monique, Alexa, Alycia, Jacob, Penny, Tiffany, Robbie, Flannery and Jen—thank you for the invaluable gift of your stories.

My family puts up with me and makes me think and laugh, and I cherish them: My parents, Rick and Eileen, my sisters, Lara, Jill, Dana, their husbands, Matt, Joel, and David, and their delightful children, Harper, Trevor, Carter, and Ella. Bob Knox will always be part of our tribe. I am also wonderfully blessed in my husband's family: Margery, Jim, Michael, Debbie, Zack, Matt, and Elena.

Paul, thank you for your boundless love and support, and for laughing when I missed my train stop. You are the best choice I ever made. Eli and Simon, thank you for your love of adventure and sense of humor, and for not bullying anyone. My grandmother Mickey was alive at the birth of this book but isn't here for its publication. She told us that she would find a way to keep reading the *New York Times*, so maybe she can include these pages, too. Gamma, I miss you, and your memory will always be for me a blessing.

Notes

THE CHARACTERS YOU'LL READ ABOUT IN THESE PAGES ARE REAL people I met and talked to in reporting this book. To tell Monique's, Jacob's, and Flannery's stories, I've relied on school and court documents and dozens of interviews with the kids, their families and friends, the kids accused of bullying and their families, other parents and students, school officials, police, and lawyers. For the most part, I have been able to verify one person's account by checking it against other sources. I've found that it's imperative to talk to people on all sides of a conflict over bullying, and I've done my best to account for multiple perspectives.

For Chapters 7, 8, and 9, I visited Freedom Middle School, Old Mill Middle School, Irving Middle School, Mary Louis Academy, and the offices of Facebook. The schools let me talk freely to students, parents, teachers, guidance counselors, and administrators, and shared with me surveys and other data. Facebook let me talk to several staff members, whom I've quoted. I've also spoken extensively to the experts I've relied on throughout.

I have changed the names of many of the teenagers in this book (including in the Prologue) to protect their privacy, and in a few cases, for the same reason, the names of their parents.

Prologue

6 **the concept that children deserve** Karen Sánchez-Eppler, *Dependent States: The Child's Part in Nineteenth-Century American Culture* (Chicago: University of Chicago Press, 2005), xvii–xxi.

7 **"He bullied and punished me"** Charlotte Brontë, *Jane Eyre*, 2nd ed. (London: Smith, Elder, 1848), 7.

7 **"Very well then; let's roast him"** Thomas Hughes, *Tom Brown's School Days* (New York: Harper and Brothers, 1911), 176.

7 **" 'Hm!' she said. 'Country girls!' "** Laura Ingalls Wilder, *On the Banks of Plum Creek* (New York: HarperCollins, 2004), 148, 242–43.

8 **And then on April 20, 1999** Dave Cullen, *Columbine* (New York: Twelve, 2009).

8 **a subsequent nationwide investigation** Bryan Vossekuil et al., *The Final Report and Finding of the Safe School Initiative: Implications for the Prevention of School Attacks in the United States,* United States Secret Service and United States Department of Education, May 2002, 21, www.secretservice.gov/ntac/ssi_final_report.pdf.

9 **while child seductions and abductions** Janis Wolak et al., "Online 'Predators' and Their Victims: Myths, Realities and Implications for Prevention and Treatment," *American Psychologist* 63 (2008): 111–28.

9 **more time social networking** Victoria J. Rideout, Ulla G. Foehr, and Donald F. Roberts, *Generation M^2: Media in the Lives of 8- to 18-Year-Olds,* Kaiser Family Foundation, January 2010, www.kff.org/entmedia/upload/8010.pdf.

10 **ninety a day compared to** Amanda Lenhart, *Teens, Smartphones and Texting,* Pew Internet and American Life Project, March 19, 2012. www.pewinternet.org/~/media/Files/Reports/2012/PIP_Teens_Smart phones_and_Texting.pdf.

10 **as scare-mongering headlines** "Out of Nowhere Comes the Shadowy Cyberbully," *Brisbane Times,* September 27, 2007.

10 **bullying, wherever it takes place, isn't** Perhaps you've heard the statistic that 160,000 kids miss school every day because they've been bullied? It's not true. It came from the National Association of School Psychologists twenty years ago. "The statistic is extremely old and not valid in 2011," a spokesperson for the organization said. "It's one of those things that the media really loved and grabbed onto and took on a life of its own." See "Assemblywoman Valerie Vainieri Huttle Says 160,000 Students Stay Home from School Every Day Because They're Afraid of Being Bullied," *PolitiFact*, September 15, 2011, www.politifact.com/new-jersey/statements/2011/sep/15/valerie-vainieri-huttle/assemblywoman-valerie-vainieri-huttle-says-160000-.

11 **Before 1999, no states** Victoria Stuart-Cassel et al., "Analysis of State Bullying Laws and Policies," U.S. Department of Education (2011). The only state without an anti-bullying law currently is Montana. See Greg Toppo, "Should Bullies Be Treated As Criminals?" *USA Today*, June 12, 2012.

11 **bullying has been linked with** Tonja R. Nansel et al., "Bullying Behaviors Among U.S. Youth: Prevalence and Association with Psychosocial Adjustment," *Journal of the American Medical Association* 285 (April 25, 2001): 2094–100; Tonja R. Nansel et al., "Cross-National Consistency in the Relationship Between Bullying Behaviors and Psychosocial Adjustment," *Archives of Pediatrics and Adolescent Medicine* 158 (August 2004): 730–36; Kisha M. Radliff et al., "Illuminating the Relationship Between Bullying and Substance Use Among Middle and High School Youth," *Addictive Behaviors* 37 (April 2012): 569–72; Catherine Winsper et al., "Involvement in Bullying and Suicide-Related Behavior at 11 Years: A Prospective Birth Cohort Study," *Journal of the American Academy of Child and Adolescent Psychiatry* 51 (March 2012): 271–82; Jennifer S. Wong, *No Bullies Allowed: Understand Peer Victimization, the Impacts on Delinquency, and the Effectiveness of Prevention Programs*, RAND Corporation, 2009, www.rand.org/pubs/rgs_dissertations/2009/RAND_RGSD240.pdf.

12 **Rates have fallen for teen pregnancy** Kathryn Kost and Stanley Henshaw, *U.S. Teenage Pregnancies, Births and Abortions, 2008: National Trends by Age, Race and Ethnicity*, Guttmacher Institute, February 2012, www.guttmacher.org/pubs/USTPtrends08.pdf.

12 **smoking, alcohol abuse, drug abuse (except for marijuana)** Lloyd D. Johnson et al., *Monitoring the Future: National Results on Adoles-*

cent Drug Use: Overview of Key Findings, 2011, University of Michigan Institute for Social Research, 2012, www.monitoringthefuture .org/pubs/monographs/mtf-overview2011.pdf.

12 **drunk-driving fatalities** *2010 State of Drunk Driving Fatalities in America,* Century Council, 2012, www.centurycouncil.org/drunk-driving/materials.

12 **less likely to commit crimes** Juvenile Arrest Rate Trends, Office of Juvenile Justice and Delinquency Protection Statistical Briefing Book, October 16, 2011, www.ojjdp.gov/ojstatbb/crime/JAR_Display.asp?ID =qa05201.

12 **and to commit suicide** "Suicide Rates Among Persons Aged 15–19 Years—United States, 1981–2009," Centers for Disease Control Vital Statistics.

13 **Mass media campaigns have had** Randy W. Elder et al., "Effectiveness of Mass Media Campaigns for Reducing Drinking and Driving and Alcohol-Involved Crashes: A Systematic Review," *American Journal of Preventive Medicine* 27 (2004) 57–65.

13 **so have school-based programs** Randy W. Elder et al., "Effectiveness of School-Based Programs for Reducing Drinking and Driving and Riding with Drinking Drivers: A Systematic Review," *American Journal of Preventive Medicine* 28 (2005) 288–304.

13 **students often overestimate** H. Wesley Perkins and Alan D. Berkowitz, "Perceiving the Community Norms of Alcohol Use Among Students: Some Research Implications for Campus Alcohol Education Programming," *International Journal of the Addictions* 21 (1986): 961–76.

13 **And when kids understand** H. Wesley Perkins, Daniel Craig, and Jessica M. Perkins, "Using Social Norms to Reduce Bullying: A Resarch Intervention Among Adolescents in Five Middle Schools," *Group Processes & Intergroup Relations* (2011).

14 **The frontal lobe, which governs** Jay N. Giedd et al., "Brain Development During Childhood and Adolescence: A Longitudinal MRI Study," *Nature Neuroscience* 2 (1999): 861–63.

14 **The Supreme Court began relying** *Roper v. Simmons,* 543 U.S. 551 (2005).

14 **and invoked it again** *Graham v. Florida,* 130 S. Ct. (2011) and *Miller v. Alabama,* 130 S. Ct. 1733 (2012).

15 **way they respond to the environments** In her 2003 book *Girlfighting* (New York: New York University Press, 2003), Lyn Mikel Brown

points out that "we risk becoming hopelessly mired in the personal, writing new versions of old self-help books that put all the blame and responsibility for change on girls." Brown quotes the psychologist Carol Tavris, who wrote in 2002, as awareness dawned of mean girls, "The psychologizing of social problems is so much easier, because psychology directs us to look inward, to personal solutions rather than institutional changes."

Chapter 1: Monique

25 **She recommended a mediation meeting** I tried to ask Diane Niles about the mediation meeting, and about other decisions she made with regard to Monique, but the school district wouldn't let me speak with her.

26 **One review of anti-bullying** David P. Farrington and Maria M. Ttofi, "School-Based Programs to Reduce Bullying and Victimization," *Campbell Systematic Reviews* 6 (December 2009): 1–148.

26 **And if intervention isn't skillful** Debra Pepler, Wendy Craig, and Paul O'Connell, "Peer Processes in Bullying: Informing Prevention and Intervention Strategies," in *Handbook of Bullying in Schools: An International Perspective,* ed. Shane R. Jimerson, Susan M. Swearer, and Deborah L. Espelage, 469–79 (New York: Routledge, 2010). See also Thomas J. Dishion and Jessica M. Tipsord, "Peer Contagion in Child and Adolescent Social and Emotional Development," *Annual Review of Psychology* 62 (January 2011): 189–214.

28 **A Swedish graduate student** Dan Olweus, *Aggression in the Schools: Bullies and Whipping Boys* (Washington, D.C.: Hemisphere, 1978).

28 **Bullying, he said, had to satisfy three** Ibid., 142–52. Olweus crystallized this definition in later writings. See Dan Olweus, *Bullying at School: What We Know and What We Can Do* (Oxford: Blackwell, 1993).

29 **an English word that dates** In the seventeenth century, the word *bully* actually meant "sweetheart" or "darling." "From my hart strings I love the lovely bully," Shakespeare wrote in *Henry V,* and in *A Midsummer Night's Dream,* "What saiest thou, bully, Bottome?" The definition of *bully* expanded over the next hundred years to encompass the other meaning that for us is familiar: as a noun, "ruffian"; as a verb, "to overawe, intimidate, or violently threaten." "What ail you, to Bully away our Customers so?" Daniel Defoe, author of *Robinson Crusoe,* wrote in 1723. Oddly, the word held on to both its positive and negative

meanings for centuries—Teddy Roosevelt said "bully" when he especially enjoyed himself, and the congratulatory "bully for you" is a
remnant—before settling into its unpleasant, surly self.

29 **He found that about 5 percent** Olweus, *Aggression in the Schools,* 47–
50, 109–17, 139.

29 **For victims, both boys and girls** Tonja R. Nansel et al., "Bullying Behaviors Among U.S. Youth: Prevalence and Association with Psychosocial Adjustment," *Journal of the American Medical Association* 285
(April 25, 2001): 2094–100.

29 **One analysis of bullying in twenty-five** Tonja R. Nansel et al., "Cross-
National Consistency in the Relationship Between Bullying Behaviors
and Psychosocial Adjustment," *Archives of Pediatrics and Adolescent
Medicine* 158 (August 2004): 730–36.

31 **This type helps account for** Dan Olweus, "Bullying Among Schoolchildren: Intervention and Prevention," in *Aggression and Violence
Throughout the Life Span,* ed. Ray DeV. Peters, Robert J. McMahon,
and Vernon L. Quinsey, 100–125 (London: Sage Publications, 1992).
See also Nansel, "Bullying Behaviors," and Maria Ttofi, David Farrington, and Friedrich Losel, eds., "Criminal Consequences of School
Bullying," special issue of *Criminal Behaviour and Mental Health* 21
(2011).

31 **Bullies are also more likely** Kisha M. Radliff et al., "Illuminating the
Relationship Between Bullying and Substance Use Among Middle and
High School Youth," *Addictive Behaviors* 37 (April 2012): 569–72;
Clayton R. Cook et al., "Predictors of Bullying and Victimization in
Childhood and Adolescence: A Meta-Analytic Investigation," *School
Psychology Quarterly* 25 (2010): 65–83.

31 **"Many bullies seem"** Philip C. Rodkin, "Bullying and Children's Peer
Relationships," materials for the White House Conference on Bullying
Prevention, March 10, 2011, 33–42.

31 **These kids experience "the worst of both worlds"** Cook et al., "Predictors of Bullying."

31 **Bully-victims, as they're often** Susan M. Swearer et al., "Psychosocial
Correlates in Bullying and Victimization: The Relationship Between
Depression, Anxiety, and Bully/Victim Status," *Journal of Emotional
Abuse* 2 (2001): 95–121.

32 **they're more likely to consider suicide** Catherine Winsper et al., "Involvement in Bullying and Suicide-Related Behavior at 11 Years: A Pro-

spective Birth Cohort Study," *Journal of the American Academy of Child and Adolescent Psychiatry* 51 (March 2012): 271–82.

32 **Bully-victims are more likely** Philip C. Rodkin and Christian Berger, "Who Bullies Whom? Social Status Asymmetries by Victim Gender," *International Journal of Behavioral Development* 32 (2008): 473–85.

32 **They tend to see themselves** Cook et al., "Predictors of Bullying."

32 **They're more likely to report physical** Renae Duncan, "Family Relationships of Bullies and Victims," in *Bullying in North American Schools,* 2nd ed. (New York: Routledge, 2011), 191–204; Susan M. Swearer and Paulette Tam Cary, "Perceptions and Attitudes Toward Bullying in Middle School Youth: A Developmental Examination Across the Bully/Victim Continuum," *Journal of Applied School Psychology* 19 (2003): 63–79.

32 **Sometimes they have a disability** Kirsti Kumpulainen, Eila Räsälen, and Kaija Puura, "Psychiatric Disorders and the Use of Mental Health Services Among Children Involved in Bullying," *Aggressive Behavior* 27 (March 2001): 102–10.

32 **"hot tempered and generally irritating"** Olweus, *Aggression in the Schools,* 122.

32 **These kids tend to score higher** Susan P. Limber, "Peer Abuse: Consequences of Bullying," *Addiction Professional,* July 1, 2004.

32 **They report more, not less** Nansel et al., "Bullying Behaviors Among U.S. Youth."

32 **as early as preschool, kids** Patricia H. Hawley et al., "Physical Attractiveness in Preschoolers: Relationships with Power, Status, Aggression and Social Skills," *Journal of School Psychology* 45 (2007): 499–521, cited in Cook et al., "Predictors of Bullying."

32 **Still, as they grow up** Thomas Farmer et al., "Rejected Bullies or Popular Leaders? The Social Relations of Aggressive Subtypes of Rural African American Early Adolescents," *Developmental Psychology* 39 (2003): 992–1004.

32 **Their methods of choice are whispered** H. Xie et al., "Aggressive Behaviors in Social Interaction and Developmental Adaptation: A Narrative Analysis of Interpersonal Conflicts During Early Adolescence," *Social Development* 11 (2002): 205–24.

33 **most victims—boys and girls** Dan Olweus, "Understanding and Researching Bullying: Some Critical Issues," in *Handbook of Bullying in Schools: An International Perspective,* ed. Shane R. Jimerson, Susan

M. Swearer, and Dorothy L. Espelage (New York: Routledge, 2010), 29. Some research points to a different kind of gender divide: when boys bully boys, the bullies tend to be popular and the victims unpopular, but when boys bully girls, it's the reverse. See Philip Rodkin and Ramin Karimpour, "What's a Hidden Bully?" Education.com, www.education.com/reference/article/hidden-bully-popular-aggressive-children.

33 **Most researchers would in fact say** Kaj Björkqvist, "Sex Differences in Physical, Verbal, and Indirect Aggression: A Review of Recent Research," *Sex Roles* 30 (1994): 177–88. Nicki Crick at the University of Minnesota has been studying relational aggression for decades, and Marion Underwood at the University of Texas at Dallas has been studying social aggression for decades. They would argue that girls are just as "aggressive"; it's simply that the aggressive behavior has a different expression. See Marion Underwood, *Social Aggression Among Girls* (New York: Guilford Press, 2003), and Nicki Crick et al., "Aggression and Peer Relationships in Middle Childhood and Early Adolescence," in *Handbook of Peer Interactions, Relationships, and Groups,* ed. K. H. Rubin, W. Bukowski, and B. Laursen (New York: Guilford Press, 2009). Dan Olweus disagrees with these findings about girls. Based on his own work, he wrote in 2010, "The male gender is the more aggressive gender." Olweus, "Understanding and Researching Bullying."

33 **"Girls can better understand"** Margaret Talbot, "Girls Just Want to Be Mean," *New York Times Magazine,* February 24, 2002.

33 **"threats, blackmail, destroying friendships"** Patricia A. Snell and Elizabeth K. Englander, "Cyberbullying Victimization and Behaviors Among Girls: Applying Research Findings in the Field," *Journal of Social Sciences* 6 (2010): 510–14.

33 **The stupid risks boys** A 2009 Pew Center survey found that about 15 percent of kids ages twelve to seventeen receive sext messages or nude images of people they know, while only about 4 percent send these messages. The survey defined sexting as sexually explicit images sent electronically. See Amanda Lenhart, *Teens and Sexting: How and Why Minor Teens Are Sending Suggestive Nude or Nearly Nude Images via Text Messaging,* Pew Internet and American Life Project, December 15, 2009.

33 **Girls socialize more via the Internet** Victoria J. Rideout, Ulla G. Foehr,

and Donald F. Roberts, *Generation M²: Media in the Lives of 8- to 18-Year-Olds,* Kaiser Family Foundation, January 2010.

33 **send and receive more text messages** Amanda Lenhart, *Teens, Smartphones and Texting,* Pew Internet and American Life Project, March 19, 2012.

39 **Cyberbullying, it was becoming clear, was** In *Bullying Beyond the Schoolyard* (Thousand Oaks, CA: Corwin Press, 2009), Sameer Hinduja and Justin W. Patchin define cyberbullying as "the intentional and repeated harm of others through the use of computers, cell phones, and other electronic devices."

40 **Most kids who report being bullied** Jaana Juvonen and Elisheva F. Gross, "Extending the School Grounds? Bullying Experiences in Cyberspace," *Journal of School Health* 78 (September 2008): 496–505.

40 **Since Olweus' foundational work** Susan P. Limber and Maury M. Nation, "Bullying Among Children and Youth," *Juvenile Justice Bulletin,* April 1998; Nansel et al., "Bullying Behaviors Among U.S. Youth."

40 **When the surveys include questions** Michele L. Ybarra, Marie Diener-West, and Philip J. Leaf, "Examining the Overlap in Internet Harassment and School Bullying: Implications for School Intervention," *Journal of Adolescent Health* 41 (2007): S42–S50; Jill DeVoe and Christina Murphy, *Student Reports of Bullying and Cyber-Bullying: Results from the 2009 School Crime Supplement to the National Crime Victimization Survey,* NCES 2011–336, U.S. Department of Education, August 2011, http://nces.ed.gov/pubs2011/2011336.pdf.

40 **no one knows whether the Internet** Some researchers argue that it's not even clear that the online aspect of bullying makes the whole experience worse than the cruelty of a generation or two ago, which could be severe and violent. See Janis Wolak, Kimberly J. Mitchell, and David Finkelhor, "Does Online Harassment Constitute Bullying? An Exploration of Online Harassment by Known Peers and Online-Only Contacts," *Journal of Adolescent Health* 41 (2007): S41–S58.

42 **The Web is toughest on subgroups** Amanda Lenhart et al., *Teens, Kindness and Cruelty on Social Network Sites,* Pew Internet and American Life Project, November 9, 2011, http://pewinternet.org/~/media/Files/Reports/2011/PIP_Teens_Kindness_Cruelty_SNS_Report_Nov_2011_FINAL_110711.pdf.

42 **Another study by two Stanford researchers** Roy Pea and Clifford Nass, "Media Use, Face-to-Face Communication, Media Multitasking, and

Social Well-Being Among 8- to 12-Year-Old Girls," *Developmental Psychology* 48 (March 2012): 327–36.

42 **"Girls who spend more time interacting"** Clifford Nass, "The Keyboard and the Damage Done," *Pacific Standard,* May/June 2012, www.psmag.com/culture/is-facebook-stunting-your-childs-growth-40577.

43 **80 percent of thirteen-year-olds** Lenhart et al., *Teens, Kindness and Cruelty.*

45 **"the young are heated by Nature"** Aristotle, *Rhetoric,* trans. J. E. C. Welldon (London: Macmillan, 1886).

45 **In the eighteenth century, Rousseau observed** Jean-Jacques Rousseau, *Émile* (London: Dent, 1911), 175.

45 **The prefrontal cortex** Jay N. Giedd et al., "Brain Development During Childhood and Adolescence: A Longitudinal MRI Study," *Nature Neuroscience* 2 (1999): 861–63.

45 **And a key part of the brain's reward circuitry** Leah H. Somerville, Rebecca M. Jones, and B. J. Casey, "A Time of Change: Behavioral and Neural Correlates of Adolescent Sensitivity to Appetitive and Aversive Environmental Cues," *Brain and Cognition* 72 (February 2010): 124–33.

45 **"Teens take more risks"** David Dobbs, "Beautiful Brains," *National Geographic,* October 2011.

46 **The drive to seek out novelty** Laurence Steinberg, "A Social Neuroscience Perspective on Adolescent Risk-Taking," *Developmental Review* 28 (2008): 78–106.

46 **Peer pressure is a real force** Ibid.; see also Laurence Steinberg, "Risk-Taking in Adolescence: What Changes, and Why?" *Annals of the New York Academy of Sciences* 1021 (June 2004): 51–58. One of the hallmarks of reckless driving, as well as drug abuse and crime, is that teenagers take these risks far more often in a group than adults do.

46 **In 2010, he and his colleagues** Jason Chein et al., "Peers Increase Adolescent Risk Taking by Enhancing Activity in the Brain's Reward Circuitry," *Developmental Science* 14 (2011): F1–F10.

47 **Steinberg called this "one very plausible"** Tara Parker-Pope, "Teenagers, Friends and Bad Decisions," *New York Times,* February 3, 2011.

47 **a behavior that peaks in middle** A. D. Pellegrini and Maria Bartini, "A Longitudinal Study of Bullying, Victimization, and Peer Affiliation During the Transition from Primary School to Middle School," *American Educational Research Journal* 37 (Fall 2000): 699–725; Debra J.

Pepler et al., "A Developmental Perspective on Bullying," *Aggressive Behavior* 32 (2006): 376–84.

51 **"I almost want to put some"** Bari M. Schwartz, "Hot or Not? Website Briefly Judges Looks," *Harvard Crimson,* November 4, 2003.

52 **For a study about teen conflict** Alice E. Marwick and danah boyd, "The Drama! Teen Conflict, Gossip, and Bullying in Networked Publics," paper presented at A Decade in Internet Time: Symposium on the Dynamics of the Internet and Society, Oxford Internet Institute, September 22, 2011.

53 **"most likely to succeed"** Robert Faris and Diane Felmlee, "Status Struggles: Network Centrality and Gender Segregation in Same- and Cross-Gender Aggression," *American Sociological Review* 76 (2011): 48–73. See also Robert Faris, "Aggression, Exclusivity, and Status Attainment in Interpersonal Networks," *Social Forces* (in press).

54 **In other words, drama** Faris also noted a telling exception to his rule of social climbing: aggression was low at the very center of the social network—just as low, in fact, as it was among the kids on the outermost edge. About this, he mused in a paper, "Kindness may be a luxury most easily enjoyed from a secure position at the pinnacle of a hierarchy, or by individuals who have no hope (or desire) to reach such heights." Faris and Felmlee, "Status Struggles."

56 **This is sadly true** Catherine P. Bradshaw, Anne L. Sawyer, and Lindsey M. O'Brennan, "Bullying and Peer Victimization at School: Perceptual Differences Between Students and School Staff," *School Psychology Review* 36 (2007): 361–82.

56 **Only at schools that have** Stan Davis, "What Works in Bullying Prevention in Schools?" presented at the Sixth Annual National Ted and Dr. Roberta Mann Foundation Symposium About Children and Young Adults with Mental Health and Learning Disabilities, 2011, www.pacer .org/help/symposium/2011/pdf/handouts/StanDavis/What-works-in -bullying-prevention.pdf.

Chapter 2: Jacob

57 **Gay teens often report feeling** Caitlin Ryan et al., "Family Rejection as a Predictor of Negative Health Outcomes in White and Latino Lesbian, Gay, and Bisexual Young Adults," *Pediatrics* 123 (January 2009): 346–52.

65 **A 2009 national survey found** Joseph G. Kosciw et al., *The 2009 National School Climate Survey: The Experiences of Lesbian, Gay, Bisexual and Transgender Youth in Our Nation's Schools,* Gay, Lesbian and Straight Education Network, September 2010, www.glsen.org/cgi-bin/iowa/all/library/record/2624.html.

65 **The rate of harassment online** Sameer Hinduja and Justin W. Patchin, "Cyberbullying Research Summary: Bullying, Cyberbullying, and Sexual Orientation," Cyberbullying Research Center, 2011, www.cyberbullying.us/cyberbullying_sexual_orientation_fact_sheet.pdf. In another survey that put the questions a little differently, the National Mental Health Association found that 78 percent of gay twelve- to seventeen-year-olds have been teased or bullied (*What Does Gay Mean?*, NMHA, 2002, www.nmha.org/whatdoesgaymean).

65 **Boys who are the targets** V. Paul Poteat and Dorothy Espelage, "Predicting Psychosocial Consequences of Homophobic Victimization in Middle School Students," *Journal of Early Adolescence* 27 (May 2007): 175–91.

65 **Students who are harassed because** Kosciw et al., *The 2009 National School Climate Survey.*

65 **Other research has shown that** Daniel E. Bontempo and Anthony R. D'Augelli, "Effects of At-School Victimization and Sexual Orientation on Lesbian, Gay, or Bisexual Youths' Health Risk Behavior," *Journal of Adolescent Health* 30 (May 2002): 364–74.

65 **In a study of young gay adults** Stephen T. Russell et al., "Lesbian, Gay, Bisexual, and Transgender Adolescent School Victimization: Implications for Young Adult Health and Adjustment," *Journal of School Health* 81 (May 2011): 223–30.

65 **And a study in Oregon showed** Mark L. Hatzenbuehler, "The Social Environment and Suicide Attempts in a Population-Based Sample of LGB Youth," *Pediatrics* (2011).

65 **The important distinction here** John Schwartz makes this point vividly in his memoir *Oddly Normal: One Family's Struggle to Help Their Teenage Son Come to Terms with His Sexuality* (New York: Gotham Books, 2012). See especially Chapter 9.

66 **Ryan published a study in 2010** Caitlin Ryan et al., "Family Acceptance in Adolescence and the Health of LGBT Young Adults," *Journal of Child and Adolescent Psychiatric Nursing* 23 (November 2010): 205–13. See also Caitlin Ryan, "Supportive Families, Healthy Children:

Helping Families with Lesbian, Gay, Bisexual and Transgender Children," Marian Wright Edelman Institute, San Francisco State University, 2009, 5–12.

71 **they are considered especially high-risk** Susan M. Swearer et al., "Psychosocial Correlates in Bullying and Victimization: The Relationship Between Depression, Anxiety, and Bully/Victim Status," *Journal of Emotional Abuse* 2 (2001): 95–121; Catherine Winsper et al., "Involvement in Bullying and Suicide-Related Behavior at 11 Years: A Prospective Birth Cohort Study," *Journal of the American Academy of Child and Adolescent Psychiatry* 51 (March 2012): 271–82; Clayton R. Cook et al., "Predictors of Bullying and Victimization in Childhood and Adolescence: A Meta-Analytic Investigation," *School Psychology Quarterly* 25 (2010): 65–83.

71 **Sometimes they lash out** David Schwartz et al., "The Aggressive Victim of Bullying: Emotional and Behavioral Dysregulation as a Pathway to Victimization by Peers," in *Peer Harassment in School: The Plight of the Vulnerable and Victimized,* ed. Jaana Juvonen and Sandra Graham, 147–74 (New York: Guilford, 2001).

71 **patterns of "reciprocated dislike and animosity"** Philip C. Rodkin, "Bullying and Children's Peer Relationships," materials for the White House Conference on Bullying Prevention, March 10, 2011, 33–42.

72 **It was Jacob's insistent** In her book *The Bully Society* (New York: New York University Press, 2012), Jessie Klein discusses the pressure boys feel to prove their masculinity by showing their "flamboyant heterosexuality."

76 **Gay student organizations got started** Tina Fetner and Kristin Kush, "Gay-Straight Alliances in High Schools: Social Predictors of Early Adoption," *Youth Society* 40 (2008): 114–30.

77 **more than four thousand schools** "About Gay-Straight Alliances," Gay, Lesbian and Straight Education Network, www.glsen.org/cgi-bin/iowa/all/library/record/2342.html.

77 **studies show that LGBT students** Hinduja and Patchin, "Bullying, Cyberbullying, and Sexual Orientation"; *Gay-Straight Alliances: Creating Safer Schools for LGBT Students and Their Allies,* Gay, Lesbian and Straight Education Network Research Brief, 2007, www.glsen.org/binary-data/GLSEN_ATTACHMENTS/file/000/000/930-1.pdf.

79 **"The district believes that all"** Renee Gamela, "Mohawk School Board Won't Recognize Club," *Utica Observer-Dispatch,* 2006, 1A.

Chapter 3: Flannery

Some of the reporting in this chapter and in Chapter 6 comes from a series I did for Slate, "What Really Happened to Phoebe Prince?" Slate, July 20, 2010.

85 **Cutting is an increasingly common** K. Hawton et al., "Trends in Deliberate Self-Harm in Oxford, 1985–1995. Implications for Clinical Services and the Prevention of Suicide," *British Journal of Psychiatry* 171 (1997): 556–60. See also Penelope A. Hasking et al., "Brief Report: Emotion Regulation and Coping as Moderators in the Relationship Between Personality and Self-Injury," *Journal of Adolescence* 33 (October 2010): 767–73.

85 **linked with depression** Joan Rosenbaum Asarnow, "Suicide Attempts and Nonsuicidal Self-Injury in the Treatment of Resistant Depression in Adolescents: Findings from the TORDIA Study," *Journal of the American Academy of Child and Adolescent Psychiatry* 50 (August 2011): 772–81.

85 **as well as borderline personality disorder** "What Are the Symptoms of Borderline Personality Disorder?" National Institute of Mental Health, www.nimh.nih.gov/health/publications/borderline-personality -disorder/what-are-the-symptoms-of-borderline-personality-disorder .shtml.

85 **Teenagers typically say that they cut** Alexandra DeGeorge, "Why Do Teens Cut Themselves?" on the website of Alexandra L. Barzvi, PhD, June 21, 2010, www.drbarzvi.com/2010/06/21/why-do-teens-cut- themselves.

85 **"Cutting was a release"** "Inside the Mind of a Cutter . . . and How to Help," Parentingtodayskids.com, March 28, 2012.

86 **Some researchers think the behavior** Thomas Joiner, *Why People Die by Suicide* (Cambridge, MA: Harvard University Press, 2005).

86 **and attempting it** Colleen Jacobson and Madelyn Gould, "The Epidemiology and Phenomenology of Non-Suicidal Self-Injurious Behavior Among Adolescents: A Critical Review of the Literature," *Archives of Suicide Research* 11 (2007): 129–47.

89 **in this guise, it can actually represent** Barent W. Walsh, *Treating Self-Injury: A Practical Guide* (New York: Guilford Press, 2006), 15.

89 **a book she'd read** Steven Levenkron, *Cutting: Understanding and Overcoming Self-Mutilation* (New York: W. W. Norton, 1999).

89 **But if cutting offers a respite** Jacobson and Gould, "Epidemiology and Phenomenology."

95 **girls who stand out as "too sexual"** Catherine Hill and Holly Kearle, *Crossing the Line: Sexual Harassment at School,* American Association of University Women, November 2011, www.aauw.org/learn/research/upload/CrossingTheLine.pdf.

96 **for girls, the most upsetting** James Gruber and Susan Fineran, "Comparing the Impact of Bullying and Sexual Harassment Victimization on the Mental and Physical Health of Adolescents," *Sex Roles* 58 (2008): 13–14.

96 **"Kids who are bullied in this way"** Rachel Rabbit White, "Why Do Girls Slut-Shame Each Other?" *The Frisky,* July 6, 2011, www.thefrisky.com/2011-07-06/girl-talk-why-do-girls-slut-shame-each-other.

97 **"Know what I hate?"** Kayla admitted to writing a post like that, though I don't have the exact quote.

101 **making bullying a crime** Wendy Murphy, "Bullying Bill Is a Bunch of Bull," *Patriot Ledger,* March 10, 2010, www.patriotledger.com/topstories/x2102348779/WENDY-MURPHY-Bullying-bill-is-bunch-of-bull.

102 **Under the headline** Kevin Cullen, "Untouchable Mean Girls," *Boston Globe,* January 24, 2010.

103 **Phoebe looked like a girl** It probably mattered, too, that she was white and middle class. In June 2010, a local news article counted 811 stories about Phoebe in 45 countries compared with 74 stories about Carl Walker-Hoover, a black eleven-year-old from Springfield who killed himself nine months earlier after classmates taunted him for being gay. Stephanie Bergman, "Why Is Phoebe Prince a Household Name, While Not Many Have Heard of Carl Walker-Hoover?" *Lowell Sun,* June 7, 2010.

104 **two cover stories** Liz McNeil, "Bullied to Death?" *People,* February 22, 2010; "Why Was Phoebe Prince Bullied?" *People,* April 15, 2010.

107 **30 percent reported** James E. Byrne, *Report on the 2005 Youth Risk Behavior Survey for Students in Grades 9, 10, 11, and 12 for the South Hadley Public Schools* (Haverhill, MA: Northeast Health Resources, August 2005), http://media2.wwlp.com/storydocuments/SHHS_2005_Survey.pdf.

107 **higher rate than the state average** Massachusetts Department of Education, *2005 Massachusetts Youth Risk Behavior Survey Results Execu-*

tive Summary, June 2006, www.doe.mass.edu/cnp/hprograms/yrbs/05/summary.pdf.

107 **"How long can the school department"** Matthew Caron and Caitlin McCarron, *Spotlight South Hadley High School,* 2005, cited in Frank D. LoMonte, "States Should Protect Student Journalists," *Philadelphia Inquirer,* August 11, 2010.

109 **it is depression that predicts** David A. Brent, "Psychiatric Risk Factors for Adolescent Suicide: A Case-Control Study," *Journal of the American Academy of Child and Adolescent Psychiatry* 32 (May 1993): 521–29; Iris Wagman Borowsky, Marjorie Ireland, and Michael D. Resnick, "Adolescent Suicide Attempts: Risks and Protectors," *Pediatrics* 107 (March 2001): 485–93; Jørgen G. Bramness et al., "Self-Reported Mental Health and Its Gender Differences as a Predictor of Suicide in the Middle-Aged," *American Journal of Epidemiology* 172 (2010): 160–66.

110 ***Boston Herald* article quoting an anonymous** Marie Szaniszlo and Laura Crimaldi, "Parent Details Phoebe's Agonizing Final Moments," *Boston Herald,* April 2, 2010.

110 **"she deserved it" and "mission accomplished"** Alyssa Giacobbe, "Who Failed Phoebe Prince?" *Boston Magazine,* June 2010.

Chapter 4: Monique

117 **So did the *Middletown Press*** Jason Siedzik, "Bullying Nightmare: Middletown Teen 'Used to Love to Go to School,' " *Middletown Press,* February 16, 2011.

119 **a "strict" anti-bullying policy** Hillary Federico, "Official: Schools Can't Tackle Bullies on Their Own," *Middletown Press,* November 23, 2010.

122 **bullying involved an audience of peers** Wendy M. Craig and Deborah J. Pepler, "Observations of Bullying and Victimization in the School Yard," *Canadian Journal of School Psychology* 13 (1997): 41–60.

123 **When they just stood around** Wendy M. Craig and Deborah J. Pepler, "Peer Processes in Bullying and Victimization: An Observational Study," *Exceptionality Education Canada* 5 (1995): 81–95.

123 **most kids who are bystanders** Ken Rigby and Phillip T. Slee, "Bullying Among Australian School Children: Reported Behavior and Attitudes Toward Victims," *Journal of Social Psychology* 131 (October 1991): 615–27.

123 **when bystanders do stand up** Craig and Pepler, "Observations of Bullying."

124 **Some prevention efforts** Karin S. Frey et al., "Reducing Playground Bullying and Supporting Beliefs: An Experimental Trial of the Steps to Respect Program," *Developmental Psychology* 41 (2005): 479–91.

124 **In one important survey, high school students** Stan Davis and Charisse Nixon, "Preliminary Results from the Youth Voice Research Project: Victimization and Strategies," Youth Voice Project, March 2010, www .youthvoiceproject.com/YVPMarch2010.pdf.

124 **"It made me feel more confident"** Stan Davis, "Supporting Positive Peer Action," Stop Bullying Now, www.stopbullyingnow.com/peeraction .htm.

124 **a map of the social networks** Dorothy Espelage, Harold Green, and Joshua Polanin, "Willingness to Intervene in Bullying Episodes Among Middle School Students: Individual and Peer-Group Influences," *Journal of Early Adolescence,* published online November 17, 2011, 1–26.

130 **"extreme reactions due to"** Melissa M. Mahady Wilton, Wendy Craig, and Debra J. Pepler, "Emotional Regulation and Display in Classroom Victims of Bullying: Characteristic Expressions of Affect, Coping Styles and Relevant Contextual Factors," *Social Development* 9 (2000): 226–45.

130 **bullies often have a physical advantage** Dan Olweus, "Bullying at School: Knowledge Base and an Effective Intervention Program," *Annals of the New York Academy of Sciences* 794 (September 1996): 265–76.

131 **The story mocks aggression** Munro Leaf, *The Story of Ferdinand* (New York: Viking, 1936). My favorite line: "The Matador was so mad he cried because he couldn't show off with his cape and sword."

132 **"It's like they're the bullies now"** Claire Michalewicz, "Marshal Sent to Pick Up Homework for Bullied Teen Comes Back Empty-Handed," *Middletown Press,* March 30, 2011.

132 **were there to catch the marshal** Doug Green, "Bullied Student Can't Get Homework," NBC Connecticut, March 30, 2011, www.nbc connecticut .com/news/Bullied-Student-Cant-Get-Homework-118868834.html; Michalewicz, "Marshal Sent to Pick Up Homework."

138 **Asked about Monique on his way out** Claire Michalewicz, "Woodrow Wilson Principal Stepping Down," *Middletown Press,* June 8, 2011.

Chapter 5: Jacob

145 **Back in 1936, the American Law Institute** First Restatement of Torts, 1936.

146 **The first gay student to invoke** Details of Jamie Nabozny's story come from my interview with Nabozny, the transcript of the trial in his case, the documentary film *Bullied: A Student, a School and a Case That Made History,* and Carlos A. Ball, *From the Closet to the Courtroom* (Boston: Beacon Press, 2010).

148 **The suit made two claims** *Nabozny v. Podlesny,* 92 F.3d 446, 453 (7th Cir., 1996).

148 **based on the Fourteenth Amendment's** Since the 1970s, courts have read the Fourteenth Amendment to mean that a public school (like any other part of government) has to have a good reason for treating someone differently because of his or her sex. (In legal terms, courts give "heightened scrutiny" to sex discrimination claims.) When you sue for discrimination on the basis of sexual orientation, on the other hand, a school just has to show it had a "rational basis" for treating you differently. In bullying cases, however, it's hard for schools to come up with *any* legitimate reason for letting serious abuse, like the kind Jamie suffered, go unchecked. Gay rights lawyers tend to sue on the basis of both sex discrimination *and* sexual orientation discrimination, when they can. The sex discrimination claims in these cases fit into a larger vision of gay identity, in which people have an affirmative right to live as they please, without conforming to traditional expectations about what it means to be male or female.

151 **"deliberate indifference" to harassment** *Davis v. Monroe County Board of Education,* 526 U.S. 629 (1999).

151 **One was a girl in California** *Flores v. Morgan Hill Unified School District,* 324 F.3d 1130 (9th Cir., 2003).

152 **Another was a gay student** *Henkle v. Gregory,* 150 F.Supp.2d 1067 (D. Nev., 2001).

152 **His school, the student said** Interview with Derek Henkle, supplement to *Assault on Gay America,* PBS *Frontline,* February 2000, www.pbs .org/wgbh/pages/frontline/shows/assault/interviews/henkle.html.

152 **Dylan Theno was called "pussy"** *Theno v. Tonganoxie Unified Sch. Dist. No. 464,* 394 F. Supp. 2d 1299 (D. Kan., 2005).

152 **Jacob could sue based on** Missing is a federal law that explicitly protects students from harassment because they are gay. Congress has

never passed a law providing that students can't be discriminated against in school because of their sexual orientation. Senator Al Franken (D-Minn.) has introduced the Student Non-Discrimination Act, which would protect students from harassment, bullying, and violence based on their actual or perceived sexual orientation or gender identity. A similar bill has been introduced in the House. Meanwhile, in sixteen states, including New York, it *is* against the law to discriminate against public school students on the basis of sexual orientation. The states with such laws are a mix of blue and purple: California, Colorado, Connecticut, Illinois, Iowa, Maine, Maryland, Massachusetts, Minnesota, New Jersey, New York, Oregon, Rhode Island, Vermont, Washington, and Wisconsin, as well as the District of Columbia. You could argue from this list that the push to protect gay teenagers from bullying is the sleeper success story of the gay rights movement. Same-sex marriage, after all, has been embraced by only six states.

153 **the NYCLU filed his lawsuit** *J.L. v. Mohawk Central School District,* N.D.N.Y., Index No. 09-CV-943.

153 **The local paper wrote an editorial** *Utica Observer-Dispatch,* "Mohawk Case a Lesson for Other Schools," January 21, 2010.

155 **a series of studies has linked** The American Psychological Association has found that zero-tolerance policies, which often give rise to lengthy suspensions, don't deter bad behavior or make schools safer. See American Psychological Association Zero Tolerance Task Force, "Are Zero Tolerance Policies Effective in the Schools? An Evidentiary Review and Recommendations," *American Psychologist* 63 (December 2008): 852–62.

156 **a Kentucky student who was** *Putman v. Board of Education of Somerset Independent Schools, et al.,* C.A. No. 00-145.

156 **a Missouri student who was harassed** *Lovins and United States v. Pleasant Hill Public School District, R-III,* Case No. 99-0550-CV-W-2 (W.D. Mo.), July 20, 2000.

157 **a letter, sent to every school** "Dear Colleague Letter: Harassment and Bullying," United States Department of Education Office of Civil Rights, October 26, 2010, www2.ed.gov/about/offices/list/ocr/letters/colleague-201010.pdf.

157 **laying out the responsibility** The Department of Education also warned districts that they could be held legally responsible when a girl is smeared for being a slut based on student gossip that she's having sex, or for bullying based on race, ethnicity, or ancestry. Students who are

in the ethnic minority in a school are more likely to be bullied than students who are in the majority, and since 9/11, Muslim students have faced an outbreak of bullying. So have Sikhs, whose turbans all too often are associated with Osama bin Laden. In 2008 in New York and in 2010 in the San Francisco Bay Area, the Sikh Coalition conducted a pair of surveys on bullying and harassment. The majority of Sikh boys reported being called derogatory names: "raghead," "Osama bin Laden," "terrorist," "Taliban." One New Jersey boy's turban was set on fire with a lighter by another student. A Sikh girl's braid was cut in English class after she said that she wore her hair long because of her religion. (Uncut hair is a tenet of Sikh faith.) The school returned the child's braid wadded up in a tissue.

Disabled students, for whom bullying is an endemic problem, also have a federal statute that protects their right to a free and adequate public education. The courts have just begun to interpret this to mean that such students, too, can recover damages from schools where they face a pattern of exclusion and taunting that no one makes a concerted effort to stop. In the 2011 case *L.K. v. New York City Department of Education,* Judge Jack Weinstein of the Eastern District of New York allowed a disabled girl to go ahead with such a suit against her school. Judge Weinstein noted that students with disabilities are less popular, have fewer friends, and struggle more with loneliness and peer rejection, increasing the likelihood they will become the victim of bullying.

157   **"They are making up"** Ari Shapiro, "Justice Department Intervenes in Gay Rights Suit," NPR, January 15, 2010, www.npr.org/templates/story/story.php?storyId=122620723.

158   **"We need to protect all children"** Erik Eckholm, "In Efforts to End Bullying, Some See Agenda," *New York Times,* November 6, 2010.

158   **Schools can take various steps** Susan M. Swearer, Dorothy L. Espelage, and Scott A. Naplitano, *Bullying Prevention and Intervention: Realistic Strategies for Schools* (New York: Guilford Press, 2009).

159   **a culture of nonacceptance can contribute** Joseph P. Robinson and Dorothy L. Espelage, "Inequities in Educational and Psychological Outcomes Between LGBTQ and Straight Students in Middle and High School," *Educational Researcher* 40 (October 2011): 315–30.

159   **In Helena, Montana, parents** Eckholm, "In Efforts to End Bullying."

159   **"I think it fails the memory"** Enjoli Francis, Linsey Davis, and Cath-

erine Cole, " 'License to Bully': Backlash over Matt Epling Bill Passed in Michigan Senate," ABC News, November 4, 2011, http://abcnews .go.com/US/Parenting/license-bully-backlash-lbgt-victims-father -matt-epling/story?id=14885102#.T5FXkbOm-1c.

160 **That kind of omission** The exception was also written into Missouri's anti-bullying law by a legislator who railed that "advancement of gay and lesbian lifestyles in local schools are being promoted in legislatures through bullying policies." Daniel B. Weddle and Kathryn E. New, "What Did Jesus Do? Answering Religious Conservatives Who Oppose Bullying Prevention Legislation," *New England Journal on Criminal and Civil Confinement* 37 (October 2011): 325–47.

160 **the Parents Action League pushed** Anoka-Hennepin is in Michele Bachmann's congressional district, and the Parents Action League is sponsored by a statewide group, the Minnesota Family Council, that Bachmann and Newt Gingrich have headlined fund-raisers for.

160 **because of "homosexual indoctrination"** Andy Birkey, "Minnesota Family Council Pushes Back in Anoka-Hennepin Anti-Gay Bullying Controversy," *Minnesota Independent,* October 4, 2010.

161 **the settlement was a "travesty"** Maria Elena Baca, "Anoka-Hennepin School District Settles Bullying Lawsuit," *Star Tribune,* March 6, 2012.

162 **"the vast majority of the measures"** "Statement of Superintendent Joyce M. Caputo," Mohawk Central School District, August 27, 2009, www .mohawk.k12.ny.us/news.cfm?story=37127. See also "Statement Regarding the U.S. Justice Department Motion to Intervene in the Federal Lawsuit Pending Against the Mohawk Central School District," Mohawk Central School District, January 15, 2010, www.mohawk.k12 .ny.us/news.cfm?story=46533.

163 **the Supreme Court ordered desegregation** *Brown v. Board of Education,* 347 U.S. 483 (1954).

164 **with "all deliberate speed"** *Brown v. Board of Education,* 349 U.S. 294 (1955).

Chapter 6: Flannery

170 **"The actions, or inactions"** "District Attorney's Statement on Prince Death," *Boston Globe,* March 29, 2010.

170 **"She'll have to explain what's troublesome"** Gus Sayer, interview by Matt Lauer, *Today,* April 2, 2010, www.videosurf.com/video/today -show-superintendent-speaks-out-on-bullying-suicide-129898834.

170 **"Mr. Sayer does not have access"** Dan Crowley, "Sayer Pledges Action, Questions DA's Remarks," *Daily Hampshire Gazette,* April 2, 2010.

170 **"The kids have a way of communicating"** Peter Schworm, "School Head Defends Response to Bullying," *Boston Globe,* April 1, 2010.

170 **"Rather than declare 'we did everything'"** "District's Defense Rings Hollow," *Boston Globe,* April 2, 2010.

174 **"causing suicide as criminal homicide"** Model Penal Code §210.5, American Law Institute, 1962.

174 **I ran a story in Slate** Emily Bazelon, "What Really Happened to Phoebe Prince?" Slate, July 20, 2010.

175 **threatening to sue to block publication** Scheibel had tried such a tactic before, when she subpoenaed a *Boston Globe* reporter after he wrote a story that embarrassed her (it involved a dispute between her office and a local clerk over a courthouse bathroom key, a conflict that was inevitably nicknamed "Pottygate"). The judge in the case blocked the subpoena.

175 **"Ms. Bazelon's article suggests"** Sandra Constantine, "DA Elizabeth Scheibel Defends Prosecution of Teenagers in Phoebe Prince Bullying," masslive.com, July 21, 2010, www.masslive.com/news/index.ssf/2010/07/da_elizabeth_scheibel_defends.html.

175 **I wrote back in Slate** Emily Bazelon, "Blaming the Victim," Slate, July 22, 2010.

176 **Joseph Kennedy, a criminal law professor** Kennedy also explained in Slate:

> *This is what a leading treatise says about suicide and causation:*
>
> > *What then, of suicide by the victim? If A wounds B with intent to kill, but thereafter C shoots B with intent to kill and does kill him instantly, we know that A is not the cause of B's death. If, instead, B takes his own life, we again have a deliberate act directed toward killing B that has intervened, so one might expect the same result. Such a result is certainly appropriate when B commits suicide from some motive unconnected with the fact that he is wounded, but suicide is not abnormal when B acts out of the extreme pain of wounds inflicted*

by A or when the wound has rendered him irresponsible. Although voluntary harm-doing usually suffices to break the chain of legal cause, this should not be so when A causes B to commit suicide by creating a situation so cruel and revolting that death is preferred. [From Wayne LaFave's Criminal Law *(5th ed.)]*

Note the limitations. Voluntary harm-doing ordinarily cuts off causation. If suicide is an abnormal response to the injury, then no causation exists. The egg-shell crime victim [the concept of the extra-fragile victim, from tort law] usually involves a particular susceptibility to physical injury (i.e. a hemophiliac bleeding to death). Suicide in response to insults would ordinarily be considered unforeseeable and thereby outside of proximate causation. Similar issues also arise with respect to the mental state of the defendant. A defendant who did not know of a victim's particular vulnerability might not have the mental state of knowingly (or perhaps even recklessly or negligently) causing a certain result.

See Emily Bazelon, "A Law Professor's Response to the Prosecutor in the Phoebe Prince Case," Slate, July 22, 2010.

176 **"There's an understandable wish"** John Schwartz, "Bullying, Suicide, Punishment," *New York Times,* October 2, 2010.

177 **They filed a complaint** Phoebe's parents settled with the town (representing the schools) a few months later, for an amount both sides agreed not to disclose. Massachusetts has a public records law written to ensure government transparency, however, and it requires the disclosure of settlements such as this one, so I went to court to get a copy of the agreement. The Prince family had made a grave accusation of wrongdoing against the schools, and the public had a right to know how South Hadley had responded. I won: the judge ordered the settlement agreement disclosed, and it turned out that Anne and Jeremy had settled for $225,000. It was a relatively low amount, but the settlement spared Phoebe's family years of court proceedings in which more of her history could have been made public.

177 **"I'd dearly like to see"** Emily Bazelon, "Talking to Phoebe Prince's Father," Slate, July 29, 2010.

177 **District Attorney Scheibel pursued the charges** Scheibel and one of her deputies, Elizabeth Dunphy Farris, had bonded tightly with Anne O'Brien. Scheibel also had a history of questionable crusades. She'd charged felony counts that carried a maximum sixty-year sentence against a seventeen-year-old who posted videos on YouTube in which he set off explosives in a field in South Hadley. The boy had Asperger's syndrome and had been making model rockets since he was a child. After a four-day trial, he was found not guilty of all charges. Scheibel also brought heavy charges against Jason Vassell, a black University of Massachusetts student accused of stabbing two white men who entered the lobby of his dormitory. The DA's office portrayed Vassell as the aggressor. But Vassell, who had no criminal record, said he was in his dorm room when the men yelled racial slurs at him from outside his window. Police reports cited by the defense said that the pair had a long history of violence and animal cruelty. After months of accusations of racism against Scheibel's office by a group called Justice for Jason, she dropped the charges.

184 **It's true that there's an association** Anat Brunstein Klomek, "High School Bullying as a Risk for Later Depression and Suicidality," *Suicide and Life-Threatening Behavior* 41 (October 2011): 501–16.

184 **The link is especially strong** Ann Haas et al., "Suicide and Suicide Risk in Lesbian, Gay, Bisexual, and Transgender Populations: Review and Recommendations," *Journal of Homosexuality* 58 (2010): 10–51.

184 **the research is mixed** Klomek, "High School Bullying."

185 **In a recent study of whether bullying** Ibid.

185 **Gould and her colleagues wrote** The ninety-six young adults who were at risk psychologically *and* had been involved in bullying were substantially more likely to be "functionally impaired"—meaning that they had trouble getting along with peers or handling social situations—than the other groups. See ibid.

186 **an arresting image in the *Harry Potter* books** J. K. Rowling, *Harry Potter and the Order of the Phoenix* (New York: Arthur A. Levine, 2003).

187 **The rate of teen suicide** "Suicide Rates Among Persons Aged 15–19 Years—United States, 1981–2009," Centers for Disease Control Vital Statistics.

187 **Nine other states** Victoria Stuart-Cassel et al., "Analysis of State Bullying Laws and Policies," U.S. Department of Education (2011). See

also Greg Toppo, "Should Bullies Be Treated as Criminals?" *USA Today,* June 12, 2012.

188   **the head of New Jersey's association** Winnie Hu, "Bullying Law Puts New Jersey Schools on Spot," *New York Times,* August 30, 2011.

188   **a state council ruled it unconstitutional** Legislators responded by allocating $1 million for a Bullying Prevention Fund. See www.njea.org/news/2012/03/27/christie%20signs%20anti-bullying%20fix and www.njleg.state.nj.us/2012/Bills/S2000/1789_I1.HTM.

190   **Elizabeth Scheibel had been named** Charles P. Pierce, "Bostonians of the Year—The Prosecutor: Elizabeth Scheibel," *Boston Globe,* January 2, 2011.

190   **said she had no regrets** Marie Szaniszlo, "D.A.: No Regrets on Bully Charges," *Boston Herald,* December 31, 2010.

190   **Piers Morgan** After the show, I asked the Piers Morgan producers what evidence they had for his statement. They responded to my query by email but sent no proof.

Chapter 7: Freedom

195   **In 1938, a seven-year-old boy** Sources for Peter Paul Heinemann's story include interviews with his children, David and Kajsa, and his article "Apartheid," *Liberal Debatt* 22 (1969): 3–14, translated by Natalie Engdahl, November 29, 2011.

197   **the hardest traumas are delivered** This is also the conclusion of William Golding's classic novel *Lord of the Flies* (Salisbury: Faber and Faber, 1954).

197   **He wrote an article** Heinemann, "Apartheid."

198   **In the mid-1960s, a well-known Austrian** Konrad Lorenz, *On Aggression* (New York: Bantam, 1966). See also R. E. D. Barrington, "'Bullying' Amongst Birds," *Nature* 129 (1932): 395.

200   **his first book, which came out** Dan Olweus, *Aggression in the Schools: Bullies and Whipping Boys* (Washington, DC: Hemisphere Press, 1978).

201   **calling *both* bullies and whipping boys** Ibid., 174.

201   **"It does not seem reasonable"** Ibid., 169–76.

202   **two large-scale studies** Dan Olweus, "Norway," in Peter K. Smith et al., *The Nature of School Bullying: A Cross-National Perspective* (London: Routledge, 1999), 30, 38–40.

205   **As Dave Cullen explains** Dave Cullen, *Columbine* (New York: Twelve, 2009).

206 **one of more than fifty school** Jessie Klein, *The Bully Society: School Shootings and the Crisis of Bullying in America's Schools* (New York: New York University Press, 2012), 2. The numbers of school shootings have continued to rise. Klein counts eighty-five between 1999 and 2009.

206 **an exhaustive investigation into the causes** Bryan Vossekuil et al., "The Final Report and Findings of the Safe School Initiative: Implications for the Prevention of Further Attacks in the United States," United States Secret Service and United States Department of Education, May 2002, www.secretservice.gov/ntac/ssi_final_report.pdf.

206 **in the wake of Columbine** In the initial rush to make sense of the shootings, Harris and Klebold were portrayed as disaffected members of a "trench coat mafia" at war with a band of jocks, and as bullied outcasts. In fact, they were neither. As Cullen writes, Harris and Klebold "were far more accepted than many of their schoolmates. They hung out with a tight circle of close friends and partied regularly on the weekend with a wider crowd." A better explanation is that Eric Harris was a psychopath and that Dylan Klebold was his depressed and suicidal follower. See Dave Cullen, "The Depressive and the Psychopath," *Slate*, April 20, 2004.

206 **a 2001 survey that highlighted bullying** "Talking with Kids About Tough Issues: A National Survey of Parents and Kids," Nickelodeon, the Kaiser Family Foundation, and International Communications Research, March 8, 2001, www.kff.org/mediapartnerships/upload/Talking-With -Kids-About-Tough-Issues-A-National-Survey-of-Parents-and-Kids -Chart-Pack-2.pdf.

207 **"If we could only round"** Sandy Banks, "When the Campus Bully Runs with the 'In' Crowd," *Los Angeles Times,* March 20, 2001.

207 **arguing that girls could be just as** Kaj Björkqvist, "Sex Differences in Physical, Verbal, and Indirect Aggression: A Review of Recent Research," *Sex Roles* 30 (1994): 177–88.

207 **"Unlike boys, who tend to bully"** Rachel Simmons, *Odd Girl Out* (New York: Harcourt, 2002), 3.

207 **In the same year, Rosalind Wiseman's** Rosalind Wiseman, *Queen Bees and Wannabes* (New York: Crown, 2002).

208 **Conservatives in particular were skeptical** On the left, feminists offered their own critique, arguing that the label of bullying trivialized boys' mistreatment of girls, which should be treated as illegal sexual harassment. See Lyn Mikel Brown, Meda Chesney-Lind, and Nan

Stein, "Patriarchy Matters: Toward a Gendered Theory of Teen Violence and Victimization," *Violence Against Women* 13 (December 2007): 1249–73.

208 **They especially objected to the kind of treacle** Matt Labash, "Beating Up on Bullies," *Weekly Standard,* February 24, 2003.

208 **given for free to more than** Since 2003, the number has grown to more than 150,000.

209 **The skeptics made mincemeat of Yarrow** They pointed out that in 1970, he pled guilty to taking "improper liberties" with a fourteen-year-old girl, served three months, and was later pardoned by President Jimmy Carter. See Labash, "Beating Up."

209 **"The conventional wisdom used to be"** Ann Hulbert, "Elephant in the Room," Slate, October 23, 2003.

209 **"by defining bullying so broadly"** Benjamin Soskis, "Bully Pulpit," *New Republic,* May 14, 2001.

209 **The initial results were disappointing** Dan Olweus, "Bullying/Victim Problems in School: Facts and Intervention," *European Journal of Psychology of Education* 12, no. 4 (1997): 495–510; Susan P. Limber, "Implementation of the Olweus Bullying Prevention Program in American Schools: Lessons Learned from the Field," in *Bullying in American Schools: A Social-Ecological Perspective on Prevention and Intervention,* ed. Dorothy L. Espelage and Susan M. Swearer (Mahwah, NJ: Lawrence Erlbaum Associates, 2004), 351–63; Maria M. Ttofi, David P. Farrington, and Anna C. Baldry, *Effectiveness of Programs to Reduce School Bullying: A Systematic Review* (Stockholm: Swedish National Council for Crime Prevention, 2008).

210 **The first two years of results** *Bullying Prevention: The Impact on Pennsylvania Schoolchildren,* Highmark Foundation, 2011, www.high markfoundation.org/publications/12_7_2011_Revised_Bullying _Report.pdf.

210 **"It used to be a pretty rough place"** Jodi Weigland, "Anti-Bullying Efforts Credited with Reducing Violence in Schools," *Pittsburgh Tribune-Review,* November 13, 2011.

210 **how much the method demands** In response, Olweus points to a recent review, by a team of Cambridge University researchers, which looked at established anti-bullying programs in thirty schools, thirteen of which followed the Olweus model, and found that bullying and victimization fell by an average of 17 percent to 23 percent. See Ttofi et al.,

Effectiveness of Programs to Reduce School Bullying; Dan Olweus and
Sue Limber, "A Misunderstanding of 'Whole-School' Problems," South
Carolina Association of School Administrators, 2010, www.scasa.org/
displaycommon.cfm?an=1&subarticlenbr=311. By contrast, another
recent review of sixteen anti-bullying programs, which varied in quality and longevity, found no change in bullying rates, on average, among
fifteen thousand students in the United States, Canada, and Europe.
See K. W. Merrell, "How Effective Are School Bullying Intervention
Programs? A Meta-Analysis of Intervention Research," *School Psychology Quarterly* 23 (March 2008): 26–42. Also see Susan M. Swearer
et al., "What Can Be Done About School Bullying? Linking Research
to Educational Practice," *Educational Researcher* 39 (January 2010):
38–47, and J. David Smith et al., "The Effectiveness of Whole-School
Antibullying Programs: A Synthesis of Evaluation Research," *School
Psychology Review* 33 (2004): 547–60 (fourteen studies of intervention
programs revealed small to negligible effect sizes for desired changes in
victimization and perpetration). Espelage points out that the Olweus
programs in Europe showed better results than the ones in the United
States.

211 **program is also less expensive** The cost of the Olweus materials, initial
two-day training, and questionnaires for Olweus runs over $4,000, and
there are ancillary expenses as well. See http://www.bullyingstatistics
.org/content/olweus-bullying-prevention-program.html. Second Step
charges $859 for its "complete school program," which includes online
training, a program guide, and curricula for grades 3 through 6. See
http://store.cfchildren.org/steps-to-respect-complete-school-program
-p193.aspx.

211 **Research has shown less acceptance** Karin S. Frey et al., "Reducing
Playground Bullying and Supporting Beliefs: An Experimental Trial of
the *Steps to Respect* Program," *Developmental Psychology* 41 (2005):
479–91.

212 **schools use nine different strategies** Gary D. Gottfredson et al., "Chapter 3: Activities to Create and Maintain Safe and Orderly Schools,"
National Study of Delinquency Prevention in Schools, Gottfredson Associates, July 2000, www.gottfredson.com/Delinquency%20Prevention
%20in%20Schools/chap3.pdf.

214 **"If it's mean, intervene"** Dan Olweus, "Bully/Victim Problems in

School: Facts and Intervention," *European Journal of Psychology of Education* 12 (1997): 495–510.

215 **results of an exciting study** H. Wesley Perkins, Daniel Craig, and Jessica M. Perkins, "Using Social Norms to Reduce Bullying: A Research Intervention Among Adolescents in Five Middle Schools," *Group Processes & Intergroup Relations* (2011).

Chapter 8: Old Mill

231 **A British doctor named John Snow** Kathleen Tuthill, "John Snow and the Broad Street Pump: On the Trail of an Epidemic," *Cricket* 31, no. 3 (November 2003): 23–31; John Snow, *On the Mode of Communication of Cholera* (London: John Churchill, 1855), 40.

234 **Sugai and his colleagues decided** George Sugai, "Multi-tiered Systems of Support and Bullying Behavior," Center for Behavioral Education and Research, presentation to the Phi Delta Kappan at University of Connecticut, February 9, 2012, www.pbis.org.

234 **In 1997 and again in 2004** Individuals with Disabilities Education Act, 20 U.S.C. §1401(c)(5)(F).

236 **The cost of the program varies** PBIS isn't purchased the way that Olweus and Second Step are. Estimates for trainings, assessments, manuals, and data collection can vary from $22,000 for the first year to $5,800 for the third year, depending on how many schools in a district are involved. See http://www.nhcebis.seresc.net/document/filename/265/General_PBIS_Proposal_for_School_Districts.pdf.

239 **teachers in PBIS schools reported less** Tracy E. Waasdorp, Catherine P. Bradshaw, and Philip J. Leaf, "The Impact of Schoolwide Positive Behavioral Interventions and Supports on Bullying and Peer Rejection," *Archives of Pediatrics and Adolescent Medicine* 166 (2012): 149–56.

240 **In 2006, 31 percent** "2006 Bullying Study," Old Mill Middle North School.

240 **All of these numbers dropped** "2011 Bullying Study—Fall," Old Mill Middle North School, www.aacps.org/surveyresults/bullying2011/middle/oldMillMiddleNorth.pdf.

240 **By 2007, Old Mill North's** "2007 Bullying Study," Old Mill Middle North School.

242 **fifth graders at schools randomly** Catherine P. Bradshaw, Christine W. Koth, Leslie A. Thornton, and Philip J. Leaf, "Altering School Climate

Through School-Wide Positive Behavioral Interventions and Supports: Findings from a Group-Randomized Effectiveness Trial," *Prevention Science* 10 (2009): 100–115; Catherine P. Bradshaw, Mary M. Mitchell, and Philip J. Leaf, "Examining the Effects of Schoolwide Positive Behavioral Interventions and Supports on Student Outcomes: Results from a Randomized Controlled Effectiveness Trial in Elementary Schools," *Journal of Positive Behavior Interventions* 12 (July 2010): 133–48.

Chapter 9: Delete Day

256 **I was on a small campus** Facebook has since moved to a larger campus in nearby Menlo Park, taking over the former headquarters of Sun Microsystems.

258 **In 2011, *Consumer Reports* estimated** "That Facebook Friend Might Be 10 Years Old, and Other Troubling News," *Consumer Reports,* June 2011.

259 **A Pew Center survey from** Amanda Lenhart et al., *Teens, Kindness and Cruelty on Social Network Sites,* Pew Internet and American Life Project, November 2011, http://pewinternet.org/~/media/Files/Reports/2011/PIP_Teens_Kindness_Cruelty_SNS_Report_Nov_2011 _FINAL_110711.pdf.

263 **In a 2009 study, researchers asked** Ellen M. Kraft and Jinchang Wang, "Effectiveness of Cyber Bullying Prevention Strategies: A Study on Students' Perspectives," *International Journal of Cyber Criminology* 3 (July– December 2009): 513–35, www.cybercrimejournal.com/Kraftwang JulyIJCC2009.pdf.

266 **accounts that aren't attached to real names** Facebook is firmly committed to this position even though it is controversial on the Web, where countless debates are devoted to whether "real name culture" helps or hurts the Internet. When Google launched its own social network, Google+, it followed Facebook in requiring real names for users. This sparked a mini-revolt (with its own hashtag, #Nymwars). "Many voices are silenced in the name of shutting up trolls: activists living under authoritarian regimes, whistleblowers, victims of violence, abuse, and harassment, and anyone with an unpopular or dissenting point of view that can legitimately expect to be imprisoned, beat-up, or harassed for speaking out," one blogger wrote. Facebook weighed in against anonymity. "I think anonymity on the Internet has to go away. People behave a lot better when they have their real names down," said

Randi Zuckerberg, Facebook's marketing director (and Mark Zucker-berg's sister). She has a point: anonymous Internet trolls can ruin the reputations of the people they trash and are hard to trace. On the other hand, outside the United States the anonymity afforded by Twitter han-dles has helped the site become a hub of anti-authoritarian protest.

It's also worth noting that real names have a higher financial value than fake ones for social media sites. They bring in more ad revenue because they make it possible to link your account to the purchases you make online, recorded by the cookies that track your online paths. See Tim Carmody, "Google+ Identity Crisis: What's at Stake with Real Names and Privacy," *Wired*, July 26, 2011.

269 **"Someone made a mistake"** News reports show that other Facebook users have struggled to get anonymous or harassing pages taken down. See George Hesselberg, "SOS: 13-Year-Old Victimized by False Face-book Page," *Wisconsin State Journal*, April 24, 2011, and Jessica Cain, "More Facebook Pages Taken Down After Complaints," *CNY Cen-tral*, October 25, 2010. In April 2012, a Georgia teenager sued two classmates and their parents for libel over a fake Facebook page. The company did not respond to her requests to remove the page until a story about the lawsuit aired on CNN, the girl's lawyer said. Kim Zetter, "Teen Sues over Facebook Bullying," *Wired*, April 27, 2012.

269 **Lori Drew was seen as "slightly annoying"** Lauren Collins, "Friend Game," *New Yorker*, January 21, 2008.

270 **Drew later told the police** Christopher Maag, "A Hoax Turned Fatal Draws Anger but No Charges," *New York Times*, November 28, 2007.

270 **the Meiers told their story** Steve Pokin, "'My Space' Hoax Ends with Suicide of Dardenne Prairie Teen," *St. Charles Suburban Journals*, No-vember 11, 2007.

271 **When the police dismissed Drew's** Maag, "Hoax Turned Fatal."

271 **A jury convicted Drew** *United States v. Drew*, 259 F.R.D. 449, 453 (C.D. Cal., 2009).

271 **a wave of tougher cyberbullying laws** Sameer Hinduja and Justin W. Patchin, *State Cyberbullying Laws: A Brief Review of State Cyberbul-lying Laws and Policies*, Cyberbullying Research Center, April 2012, www.cyberbullying.us/Bullying_and_Cyberbullying_Laws.pdf.

271 **Tony Orsini, a middle school principal** Jan Hoffman, "Online Bullies Pull Schools into the Fray," *New York Times*, June 27, 2010.

272 **The Supreme Court first took** *Tinker v. Des Moines Independent Community School District,* 393 U.S. 503 (1969).

273 **making "lewd" remarks** *Bethel School District No. 403 v. Fraser,* 478 U.S. 675 (1986).

273 **delete articles from a school-sponsored** *Hazelwood School District v. Kuhlmeier,* 484 U.S. 260 (1998).

273 **they can restrict speech** *Morse v. Frederick,* 551 U.S. 393 (2007).

274 **J.'s misadventures began** *J.C. v. Beverly Hills Unified School District,* 711 F.Supp.2d 1094 (C.D.CA. 2010).

274 **"What incensed me"** Hoffman, "Online Bullies Pull Schools."

274 **Kara Kowalski brought the same** *Kowalski v. Berkeley County Schools,* 652 F.3d 565 (2011).

278 **"Suppose a high school student"** *J.S. v. Blue Mountain School District,* 650 F.3d 915 (2011).

281 **seven and a half million kids** "That Facebook Friend Might Be 10 Years Old, and Other Troubling News," *Consumer Reports,* June 2011.

283 **There's a lively debate** The Stanford researchers Roy Pea and Clifford Nass and James Steyer, the head of Common Sense Media, suggest that texting and social networking can have negative effects on teenagers. See Roy Pea and Clifford Nass, "Media Use, Face-to-Face Communication, Media Multitasking, and Social Well-Being Among 8- to 12-Year-Old Girls," *Developmental Psychology* 48 (March 2012): 327–36, and James Steyer, *Talking Back to Facebook* (New York: Scribner, 2012). Cultural anthropologist Mizuko Ito of the University of California at Irvine gives a more positive take on teenagers and Internet use in her book *Hanging Out, Messing Around, and Geeking Out* (Cambridge, MA: MIT, 2009). See also "Educational Benefits of Social Networking Sites Uncovered," *ScienceDaily,* June 20, 2008; Matt Richtel, "Wasting Time Is New Divide in Digital Era," *New York Times,* May 30, 2012.

283 **two-thirds of the time, underage kids** danah boyd et al., "Why Parents Help Their Children Lie to Facebook About Age: Unintended Consequences of the 'Children's Online Privacy Protection Act,'" *First Monday* 16 (November 2011), www.uic.edu/htbin/cgiwrap/bin/ojs/index .php/fm/article/view/3850/3075.

283 **45 percent of twelve-year-olds** Lenhart et al., *Teens, Kindness and Cruelty.*

284 **research suggests that lots of** Pea and Nass, "Media Use"; Lenhart et al., *Teens, Kindness and Cruelty.* See also Steyer, *Talking Back to Facebook,* 22–23. For more on the effects of social networking and the Internet on the social lives of adults as well as kids, see Sherry Turkle, *Alone Together* (New York: Basic Books, 2011), and Jaron Lanier, *You Are Not a Gadget* (New York: Knopf, 2010).

285 **I made this argument** Emily Bazelon, "Why Facebook Is After Your Kids," *New York Times Magazine,* October 12, 2011.

285 **more than fifty privacy buttons** Nick Bilton, "Price of Facebook Privacy? Start Clicking," *New York Times,* May 12, 2010.

285 **When the company went public** Somini Sengupta, "Facebook Delivers an Earnings Letdown," *New York Times,* July 26, 2012, and Somini Sengupta, "To Settle Lawsuit, Facebook Alters Policy for Its Like Button," *New York Times,* June 21, 2012.

286 **"the very idea of making"** Farhad Majoo, "It's Not All Facebook's Fault," Slate, November 30, 2011.

287 **Cookies are even more prevalent** Steve Stecklow, "On the Web, Children Face Intensive Tracking," *Wall Street Journal,* September 17, 2010.

287 **announced a settlement with Facebook** Federal Trade Commission, "Facebook Settles FTC Charges That It Deceived Consumers by Failing to Keep Privacy Promises," November 29, 2011, http://ftc.gov/opa/2011/11/privacysettlement.shtm. Twitter and Google have also settled with the FTC over privacy complaints.

Conclusion

298 **an episode in Mitt Romney's** Jason Horowitz, "Mitt Romney's Prep School Classmates Recall Pranks, but Also Troubling Incidents," *Washington Post,* May 10, 2012.

298 **Olweus found that 15 percent** Dan Olweus, "Norway," in Peter K. Smith et al., *The Nature of School Bullying: A Cross-National Perspective* (London: Routledge, 1999), 32.

298 **Research consistently shows** Susan P. Limber and Maury M. Nation, "Bullying Among Children and Youth," *Juvenile Justice Bulletin,* April 1998; Tonja R. Nansel et al., "Bullying Behaviors Among U.S. Youth: Prevalence and Association with Psychosocial Adjustment," *Journal of the American Medical Association* 285 (April 25, 2001): 2094–100. As noted in Chapter 1, including reports of cyberbullying tends to raise the

rate of reported bullying slightly. See Jill DeVoe and Christina Murphy, *Student Reports of Bullying and Cyber-Bullying: Results From the 2009 School Crime Supplement to the National Crime Victimization Survey,* NCES 2011-336, U.S. Department of Education, August 2011, http://nces.ed.gov/pubs2011/2011336.pdf.

299 **good research tells us** H. Wesley Perkins, Daniel Craig, and Jessica M. Perkins, "Using Social Norms to Reduce Bullying: A Research Intervention Among Adolescents in Five Middle Schools," *Group Processes & Intergroup Relations* (2011).

299 **We also should rethink** Victoria Stuart-Cassel et al., "Analysis of State Bullying Laws and Policies," U.S. Department of Education (2011).

300 **In the initial reports** Dave Cullen, *Columbine* (New York: Twelve, 2009). Today, when Cullen goes to schools to talk about what happened at Columbine, he asks students and parents why they think the shootings happened. Bullying is the number one answer they give.

300 **In 2007, when a senior** Dave Cullen, "Mean Kids: 'The Bully Society,' by Jesse Klein," *New York Times,* April 27, 2012.

300 **we just don't know how** On Clementi's computer, the police found three documents, called sorry.docx, gah.docx, and why is everything so painful.docx, which were not made public. Clementi's suicide note also wasn't released. Emily Bazelon and Kevin Lerner, "Dharun Ravi Should Cut a Deal," Slate, February 14, 2012; Emily Bazelon, "Make the Punishment Fit the Cyber-Crime," *New York Times,* March 19, 2012.

300 **You'd never know from the film** Emily Bazelon, "The Problem with *Bully,*" Slate, March 29, 2012; Emily Bazelon, "More Problems for *Bully,*" Slate, May 22, 2012.

300 **which is linked to suicide** Michael Fitzgerald, "Suicide and Asperger's Syndrome," *Crisis: The Journal of Crisis Intervention and Suicide Prevention* 28 (2007): 1–3, http://psycnet.apa.org/journals/cri/28/1/1.

301 **In 1999, a girl who was** *Davis v. Monroe County Board of Education,* 526 U.S. 629 (1999).

301 *Bullying,* **by contrast, is a term** Lyn Mikel Brown, Meda Chesney-Lind, and Nan Stein, "Patriarchy Matters: Toward a Gendered Theory of Teen Violence and Victimization," *Violence Against Women* 13 (December 2007): 1249–73. Another veteran in the field, the sociologist David Finkelhor, has expressed frustration at how the "bullying" label can diminish the significance of onetime physical attacks. He gives the

example of a child who whacks a classmate with a baseball bat and sends him to the hospital, and asks why anyone who wants to ensure kids' safety would deemphasize such an act. See David Finkelhor, Heather A. Turner, and Sherry Hamby, "Let's Prevent Peer Victimization, Not Just Bullying," *Child Abuse and Neglect*, 2012.

303 **It's far too simple** Some studies suggest a connection between TV viewing and behavior—particularly violence—but the validity of these findings is debated. See Lynette Friedrich-Cofer and Aletha C. Huston, "Television Violence and Aggression: The Debate Continues," *Psychological Bulletin* 100 (November 1986): 364–71; Richard Rhodes, "Hollow Claims about Fantasy Violence," *New York Times*, September 17, 2000.

304 **Mark Zuckerberg likes to say** Letter from Mark Zuckerberg, included in Facebook's filing to the U.S. Securities and Exchange Commission, February 1, 2012.

305 **I sometimes fear that parents go** The loss of physical "room to roam," as the British group Natural England calls it, is a generational shift, which the researcher William Bird neatly captured in a report for Natural England and the Royal Society for the Protection of Birds (*Natural Thinking*, June 2007, www.rspb.org.uk/Images/naturalthinking_tcm9-161856.pdf). The movements of four generations of a family in the city of Sheffield in South Yorkshire, which has a population of about half a million today, reflect this gradual distancing from nature. When George Thomas was eight years old in 1926, he routinely walked six miles on his own to his favorite fishing spot. At the same age in 1950, his son-in-law could walk about a mile to the local woods. By 1979, when Thomas' granddaughter was eight, she could go only to the swimming pool alone, half a mile from her house. And now that Thomas' great-grandson Edward is that age, his freedom extends only to the end of his street. Where George Thomas had six miles to himself, his great-grandson Edward Grant has three hundred yards. See David Derbyshire, "How Children Lost the Right to Roam in Four Generations," *Daily Mail*, June 15, 2007. See also Lenore Skenazy, *Free-Range Kids* (San Francisco: Jossey-Bass, 2009), and Dalton Conley, *Elsewhere, USA* (New York: Pantheon, 2009), xii.

306 **"Childhood is, or has been"** Michael Chabon, "The Wilderness of Childhood," in *Manhood for Amateurs* (New York: HarperCollins, 2009), 61.

Frequently Asked Questions About Bullying

318 **"If it's mean, intervene"** Dan Olweus, "Bully/Victim Problems in School: Facts and Intervention," *European Journal of Psychology of Education* 12 (1997): 495–510.

319 **They have authority to address** Sameer Hinduja and Justin W. Patchin, *State Cyberbullying Laws: A Brief Review of State Cyberbullying Laws and Policies,* Cyberbullying Research Center, April 2012, www .cyberbullying.us/Bullying_and_Cyberbullying_Laws.pdf.

Index

About the Author

Emily Bazelon is a senior editor at Slate, a contributing writer at *The New York Times Magazine,* and the Truman Capote Fellow at Yale Law School. Before joining Slate, she worked as a law clerk on the U.S. Court of Appeals for the First Circuit. She is a graduate of Yale College and Yale Law School, and lives in New Haven with her husband and two sons. This is her first book.

About the Type

This book was set in Sabon, a typeface designed by the well-known German typographer Jan Tschichold (1902–74). Sabon's design is based upon the original letter forms of Claude Garamond and was created specifically to be used for three sources: foundry type for hand composition, Linotype, and Monotype. Tschichold named his typeface for the famous Frankfurt typefounder Jacques Sabon, who died in 1580.